Contents

Preface

This book is intended to provide practising engineers, technologists, engineering students and researchers with a handbook on engineering-related Internet resources which they can use in their daily engineering work, study and research.

Since its advent, the Internet has been the topic of numerous books. Many are introductory and some are on the Internet's technical aspects. There are few books written with its interests focused on a discipline or targeted to a chosen profession. This book intends to fill that gap for people studying, researching and working in engineering and technology.

This book originated from my experience in teaching engineering undergraduates and supervising postgraduate students. My academic career spans the period when the Internet was introduced into the university campus and began to flourish, and the momentous changes it has brought about in communication, teaching and learning. The application of the Internet within the engineering community is being felt, and pursued with great enthusiasm. Its potential to influence the engineering community is immeasurable. The Internet introduces a new dimension in providing common access to information, library resources and education.

Resources relating to engineering and technology are scattered all over the Internet. They may cover professional societies, conferences, computer software, library access, bibliographic databases, newsletters, journals, discussion groups and more. For example, the Internet enables an engineer, without being a member of the American Society of Mechanical Engineers, to be informed about its recent activities from its Internet site. The Internet also enables users to access the vast information resources on engineering literature and publications from libraries world-wide .

Engineering resources available on the Internet are as yet not fully utilised. At present, many engineering researchers still conduct their literature survey the way it was done a decade ago: from the reference list in a recent publication to more reference lists. Practising engineers and scientists are still accustomed to seeking information only from

Internet Resources
for Engineers

Jimin He

To my family

Australia
Butterworth-Heinemann, 18 Salmon Street, Port Melbourne, Vic. 3207
Singapore
Butterworth-Heinemann Asia
United Kingdom
Butterworth-Heinemann Ltd, Oxford
USA
Butterworth-Heinemann, Newton

National Library of Australia Cataloguing-in-Publication entry

He, Jimin.
Internet resources for engineers : a practical handbook for engineers and students.

Includes index.
ISBN 0 7506 8949 8

Enquiries should be addressed to the publisher.
Typeset by Keyword Editorial Services.
Printed by Kin Keong Printing Co. Pte. Ltd.

peers or printed publications. Educators and academics by and large have not been comfortable with using the Internet.

However, finding engineering-related resources on the Internet may lead to only limited success, due to the enormous dispersal of information. A cursory visit to the Internet is not efficient. Curiosity alone is insufficient. Some guidance is essential. This book attempts to help readers to learn how to use and to find engineering resources on the Internet.

Chapters 1 and 2 present an introduction to the Internet; regular users may simply scan through these chapters. Chapter 3 discusses the non-Web search capacities the Internet offers, essential for accessing information in Gopher, Telnet, Archie and WAIS protocols. Chapter 4 covers the Web search engines and Internet directories. The Web search engine is the main search tool for finding engineering- and technology-related resources, and Internet directories are classified information sources. Chapter 5 is concerned with using library resources world-wide—in this context, the Internet has become a global library that consists of libraries from different parts of the world. In Chapter 6, a comprehensive list of databases of engineering relevance is introduced, which can be used by researchers to locate the latest publications on a topic, or by practising engineers discovering patents pertinent to their design projects. Chapter 7 deals with education-related Internet engineering resources and engineering societies. Chapter 8 encompasses engineering publication on the Internet, including online engineering journals, magazines and books. The Appendix contains some additional topics of interest. Those of general interest for Internet users are a glossary, a list of file and data formats, a description of Boolean operators, country codes and Internet domain names. Those specifically for engineers are engineering career information and computer software resources.

The objective of this book is to provide readers with an awareness of engineering resources on the Internet and also to foster in readers the ability to find relevant information. In this it differs from some other books that tend to muster lists of catalogues or Web sites of engineering resources. Web sites are dynamic, and thus often subject to changes. It is the users' ability to locate up-to-date information by themselves that will bring them the maximum benefits from using the Internet. In addition, with some exceptions, resources mentioned in this book are based on the World Wide Web. This accords with the reality that most of the non-Web Internet protocols can now be accessed from their Web gateways, and the future of the Internet is seen to be exclusively a Web environment.

It is not possible to acknowledge individually each of the organisations and people whose Web sites and the information they contain have been included in this book. I have sought to use the latest image and Internet address of each Web site presented.

I am most thankful to the book's editor Michael Wyatt, without whose excellent editorial skills this book would not have been able to meet its readers' needs. I am also thankful to Jonathan Glasspool and Rosemary Peers for many valuable suggestions and reminders, and for their patience during the entire preparation of the manuscript.

I am grateful to my colleagues whose help ensured the manuscript was ready for editing. Professor Geoff Lleonart and Ms Coral Ware kindly read the manuscript and suggested many helpful changes, which have been incorporated into this book. Ms Denise Colledge and Ms Annabel McCooke also reviewed a few chapters and made many helpful comments.

A Web site has been established at **http://dingo.vut.edu.au/~jimin/book.html** specifically for this book. Many of the Internet resources listed in this book are available there for easy access and downloading. It will be updated with the latest Internet information and addresses. Typing URLs (Internet addresses) can be a laborious and error-prone exercise—why not add our site to your bookmark file and use it to click your way through the Internet's amazing resources? I look forward to receiving your comments and suggestions on this book and the Web site—simply click "Mail me" on the site's home page. I hope to incorporate your comments and suggestions in the next edition.

Jimin He
Ivanhoe East, Vic.

1

Introduction to the Internet and World Wide Web

What is the Internet?

A brief history of the Internet

The World Wide Web (WWW)

What is a database?

Why do we need to search the Internet?

Why search remote databases online?

Information retrieval on the Internet

Hypertext

Online training and learning

What is the Internet?

The Internet, and the name by which it is sometimes known, the Information Superhighway, have become popular buzz words. Whether you are already an avid Internet user or still a novice, the growing relevance of the Internet to your work, study, research, social life and recreational activities is irresistible. In particular, the Internet is becoming more meaningful for engineers, scientists and technologists.

The Internet is a computer network interconnecting numerous computer hardware or local computer networks. These networks are linked by a set of common technical 'protocols' that enable users of any one of the networks to communicate with or use the services located on other networks. A protocol can be seen as a formal description of message formats and the rules that two communicating computers must follow to exchange data. Protocols can describe the low-level details of machine-to-machine interfaces (i.e., the order in which bits and bytes are sent across a wire) or high-level exchanges between allocation programs (i.e., the way in which two programs transfer a file across the Internet). These protocols are referred to as the Transmission Control Protocol/Internet Protocol, or TCP/IP protocol, suite. The number of these computer networks for the Internet is growing astronomically. A recent (July 1995) Internet domain survey shows that there are 6.6 million computers connected to the Internet. The rapid growth of the Internet in the next decade or two is widely anticipated.

The TCP protocol for data transmission is a group of over 100 data-communications protocols currently being used to link computers and data-communications equipment into computer networks. Originally designed to interconnect hosts on ARPAnet, an early computer network located at the US Department of Defense, TCP/IP has now been adopted by a large number of universities, research institutions, government agencies and corporations as their computer communication network protocol for the Internet.

The Internet would not have developed without a technology called packet-switching. The technology preceding packet-switching was capable of transmitting large quantities of data from one computer to another only in a single continuous stream. This is like a telephone call in which only one line can be connected to one telephone at a time. So it was not possible for different network segments to 'share' a common transmission medium. Packet-switching technology breaks the data into small fragments—each fragment is 'packed', marked with its source and destination, and pushed into the transmission line. This allows packets from different sources to pour into the transmission and arrive at each destination. After reaching its destination, each packet is unpacked and re-assembled with other packets to recover the original data.

Though information provided by the Internet can be of many kinds, the Internet only transmits data. Of course, the data can be of texts, pictures, graphs, publications, sounds, video and more. In order for your computer to interpret correctly different types of data, you need not only the right hardware such as a modem, sound card, etc., but also the right software. There are plenty of books that address the hardware side of linking to the Internet. For people engaged in engineering study and research, the computer hardware is often readily available. What you require now are the skills to exploit the Internet to your own maximum benefit. The purpose of this book is to teach you those skills.

The Internet provides various services for interacting with computers, and data are transferred by different protocols. Among the most commonly used protocols between computers on the Internet are:

- mailing and receiving electronic text to each other (email)
- retrieving and sending documents or groups of documents to and from each other (FTP or file transfer protocol)
- browsing each other's collections of documents (Gopher, FTP)
- requesting a search for a document on a remote system (WAIS or Wide-Area Information Server)
- exchanging messages on electronic message boards (Usenet newsgroups).

These protocols will be elaborated on in Chapter 3. There are also other more complex interactions that link computers, but many are actually combinations of these basic services.

The Internet is a worldwide communication medium. It is an information pool from where people all over the world exchange, retrieve, disseminate and store information. Never before have people had such a boundless and dynamic environment in which to do so. The information floating on the Internet can be of any kind. Given time and effort, you will be impressed by what the Internet can offer you. In this book, you will find laid open to you the richness of information related to engineering practice, studies and research, and ways of maximising the benefits that arise from them.

A brief history of the Internet

The advent of the Internet was somewhat accidental. The Internet was originally the outcome of a strategic study during the cold war years, into how US authorities could communicate and command centres function after a nuclear strike. The answer was that a special command-and-control network was needed. According to conventional wisdom, such a network would be unreliable because of a its lack of a central command system; nevertheless, it is capable of functioning in a decentralised fashion. It would be designed from the start to transcend its own unreliability. All the nodes in the network would be equal in status to all other nodes, each node with its own authority to originate, receive and pass on messages. It would also be possible to add or remove nodes without disturbing the overall functioning of the network. Such a network would serve the primary purpose of continuing to run as a network despite local malfunctions.

The first such network was created in 1969 for the US Department of Defense. Called the ARPAnet (ARPA stands for Advanced Research Project Agency), it was designed to be decentralised so that even if part of the network malfunctioned, the remainder would keep functioning. However, it was soon revealed that ARPAnet's users had 'warped' the computer-sharing network into a dedicated, high-speed, federally subsidised electronic post-office. The main traffic on ARPAnet was not long-distance computing; instead, it was news and personal messages. Researchers were using ARPAnet to collaborate on projects, to trade notes on work, and eventually, to barter gossip and rumours. People had their personal addresses for electronic mail on the ARPAnet computers. Their enthusiasm for using ARPAnet as an interpersonal communication tool greatly overshadowed the system's original objective of being a long-distance computational tool. It was not long before the invention of the mailing-list, an ARPAnet broadcasting technique in which an identical message could be sent automatically to a large number of network subscribers. Throughout the 1970s, ARPA's network grew. Its decentralised structure made expansion easy. Unlike standard corporate computer networks, the ARPA network could accommodate many different kinds of machine.

In 1984, the National Science Foundation (NSF) of the US government recognised the great potential of networking for scientific research and built its own network, known as NSFnet. The new NSFnet set a blistering pace for the Internet's technical advancement. Other US government agencies such as NASA soon joined the race. There were also other major networks, including the Australian Academic and Research Network (AARNet), the NASA Science Internet (NSI) and the Swiss Academic and Research Network (SWITCH). As the networks grew, different Internet 'domains' were generated and standardised. They are **gov** for government institutions, **mil** for military institutions, **edu** for educational institutions, **com** for commercial institutions, **net** for network operations and services, and **org** for non-profit organisations. This list is due to be expanded.

NSFnet soon expanded and overtook ARPAnet, thanks to its more advanced communication technology and became the foundation stone of what we now call the Internet. Today there are tens of thousands of nodes in the Internet, with more coming online every day. Millions of people world-wide are using this gigantic computer network. The Internet's growth rate is estimated at 10% per month. In Australia, there are over 600 000 users, and the number is growing every day. For people studying and researching in engineering and technology, the Internet is growing from a curiosity to a necessity.

The World Wide Web (WWW)

The World Wide Web, also known as the Web, the WWW or W3, was initially developed by the European Laboratory for Particle Physics, otherwise known as CERN, in order to build a distributed hypermedia system. It is an interconnected assembly of resources available on the Internet that can be displayed by means of a type of software program known as a 'Web browser' or 'Web navigator'. This system aims to provide global access to a universe of documents, most of them in the form of 'hypertext'. Hypertext is akin to regular text in many aspects—it can be stored, read, searched or edited. However, unlike regular text, it contains pointers to other text. In this way, it generates 'hyperlinks' which form a web and continue to provide you with information and documents on a particular topic.

To access the World Wide Web, you need a Web browser to read documents and retrieve them onto your computer from other sources. Information providers set up hypermedia 'servers' from which browsers access documents. The browsers can, in addition, access files by FTP, NNTP (the Internet news protocol), Gopher and a range of other protocols. Better still, if the server has search capabilities, the browsers permit you to search documents and databases.

There are over 30 different Web browsers currently in use, but only a few have gained widespread acceptance. Netscape Navigator from Netscape Communications is perhaps still the most popular browser on the Web, and is highly recommended. It is compatible with PC, Macintosh and Unix platforms. Figure 1.1 shows the 'home page' (the designated site for World Wide Web access) of Netscape Communications. Another Web browser, the Internet Explorer from Microsoft, has been gaining enormous ground in popularity.

Both the terms 'World Wide Web' and 'Internet' are frequently used, but it is important to understand that the terms are not synonymous. The Web refers to a body of information—an abstract space of knowledge—while the Internet refers to the physical side of the global network, a giant mass of cables and computers. Viewed as a hierarchy, the Web is a subset of the Internet.

What is a database?

Databases on the Internet are information warehouses. A database is a structured collection of information records. Each record is usually divided into a number of fields of a particular type and contains a collection of operations that facilitate searching and sorting. A database can be bibliographic, full-text, numeric or of some other type. Well before the advent of the Internet, there were many bibliographic databases for engineering, science and other disciplines, which could

Netscape® Netcenter™

Today's Netscape News
Netscape Launches Two
New Community Services

ABCNEWS
Clinton Aide Set to Testify
Again

Net Search: Select Your Favorite Service

[Infoseek ▼] [   ] [Search]

Join Netcenter and enter to
win exciting high-tech gear
from netMarket.

get your own
domain name
your-name.com
go!

Software	**Content**	**Commerce**
Try Internet Products	Navigate the Web	Shop for Products
· **Netscape Download**	· **Business Journal**	· **Marketplace**
Free Browsers, Servers ...	News, Companies ...	Books, Music, Flowers ...
· **SmartUpdate**	· **In-Box Direct**	· **Travel**
Upgrade to Communicator ...	Sports, Entertainment ...	Reservations, Flights ...
· **Netscape Store**	· **Internet Guide**	
Communicator, Books ...	Businesses, Computers ...	**Community**
· **Software Depot**	· **Channel Finder**	Build Relationships
Web Builder, Plug-ins ...	Business, Technology ...	· **Instant Messenger**
	· **Net Search**	· **Virtual Office**
	Specialized Searches ...	· **ISP Select**
		Switch Your Provider

inside
Netcenter
Wednesday

Does moving customer
service to the web help
business? Track the
trend with In-Box Direct
and Netscape
Enterprise Developer.

Tell us what you think of our site and how we can
make it better.

Do *Only the Paranoid
Survive*? Intel CEO
Andy Grove examines
business strategies for
survival in
Amazon.com.

Netscape
The Internet Company

· **Company** · **Support** · **Developers** · **Columns**
· **Products** · **Solutions** · **Partners**

[Netscape International ▼]

| Netcenter | Download | Site Search | Site Map | Feedback | About This Site |

Advertise With Us
Customer Service
How to Get Netscape Products

Copyright © 1998 Netscape Communications Corporation.
This site powered by Netscape SuiteSpot servers.

Figure 1.1 Netscape's home page

be accessed in various ways. With the Internet, the dimension of these
databases has been immensely increased. Old bibliographic databases
revive and evolve, new databases are born and thrive. The emergence
of multimedia is being accompanied by databases of images, sounds,
video, animation and combinations of them. All these have fostered
new meanings for the term 'database'.

The Internet has also brought into being special types of databases,
namely databases of Internet resources. Some of these not only gather
records but also categorise them. These categories are referred to as
'subject-oriented guides', 'tertiary sources' or simply 'Internet
directories'. Using the categories, you can browse the database as well
as search it, useful for seeking information on a well-defined topic
which falls into one of the categories used in a database. In general,
however, to extract information it is still necessary to search through
the database.

Before the development of the Internet, there were a number of databases available online. This used to mean using a dial-up service to remotely connect to a computer, using tailor-made software to search a foreign database. These searches were carried out on a teletype terminal, a semi-intelligent terminal or, later, on a microcomputer. The remote connection was made over telephone lines, usually using a modem. Back then, those few available databases (some of them are still alive or have been transformed) were largely of bibliographic data, with very similar structure and format. Currently on the Internet the word 'database' has assumed a new meaning: in terms of an information resource, a database can also be either a 'reference database' or a 'source database'.

A reference database is an organised collection of 'pointers' or links. A search of a reference database is often the first step in retrieving information. A source database is an organised collection of records or sources. You can think of the library's journal collection (alphabetically organised by titles) as a source database in print form. An electronic analogy would be a full-text database of that collection. Other source databases are built by organising data submitted directly or collected from other publications. For engineering and technology, the most useful databases are usually those related to journal and conference publications, patents, technical reports and industry products, many of them bibliographic. The outcome of a search is a list of references to documents, some of which may also contain abstracts. Therefore these databases can be referred to as 'abstract' databases as well as bibliographic databases. For researchers working in universities or industry research institutions, these databases are also known as 'research databases'.

Users have no control over a database. However, in order to make an intelligent selection of databases, it is worth while learning some of their characteristics. The scope of a database is of primary importance: that is, facts about its coverage and time period; the total number of records; its subject area; the types of sources; and how completely each source is presented. The cost of using it is also important. Database vendors (many of them private enterprises) charge for usage based on a combination of connect time, search performed, and information displayed. Unless you are fully aware, you can spend a small fortune searching certain legal and business databases. If you have an institutional subscription, you will not be personally liable for payment; however, unless the institution has paid a fixed annual subscription fee it usually has to foot the bill for your usage. The currency of the information in a database is also crucial. For a bibliographic database, this means the time taken for the record to appear after an article is published. The search method used is becoming less a real issue, as most databases can now be readily searched via the Internet without any special software. This does not preclude familiarity as a factor in using databases; however, search aids, documentation and online help from database providers or vendors become more important since most users are 'amateurs'.

Why do we need to search the Internet?

Anyone with some experience of finding information on the Internet will intuitively know why. It would be inconceivable to attempt to locate a particular book in a library without first consulting its catalogue. Nevertheless, the collection in a library is finite and usually does not grow dramatically month by month. Besides, you can always ask the librarians for assistance. Metaphorically, the Internet is a huge rapidly growing library with a skyrocketing collection, yet it does not have librarians ready to assist. Nor does it have an organised collection or catalogues. Finding the information you want on the Internet without help and guidance can be frustrating, if not futile. While you may enjoy hopping from one Web site to another for useful links, the Internet can only be truly useful if you can quickly search for and find sites containing the information you need.

Fortunately, the Internet possesses tools devised for information searches. Without them, we would all be wandering around in the Internet maze. Before the advent of the World Wide Web, there were already a few tools that enabled users to search through the Internet—the FTP archiver Archie, the Gopher searcher Veronica (and, later, Jughead), and the database-finding Wide Area Information Server (WAIS). All these tools, known also as 'Internet search tools', will be discussed in Chapter 3. Although they serve well the purpose they were designed for, they are not always friendly to users, and the information they retrieve and deliver is limited to their own protocols. They do not search through the information residing at World Wide Web 'servers' (computers that provide WWW service to other computers).

Since its inception, the World Wide Web has been growing so fast that it has become impracticable to find anything without a proper search tool. You can spend days or months piecing together information along the way, creating a bookmark or a little private database — in fact, many Web users have been doing just that. However, this pedestrian approach to information gathering is most inefficient, and in no way keeps up with the Web's rapid expansion and constant updating. It was this scenario that engendered the development of Web search tools, and the result is the numerous Web search engines now available throughout the WWW world, often referred to as 'Webspace'. Furthermore, many of these search engines have now embarked on compiling and indexing information, creating their own directories for subject guidance as well as databases for searching.

What exactly is a 'search engine'? It is a software program that helps you find information on numerous servers on the Internet, and also helps you filter the huge amount of information retrieved. The result of using a search engine is a list of Internet sites, usually accompanied by descriptions. A Web search engine is obviously one that operates on and extracts information from the Webspace. By now, most non-Web search engines have been provided with interfaces to the Webspace and are therefore accessible on the Web.

Usually, a search engine allows you to enter keywords (otherwise known as 'search query') that relate to the topic of your interest, and then generates a list of Web or non-Web site names or relevant document titles. Obviously, a search engine has to interpret the query and identify searched items with precision, and it often ranks the returned items. The search can be carried out on the titles of Internet sites, abstracts, or both. Some special-purpose search engines can even search full documents. The search can be either a 'keyword search', whereby keywords are exactly matched, or a 'concept search' whereby query terms are interpreted as being 'close' to terms appearing in Internet documents. In both cases, the search is usually successful in terms of the number of sites accessed, with information on some relevant sites returned. The engines are customarily placed on the Internet as a public service to the community. They attract a huge number of users every day and may occasionally be difficult to access when traffic becomes congested.

No search engine is 'meticulous' overall in searching for information. In order to carry out a thorough search for a particular topic within the vast Internet resources, you need to use several different types of search engines or several search engines of the same type. For example, the information you are looking for may reside on Archie servers, WAIS servers, WWW servers, Gopher servers, etc. For an individual protocol such as the Web, you may have to use several WWW search engines for completeness. The data available on one server may be more current than that on another. There is also the question of the quality of information. A search engine returning everything remotely linked to the search query will dilute the quality of the search and jeopardise the effective use of the search results.

Why search remote databases online?

At present, most databases for online searching are bibliographic or research databases. Methods of searching these databases are described in Chapter 6. Online search of a remote database is not a novelty for the Internet. Its history dates back to the early 60s, although at that time the service had very different forms and capabilities. Early online database searching had nowhere near the capabilities of today's Internet searches in terms of accessibility, convenience and scale. Today, remote databases available for online search have become an indispensable component of information sources in academic research work, industry, business and commerce.

An alternative to online searches of remote databases is the CD-ROM, which can be searched either on site (in your own computer) or remotely (by connecting to some other computer where the CD-ROM is installed). Modern technology allows the CD-ROM to hold an amount of information undreamed of a couple of decades ago, allowing CD-ROMs to become a real choice for accessing information provided by remote databases. However, the difference between using a CD-ROM and an online search is evident. A CD-ROM is basically a copy of a database at a certain period in time. Therefore, a complete search of information across a number of years has to be performed on several discs separately. By the same token, updating a database means acquiring new discs. In order to facilitate better access to a CD-ROM search, certain hardware may have to be purchased to house the discs or to permit a remote search. Some libraries do not have the necessary hardware in place, and as a result you can only use the CD-ROM by visiting the library and using it on site. Because of the time needed to manufacture and distribute discs, information held on CD-ROM will inevitably experience a time delay compared with online databases.

An online search of the Internet can overcome some problems of using a CD-ROM. You can access a remote database from any computer with an Internet connection. You can access a database of any size, and the search is usually carried out over the whole database. There is hardly a special need for software and hardware apart from an Internet connection and an appropriate Web browser. As for value for money, some databases offer a pay-as-you-go policy so that no upfront payment is required. For many academic institutions, online searching offers its patrons great flexibility in access to databases using a favourable institutional subscription.

Information retrieval on the Internet

Long before the advent of the Internet, information retrieval as a technology had already been established for various applications. For instance, searching through databases for legal cases, industrial products, patents and library catalogues were common information retrieval applications for some decades. In the past, these applications usually required special training and were therefore conducted only by specialists or librarians. Users had to provide the specialist with their specific information requirements, and information retrieved had to be passed back to them. This process is reminiscent of the early days of computers, when the user had to bring a bunch of punched cards to a computer operator who fed the cards into the computer for compilation and execution, and returned the program's output to the user. Sometimes a minute programming error required a complete examination of the cards and a rerun of the program. This was an awkward scenario, where the user was separated from the tool. Between the two often stood someone who understandably had little appreciation of the requester's exact requirements.

The development of personal computers and local network systems made a significant impact on information retrieval and changed this awkward scenario of separating the user from the tool. It enabled users to access directly databases from different computers rather than from the ones designated through the local computer network. From there, it was a short step for information retrieval from embracing the arrival of the Internet to where information retrieval became an interactive operation for anyone connected online. Here, little training or experience is required from users, yet the user expects continuous improvement in the accuracy, completeness, efficiency and quality of information retrieved. There is no doubt that information retrieval as a technology is facing a revival, together with new challenges.

The Internet has dramatically increased the rate of usage of databases and information retrieval. This on its own poses a challenge to the efficiency of information retrieval. Many online databases hold records containing mainly natural language terms, and many words contained in them may have different meanings in engineering and science from those used in other fields. This imposes significant vagueness or imprecision on keyword searches. A challenge like this helps to nourish new developments in information retrieval.

Traditional information retrieval was largely conducted only on document abstracts, ensuring that items were retrieved efficiently and in a uniform format. In fact, often relevant abstracts can be presented to the searcher without further explanation. However, the Internet's revolutionary capacity is accompanied by a growing demand for full document retrieval. This also poses a new task on retrieving information online. While searching on full documents is likely to retrieve more information, it may also generate imprecise results. This is because words frequently occurring in a document may not really represent the gist of the document. For instance, an article on J S Bach's music may frequently use the terms 'modal' and 'analysis', but it is completely alien to the modal analysis technology known to structural engineers.

For an Internet user seeking information within 'cyberspace', an understanding of the different information retrieval technologies used by various online databases is desirable but not essential. Instead, the relevance of retrieved information depends on quality. So it is essential that you have some basic understanding of information retrieval in order to refine a search query in such a way that the usefulness of the retrieved information can be maximised for each search.

Hypertext

The rapid growth of the Internet can be largely attributed to the development and availability of hypertext and hypermedia software. Hypertext was originally perceived as a body of written or graphic materials interconnected in a complex way that could not be conveniently represented on paper. Nowadays it can be broadly defined as 'an approach to information management in which data is stored in a network of nodes connected by links.' In other words, hypertext means nodes connected by a network of links.

A node is a fundamental unit of information in a hypertext document. It can be text, a graphic, an animation clip, a piece of audio signal, a video sequence, source codes or other forms of data and a combination of them. A node may also contain other nodes or links that point to more nodes. An aggregation mechanism can be applied in hypertext so that a composite node manages a collection of nodes. And so the web spreads. Sometimes a node may have several links, each associated with a component of the node. These components are also referred to as 'anchors' of that node; they help navigate the hypertext network.

A hypertext link is a logical connection between an 'origin node' (also known as the 'reference') from which a logical connection emanates, and a 'destination node' (also known as the 'referent') where the connection ends. Each link in hypertext constitutes a possible exploration path. A link can be either 'referential' for cross-referencing purposes or 'hierarchical' for parent-child dependence. A link can be explicit or implicit. An explicit link is an author-made connection between two nodes. An implicit link is one that is not visible: it can be activated using a word present in a node, and is not specifically created during the composition of a hypertext document. A network of links constitutes the only structure you can use to navigate in the hypertext.

Hypertext with multimedia features is called 'hypermedia'. A 'hypertext system' is a configuration of hardware and software that presents a hypertext document to users and allows them to access the information it contains.

If those descriptions of hypertext and hypermedia are too technical, then it is enough simply to accept hypertext as a tool consisting of computer-supported links within a document and between remote documents. This linking ability is responsible for the revolutionary information flow on the Internet and, in particular, in Webspace.

The concept of hypertext is not new. Dictionaries and encyclopaedias can be seen as a form of hypertext, and are indeed a network of textual nodes joined by referential links. Computer users have always been exposed to hypertext features: for example, PC users are probably familiar with Windows Help, an icon that you click on to get to the Help page. Within the Help page, coloured words link you further to specific help items—all this can be seen as a form of hypertext. Macintosh users have been acquainted with hypercards years before hypertext appeared on other computer platforms. However, today's hypertext system seen on the Internet is far more sophisticated. Because of its capacity to link and manage information, it can be seen as a database system that provides an original way of accessing and managing data. This database system technically provides a totally unrestricted way of accessing information without a regulated structure, thus giving you a free hand to explore and disseminate information.

To navigate in a hypertext document, you need a special software tool to activate links and follow paths. This tool should also be capable of dealing with different forms of data embedded in a hypertext file. Such a tool is called a 'browser'. In Chapter 3, some commonly used browsers will be discussed. Of course a browser can only activate any links that already exist in the hypertext file, whether explicit or implicit. For example, searching on the Internet for a specified word or string results in a number of links that contain the search query but were not explicitly designed when the hypertext document was being written.

Online training and learning

The Internet has brought a new era to education and learning. It is an excellent medium for storing and disseminating information, course materials and teaching materials, and for conducting discussions and tutorials. For learning how to use the Internet itself, there are

Introduction to the Internet

EFF's Guide to the Internet
http://uu-gna.mit.edu:8001/uu-gna/text/netguide/ng_cont.html

Explore the Internet (Library of Congress)
http://lcweb.loc.gov/global/

Index on We May 28
http://www.csci.csusb.edu:80/doc/

Internet Beginner's Guide from Yahoo!
http://www.yahoo.com/Computers_and_Internet/Internet/Information_and_Documentati
on/Beginner_s_Guides/

Internet Learner's Page
http://www.clark.net/pub/lschank/web/learn.html

An Internet Tutorial
http://www.msn.com/tutorial/default.html

IPL Education Documents
http://ipl.sils.umich.edu/classroom/userdocs/userdocs.html

Rob's Tutorials and Links for Newbies
http://www.mindspring.com/~icarus1/newbies.html

Teaching Students to Think Critically About Internet Resources
http://weber.u.washington.edu/~libr560/NETEVAL/index.html

Introduction to the WWW

The Internet Text Project
http://uu-gna.mit.edu:8001/uu-gna/text/internet/notes/index.html

Introduction to the Internet and WWW
http://www.c3.lanl.gov/village/WWW-intro.html

An Introduction to the World-Wide Web
http://www.man.ac.uk/MVC//SIMA/WWW/introwww.html

A Little History of the WWW
http://www.w3.org/pub/WWW/History.html

LOCAL Foilset Introduction to World Wide Web (WWW)
http://www.npac.syr.edu/users/gcf/ecs400spring96/ecs400www/fullhtml.html

WWW Introduction
http://www.robelle.com/www-paper/intro.html

WWW—Introduction, Resources and References
http://mthwww.uwc.edu/wwwmahes/wwwrefs.htm

The Internet and engineering

CORE Industrial Design Network
http://www.core77.com/

Edinburgh Engineering Virtual Library
http://www.eevl.ac.uk/

Industry.Net
http://www.industry.net/

Internet Connections for Engineering
http://www.englib.cornell.edu/ice/ice-index.html

Internet Help Page
http://www.ai.org/other/inhelp.html

Penn Library-Engineering
http://www.library.upenn.edu/resources/sciences/engineering/engin.html

Resources of Scholarly Societies—Mechanical Engineering
http://www.lib.uwaterloo.ca/society/mecheng_soc.html

The WWW Virtual Library Engineering
http://arioch.gsfc.nasa.gov/wwwvl/engineering.html

Internet online help

Helix Help
http://204.244.109.2/sub/help1.html

Internet Help!
http://ftlauderdale.vcn.net/lifegrd/lifegrd.html

Internet Help Page
http://www.ai.org/other/inhelp.html

Internet Help Page
http://www.voyager.net/msms/help.html

Internet Resources
http://www.brandonu.ca/~ennsnr/Resources/

The Internet Services List
http://www.spectracom.com/islist/

WebCrawler Internet Guide
http://www.webcrawler.com/select/internet.iug.html

Yahoo! Internet Life
http://www3.zdnet.com/yil/filters/surfjump.html

Table 1-1 Introduction to the WWW—some resources

CHAPTER
1

numerous teaching aids available online. In the bibliography at the end of this Chapter, you can find a short list of Web sites that offer online documentation on the Internet and the Web. These sites, and many more, provide general help to new and regular users alike. Many other Web sites also offer help on specific topics. An effective way of locating the Web sites for a chosen topic is to use Web search engines. After the introduction to Web search engines in Chapter 4, try locating online learning resources on the Internet.

Because of the rapid development of technology and information providers, some online information about the Internet may be updated frequently, so it is advisable to refresh your knowledge by consciously revisiting online resources. Table 1-1 provides some useful resources for specific topics, your first stop in your exploration of the Internet.

Bibliography

BrowserWatch
http://browserwatch.internet.com/

FAQs about FAQs
http://www.lib.ox.ac.uk/internet/news/faq/archive/faqs.about-faqs.html

Free Internet Guide
http://www.freenetguide.com/

A Guide to Cyberspace
http://www.hcc.hawaii.edu/guide/www.guide.html

Internet Domain Survey
http://www.nw.com/zone/WWW/top.html

Internet Related Magazines
http://www.sau.edu/CWIS/Internet/Wild/Internet/Journals/jnindex.htm

Internet Starter
http://www.glink.net.hk/~yhhui/

Internet Starter Kit Slip/PPP Internet Access
http://www.bayon.com/cstar/online/gconnect.htm

Internet Training Manual

http://clinfo.rockefeller.edu/manual/index.html

Learn the Net

http://www.learnthenet.com/english/index.html

Visionary Help Page

http://www.vcn.com/help.html

**Don't forget to visit us at
http://dingo.vut.edu.au/~jimin/book.html**

CHAPTER

1

CHAPTER

2

Getting Started

What is a URL?

Try a URL site

Text browsing

What next?

In Chapter 1, we covered several aspects of the Internet in a rudimentary way. With that basic background, we should be ready to start exploring the Internet on an Internet-connected computer. However, before doing that, we still need to learn some Internet jargon and technical terms.

Because the World Wide Web has become the standard platform for the Internet, wherever possible examples of accessing Internet are shown in this book using a Web browser. In the past, there were many types of 'client software', each enabling Internet connection to a particular protocol. Nowadays, since all protocols have their 'gateways' on the Web, the days of using specialised client software for individual protocols are fast fading away.

What is a URL?

URL stands for 'Uniform Resource Locator'. A URL represents hypermedia links or links to the Internet resources, and is in effect the Web address for any document or object on the Internet. URLs can represent nearly all files and resources on the Internet. Not only can it point to a file in a directory, but that file and directory can exist on any machine on the Internet. A URL looks like this:

file://fits.cv.nrao.edu/fits/traffic/scidataformats/faq.html
ftp://wuarchive.wustl.edu/
gopher://gopher.ncsa.uiuc.edu:70/1
http://www.yahoo.com/
news:alt.hypertext
telnet://www.lib.muohio.edu:8013

A URL is written or keyed as a single unbroken line, with no spaces, and consists of two parts. The first part of the URL, before the colon, specifies the access method (such as FTP or HTTP, explained later). The second part, after the colon, is the computer server's name together with the hierarchy of its directories and files. It may also contain specifications of the 'port' (network connection) to connect to:

Access method:	**telnet://**
Computer server:	**www.lib.muohio.edu**
Connection port:	**:8013**

The name of the Computer server follows a 'DNS' (Domain Name System). With a DNS, a template of structures of names can be clearly defined. In the example above, **www.lib.muohio.edu** is the sub-domain name and **edu** is the domain name of the computer server at the University of Ohio, USA.

FTP URLs

FTP (File Transfer Protocol) is a standard protocol for transferring information between computers on the Internet. It is most commonly used to download files that have been made publicly accessible on so-called 'anonymous FTP archives'. FTP can also be used to transfer secured information from and to other machines with protected access. An FTP URL looks like this:

ftp://ftp.doc.ic.ac.uk/

Not all the directories on an FTP server are open for public access. However, you can explore any directory without deliberately trying to decode the security of the server.

File URLs

A file URL points to a particular file or document on the Internet. Suppose there is a document called 'README' and it resides at an anonymous FTP server called **ftp.cica.indiana.edu** in directory **/pub/pc/win95**. The URL for this file is then:

file://ftp.cica.indiana.edu/pub/pc/win95/readme

Many FTP servers have a directory called **/pub** that is available for the public to visit. However, not all directories on the server are accessible by remote anonymous users. Users from different time zones need to be aware that some servers impose restrictions on access time.

Gopher URLs

The Internet Gopher is a distributed document archive and retrieval system. It combines the best features of browsing through collections of information and fully indexed databases. Gopher is a client/server protocol and it permits users on a heterogeneous mix of desktop systems to browse, search, and retrieve documents residing on multiple distributed server machines. Gopher URLs are similar to file URLs. For example, to visit a particular Gopher server on **veronica.scs.unr.edu**, use this URL:

gopher://veronica.scs.unr.edu/

However, Gopher servers may sometimes reside on unusual network connections on their host machines. The default Gopher port number is 70, so if you know that the Gopher server on the machine **mudhoney.micro.umn.edu** is on port 4326 instead of port 70, then the corresponding URL would be:

gopher://mudhoney.micro.umn.edu:4326/7

Telnet URLs

Telnet is a classic service that allows a network user on one computer to log onto a computer in a distant location in order to utilise its software programs or data files. Telnet was one of the first tools built by the architects of the Internet so that they could share software and research results more easily. One of the most common uses of Telnet today is accessing online library catalogues at universities or databases around the world. The standard network port number for Telnet is 23.

Once you have requested a connection to a Telnet site, your computer attempts to link you to a remote computer. This process may take a little time. If the Telnet site has a security system in operation, you need a password to log in. However, many Telnet sites are open to the public, and if you need a log-in name and password, the site will advise you at the beginning. A Telnet site URL commonly looks like:

telnet://ovid.unilinc.edu.au
or
telnet://www.lib.muohio.edu:8013

Some Telnet sites will disconnect you after a certain length of idle time.

News URLs

Usenet is a worldwide distributed discussion system. It consists of a set of 'newsgroups' with names that are classified hierarchically by subjects. Usenet is also a collection of computers that allow users to exchange public messages on many different topics. People with appropriate software post articles to these newsgroups which are then broadcast to other interconnected computer systems via a wide variety of networks. They are intended for public discussions rather than personal communication. There are thousands of newsgroups on Usenet. For example, to connect to Usenet newsgroup **aus.mathematics**, simply type the URL:

news:aus.mathematics

This assumes that you are connecting to newsgroups from your Internet service provider's news server. If such a server is unavailable, you can connect to a remote news server that is open for remote users, but your computer will take a little longer to respond to the server. The same newsgroup at a remote server called **news.intelinet.net** will then have a URL like:

news://news.intelinet.net/aus.mathematics

HTTP URLs

The Hypertext Transfer Protocol (HTTP) has been in use by the World Wide Web global information initiative since 1990, and is now the most commonly used protocol for serving hypertext documents. HTTP is an application-level protocol with the lightness and speed necessary for distributed and collaborative hypermedia information systems.

In computer science, object-oriented programming is a class of techniques based on the concept of a data structure ('object') encapsulated within a set of routines which operate on the data. HTTP is a generic, object-oriented protocol which can be used for many tasks. It is a very low-overhead protocol because it capitalises on the fact that Web navigation information can be embedded in hypertext documents directly. As a result, the protocol itself does not have to support full navigation features as the FTP and Gopher protocols do.

A typical HTTP URL is:

http://www.ic.ac.uk/

An HTTP URL address sometimes provides information beyond just the hypertext document it points to. For instance, the URL for the Australian WWW servers is **http://www.csu.edu.au/links/ozweb.html**. From there, you may descend in the hierarchy to explore **http://www.csu.edu.au/links/** and, likewise, **http://www.csu.edu.au/**.

A URL is normally associated with a hypertext file, except for those for Telnet. Some URL sites are attractively designed graphically, for example **http://www.zdnet.com/**. Others, especially those engineering- and technology-related sites, may not be full of gloss yet they are pragmatic. A URL can be a living address which may change or disappear without notice. Some of the URLs used in this book may be obsolete by the time you read this text. There are also many useful URLs that are created by individuals; these usually disappear when the authors leave their jobs or finish their degrees. If a URL is of particular interest to you, then you can store the hypertext file associated with the URL on your computer, so long as you do not breach copyright.

Try a URL site

Different protocols on the Internet have different client software. For instance, there are a number of client software packages for Gopher which are tailor-made to interface with Gopher servers on the Internet, and also provide customised catalogues for them. However, by far the most popular and efficient method for exploring the whole

Gopher data retrieval system, known as 'Gopherspace', is to use a WWW browser. Thanks to the WWW gateways available for various protocols, a WWW browser can now access almost any Internet protocols.

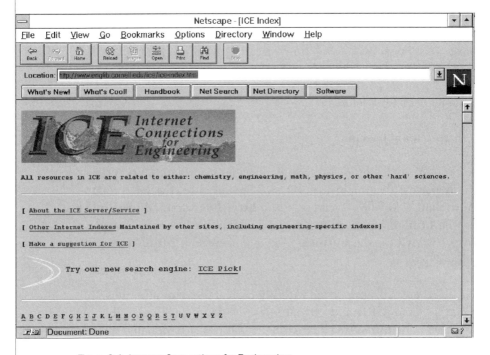

Figure 2.1. Internet Connections for Enginnering

Assume you already have a WWW browser such as Netscape. (A detailed discussion of browsers will be presented in Chapter 3.) Let's connect to a URL site called 'The Internet Connections for Engineering' at Cornell University in the USA. The URL address is **http://www.englib.cornell.edu/ice/ice-index.html** (Figure 2.1).

There is only space here to show you part of the document. Other hypertext documents used in this book may also be only partially shown, but when you view them from your computer screen you can scroll the page up and down to read the complete document.

The convention on the Internet is to display blue text to indicate hypertext links (although some documents use different colours for

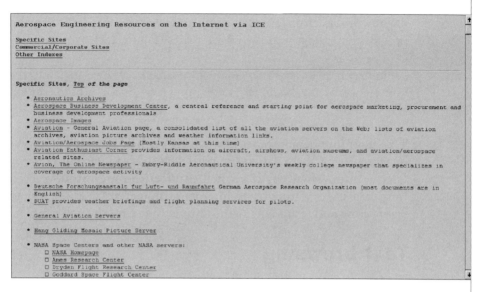

```
Aerospace Engineering Resources on the Internet via ICE

Specific Sites
Commercial/Corporate Sites
Other Indexes


Specific Sites, Top of the page
    * Aeronautics Archives
    * Aerospace Business Development Center, a central reference and starting point for aerospace marketing, procurement and
      business development professionals
    * Aerospace Images
    * Aviation - General Aviation page, a consolidated list of all the aviation servers on the Web; lists of aviation
      archives, aviation picture archives and weather information links.
    * Aviation/Aerospace Jobs Page (Mostly Kansas at this time)
    * Aviation Enthusiast Corner provides information on aircraft, airshows, aviation museums, and aviation/aerospace
      related sites.
    * Avion, The Online Newspaper - Embry-Riddle Aeronautical University's weekly college newspaper that specializes in
      coverage of aerospace activity

    * Deutsche Forschungsanstalt fur Luft- und Raumfahrt German Aerospace Research Organization (most documents are in
      English)
    * DUAT provides weather briefings and flight planning services for pilots.

    * General Aviation Servers

    * Hang Gliding Mosaic Picture Server

    * NASA Space Centers and other NASA servers:
        □ NASA Homepage
        □ Ames Research Center
        □ Dryden Flight Research Center
        □ Goddard Space Flight Center
```

Figure 2.2 A subpage of' 'Internet Connections for Engineering'

this). When you click on the coloured text, the system takes you directly to a new URL site. For instance, scroll down the 'Internet Connections for Engineering' Web page and click on the blue text 'Aerospace Engineering & Aviation' —immediately you jump to a

Figure 2.3 The NASA home page

document for aerospace engineering and aviation, which in turn also provides hyperlinks to other relevant sites (Figure 2.2).

From here let's choose the 'NASA Homepage', and we are led to the home page of the National Aeronautics and Space Administration (Figure 2.3).

This short tour demonstrates how hyperlinks help to organise various documents and sites relating to a particular subject. Starting from the URL at **http://www.englib.cornell.edu/ice/ice-index.html**, you can 'surf' and search through the Internet at numerous sites relevant to engineering and technology—the limit is your curiosity and time.

Text browsing

Web browsers with a graphical interface such as Netscape enable you to view graphics in hypertext as well as text. This is made possible at the expense of additional time taken to download the document. However, there are also text-based browsers like Lynx that permit only text viewing. For some applications, text viewing is sufficient, such as conducting a full-text literature search on the Internet. Some hypertext documents advise you that there is a text-based counterparts. Usually, text viewing is much faster, since it avoids sometimes agonisingly slow loading of graphics. If a hypertext document has a text-only counterpart, you can also view this version with a graphical-interface Web browser, but it will often be a lot quicker.

What next?

Now that you have found and viewed some interesting engineering sites, you may want to record this information for future reference. Many WWW browsers allow you to store a URL address as a 'bookmark' in a file of useful URLs. If you are concerned about losing the bookmark in the event of computer power blackout, you should create one yourself and store URL information there. A bookmark file can be just a simple text file, and is good practice for keeping track of URLs. Moreover, it will be the first step towards creating your own hypertext documents and, better still, your own WWW home page.

Mastery of one good WWW browser such as Netscape is essential for effective use of the WWW. In the next chapter, we will introduce some famous WWW browsers available on the Internet, along with the Web locations for downloading them. Although there are numerous client programs for particular Internet domains such as for Gopher, WAIS, FTP, etc., the best and most convenient way is to use a versatile Web browser to accommodate all protocols. This not only brings you the full graphics impact of the Internet, but also saves you the extraordinary amount of time and considerable computer resources required to learn and install different client programs.

Bibliography

BrowserWatch
http://browserwatch.internet.com/

Getting started on the Internet
http://www.j51.com:80/internet/newbie.html

Guide to Usenet
http://www.glink.net.hk/GuideToUsenet.html

The Internet
http://www.lib.ox.ac.uk/internet/

Internet Starter
http://www.glink.net.hk/~yhhui/

Internet Starter Kit Slip/PPP Internet Access
http://www.bayon.com/cstar/online/gconnect.htm

Internet Training Manual
http://clinfo.rockefeller.edu/manual/index.html

Starting Points for Internet Exploration
http://www.ncsa.uiuc.edu/SDG/Software/Mosaic/StartingPoints/
NetworkStartingPoints.html

**Don't forget to visit us at
http://dingo.vut.edu.au/~jimin/book.html**

CHAPTER

2

CHAPTER

3

Internet Search Tools

WWW browsers

Gopher

Gopher searchers: Veronica and Jughead

Archie

HyTelnet

WAIS

Differences between WWW, Gopher and WAIS

WWW browsers

By far the most popular means of using the Internet nowadays is by using the World Wide Web. Any Internet connection protocols such as FTP and Gopher can be accessed from the Web. To use it, you have three options:

- use a Web browser on your own machine (the best option)
- use a browser that can be remotely accessed (not as good)
- access the Web by email (the least attractive, but for some with less sophisticated hardware it may be the only option).

It is always best to run a browser on your own machine rather than one accessed via a network. Most browsers offer access to a number of different types of non-WWW servers, too. These include, but are not limited to, FTP, Gopher, WAIS, email, Telnet and newsgroups.

To use World Wide Web efficiently, you need a good browser. There are hundreds of them in use today, the most popular being Netscape Navigator.

Netscape Navigator

Netscape Navigator is a Web browser from Netscape Communications that facilitates the retrieval and viewing of World Wide Web multimedia documents. It was designed to provide the highest Web navigation performance and ease of use. Netscape Navigator features:

- progressive rendering, allowing for simultaneous text and image downloading
- native in-line JPEG, GIF and XBM image support
- scrolling with continuous display of documents as they load
- multiple independent windows
- Usenet/NNTP interface.

It is available for PC, Macintosh and Unix platforms. Netscape Navigator is highly recommended. In this book, we use Netscape Navigator in all examples. If you are not familiar with Netscape Navigator, there is a tutorial on the Web at **http://home.netscape.com/eng/mozilla/1.1/handbook/index.html**.

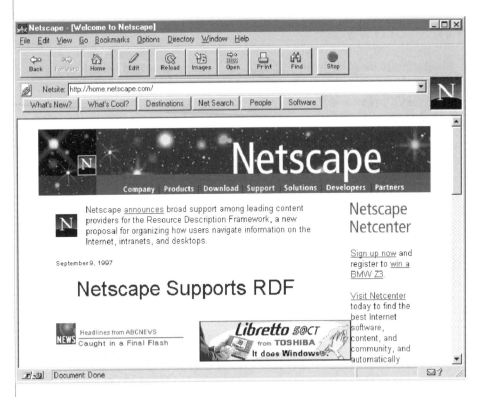

Figure 3.1 Netscape home page

Internet Explorer

Internet Explorer is the World Wide Web browser offered by Microsoft. It was designed specifically for Windows 95, but works with earlier operating systems. Internet Explorer is compatible with nearly all the Internet protocols on the Web today and appears to be powerful enough to be the browser of choice for the most demanding Web surfers. The prominence of Internet Explorer will ride on the popularity of the Windows 95 operating system.

NCSA Mosaic

NCSA Mosaic was developed at the National Center for Supercomputing Applications (NCSA) at the University of Illinois in Urbana-Champaign. As the first browser to bring a graphical, point-and-click interface to the Web, it once became almost synonymous with it. There are different versions of Mosaic for

Figure 3.2 Internet Explorer home page

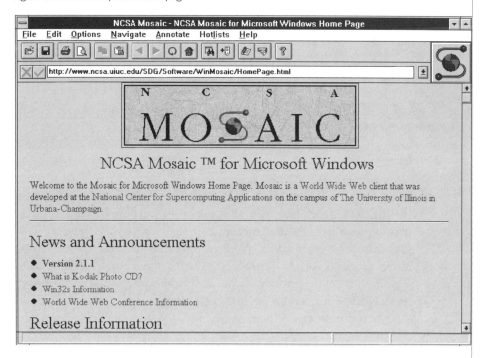

Figure 3.3 Mosaic home page

different platforms: PC, MacIntosh and Unix. However, NCSA recently decided to cease continuous development, and as a result its early popularity has begun to wane.

Cello

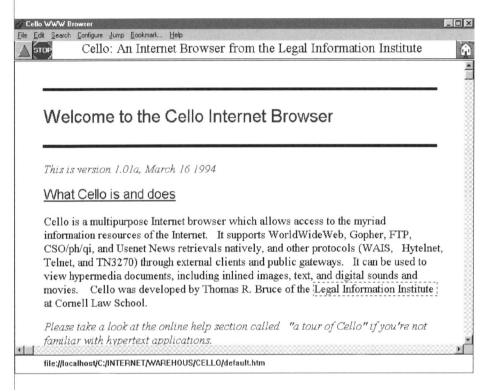

Figure 3.4 Cello home page

Cello was developed by Thomas R. Bruce of the Legal Information Institute at Cornell Law School. It is a multi-purpose Internet browser that allows access to the Internet's myriad information resources. It supports the World Wide Web, Gopher, FTP, and Usenet News retrievals, and other protocols (WAIS, HyTelnet, Telnet, and TN3270) through external clients and public gateways. It can be used to view hypermedia documents, including images, text, and digital sounds and movies.

WinWeb and MacWeb

WinWeb and MacWeb are fully featured World Wide Web browsers for Windows and the Macintosh respectively. Both were created by TradeWave. Recently, the distribution of these browsers has become restricted.

WebSurfer

Figure 3.5 WebSurfer home page

WebSurfer is a World Wide Web client application developed by NetManage. It provides high performance on LANs using multiple connections, while also allowing deferred image retrieval for fast performance on dial-up connections. The many user-definable parameters let you customise its look and operation.

Lynx

Lynx is a fully featured World Wide Web browser for users on both Unix and VMS platforms who are connected to those systems via cursor-addressable, character-cell terminals or emulators. That includes VT100 terminals and desktop-based software packages emulating VT100 terminals (such as Kermit or Procomm). Being a text-based Web browser, no graphics are visible when running Lynx. A number of Internet sites have text-only versions of their hypermedia documents, designed to cater for such text-based browsers. Since graphics take a long time to download, you can save a considerable amount of time by using a text-based browser.

Alternatively, if you are using a graphical browser, you can turn graphics off for a speedy download of hypermedia documents. In this case, only the text part of the documents is displayed and the information on your screen may be incomplete.

DosLynx

DosLynx is a text-based browser for use only on DOS systems. If your PC has an Ethernet connection, or you have SLIP connection, you should be able to use DosLynx. You can get details from the README.HTM file at the DosLynx site at **ftp://ftp2.cc.ukans.edu/ pub/WWW/DosLynx/**, and download DosLynx from the anonymous FTP server at **ftp2.cc.ukans.edu** in the directory **pub/WWW/DosLynx**.

Browsers compared

Table 3-1 summarises the commonly used WWW browsers and shows their origin and the platforms upon which they operate. You can find a complete list of WWW browsers available **http://browserwatch.internet.com/**.

Gopher

Gopher is a menu-driven computer interface on the Internet that allows users to access a large number of resources stored on the Internet. It is based on a 'client/server architecture', where the user's

Browser, company and Internet address

Arena (W3C)
http://www.w3.org/hypertext/WWW/Arena/
Windows, Macintosh and Unix

Cello (Thomas Bruce, Cornell Law School)
http://www.law.cornell.edu/cello/
Windows

HotJava (Sun Mircosystems)
http://java.sun.com/
Windows, Macintosh and Unix

Internet Explorer (Microsoft)
http://www.microsoft.com/ie/
Windows and Macintosh

Lynx (University of Kansas)
http://kuhttp.cc.ukans.edu/about_lynx/
Unix

MacWeb (EINet)
http://www.einet.net/EINet/MacWeb/MacWebHome.html
Macintosh

NCSA Mosaic (NCSA, University of Illinois)
http://www.ncsa.uiuc.edu/
Windows, Macintosh and Unix

Netscape Navigator (Netscape Communications)
http://www.netscape.com/home/welcome.html
Windows, Macintosh and Unix

Web Explorer (IBM)
http://www.ibm.net/support/web.html
Unix

WebSurfer (NetManage)
http://www.netmanage.com/netmanage/apps/websurfer.html
Windows and Macintosh

WinWeb (EINet)
http://www.einet.net/EINet/WinWeb/WinWebHome.html
Windows

Table 3-1 Some useful Web browsers

computer (the client) retrieves information from a resource host (the server) such as an FTP archive or a Web site. This provides a distributed information delivery system upon which a world information system (CWIS) can readily be constructed. While providing a delivery vehicle for local information, Gopher facilitates access to other Gopher and information servers throughout the world.

Gopher servers accommodate text and graphics. Many offer a large selection of services and files, and the contents of Gopher servers are often searchable. There are over one thousand registered Gopher servers and computer sites where information is made available through Gopher. More will undoubtedly be added to the Internet in the future.

Since Gopher caters for a simple client/server protocol, it can be conveniently used to publish and search for information held on a distributed network of hosts. Gopher clients have a seamless view of the information in Gopherspace, even though the information is distributed over many different hosts. Clients can either navigate through a hierarchy of directories and documents or ask an index server to return a list of all documents that contain one or more words. Since the index server performs full-text searches, every word in every document is a keyword.

Gopher was originally developed in April 1991 by the University of Minnesota Microcomputer, Workstation, Networks Center to help the University campus find answers to their computer questions. (Gopher, the animal, is a native inhabitant of Minnesota—the 'Gopher State'.) It has since grown into a fully fledged world-wide information system used by a large number of sites throughout the world.

To run Gopher, you may use a Gopher 'client' program that runs on your local PC, Macintosh or workstation. There are clients for Unix Curses & Emacs, Xwindows, Macintosh, DOS, and Windows. A client uses the custom features of the local machine (mouse, scroll bars, etc.) to ensure speedy and friendly operation. There are a number of Gopher client programs available on the Internet, and in the next chapter we will show you how to search for them. The main advantage of these client programs is that they usually offer an impressive list of excellent Gopher servers. Gopher can also be run remotely; there are a

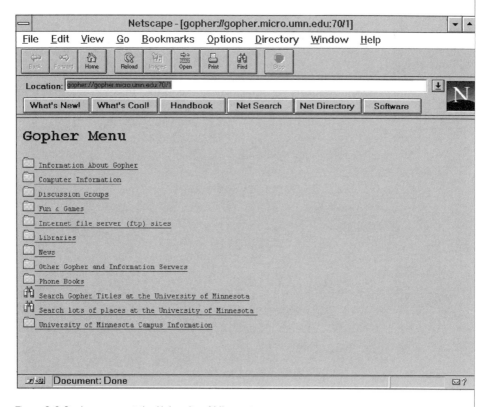

Figure 3.6 Gopher server at the University of Minnesota

number of public Telnet log-in sites available for this. The University of Minnesota operates one on the machine **gopher://consultant. micro.umn.edu**.

The most convenient way to connect to a Gopher server is to use a Web browser like Netscape Navigator. As long as you know the URL address of a Gopher server, you can use your Web browser to interface fully with the server without the aid of other programs. Of course, you have to configure it correctly so that it is able to 'talk' to a Gopher server. Figure 3.6 illustrates using Netscape Navigator to connect to the Gopher server **gopher://gopher.micro.umn.edu:70/1** at the University of Minnesota, the birthplace of Gopher.

There are currently over 6000 Gopher servers on the Internet, and the number is increasing. A good collection of Gopher servers can be

CHAPTER
3

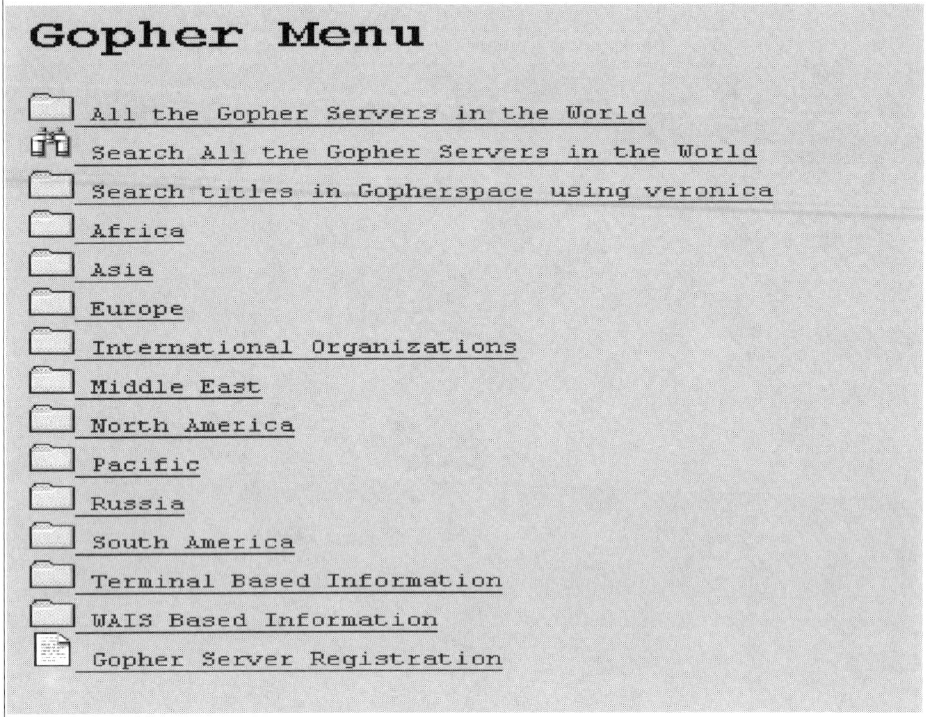

Gopher Menu

- All the Gopher Servers in the World
- Search All the Gopher Servers in the World
- Search titles in Gopherspace using veronica
- Africa
- Asia
- Europe
- International Organizations
- Middle East
- North America
- Pacific
- Russia
- South America
- Terminal Based Information
- WAIS Based Information
- Gopher Server Registration

Figure 3.7 Directory of the Gopher servers

found from the 'Other Gopher and information services' directory of the Gopher server at the University of Minnesota (Figure 3.7).

You can get online help on Gopher from numerous documents on the Internet. A good place to start is the document 'Frequently Asked Questions About Gopher', prepared by the University of Minnesota at its Gopher server at **gopher://mudhoney.micro.umn.edu:70/00/ Gopher.FAQ**.

Gopher searchers: Veronica and Jughead

Although most Gopher servers are mainly information pools, there are others that provide services for searching information through Gopherspace, 'Gopher searchers'. Veronica is the most famous Gopher searcher; the developers would have us believe that the name stands for 'Very Easy Rodent-Oriented Net-wide Index to

Computerized Archives', but, like 'Jughead', it complements the tool 'Archie' discussed below. Developed by Steve Foster and Fred Barrie at the University of Nevada Reno and launched in 1992, it offers a keyword search of most Gopher server menus in the whole of Gopherspace. The search results will connect you directly to the data sources. Veronica can be accessed through a Gopher client or a WWW browser like Netscape Navigator. In either case, it gives access to all types of data supported by the Gopher protocol.

Gopherspace is like a huge electronic library that needs a workable indexing and catalogue system. Without a searcher, it would be fruitless for the user to rummage though the space to locate the information wanted. This problem is compounded by Gopherspace's phenomenal increase in volume. Designed as a response to the problem of resource retrieval in the rapidly expanding Gopherspace, Veronica provides an effective means of finding resources through almost the whole of Gopherspace without having to know their Internet locations.

The result of a Veronica search is an automatically generated Gopher menu, customised according to the user's keyword specification. Items on this menu may be drawn from hundreds of Gopher servers, all registered with the Veronica server. These items are functional Gopher items, immediately accessible via a Gopher client or a WWW browser. You can double-click them using a computer mouse to open directories, read files, or perform other searches. You need never know which server is actually involved in filling your request for information. Items that appear to be particularly interesting can be saved in your bookmark list.

In the light of the vast scale of documents and files in Gopherspace, it is impractical for Veronica to perform full-text searches. Instead, it finds resources by searching for words in the titles of the resources as they appear on the menu of their home Gopherservers. The Veronica index contains about 10 million items from approximately 5500 Gopher servers, and new Gopher sites are constantly added to Veronica's index list.

To access Veronica, you can select it from the 'Other Gophers' menu on Minnesota's Gopher server, shown in Figure 3.8. Alternatively, you can use Netscape Navigator to connect to the Gopher server of the

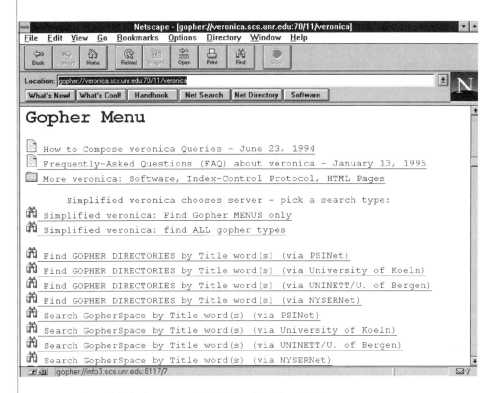

Figure 3.8 Gopher server at the University of Nevada Reno

University of Nevada Reno at **gopher://veronica.scs.unr.edu:70/11/veronica**.

Like many Veronica servers, this one offers a number of Veronica server sites. You can choose which one to use, but different Veronica servers do not give you exactly the same search results, since their indexes are not updated at the same time. Some servers will return the search results faster than others, depending on the load and network traffic.

Veronica supports Boolean operators. Using these operators together with keywords will greatly enhance its performance. If you type in more than one keyword (separated by a space) without Boolean operators, Veronica assumes there is an 'and' between them. If the search's response is 'Too many connections, try again soon', change to a different Veronica server or try again later.

To be efficient and swift, Veronica offers two types of predefined searches: 'Search Gopherspace by keywords in titles; and 'Search Gopher directories only for keywords in titles'. The first type of search will find resources whose titles contain the keywords you specified. They may be of any Gopher data type, such as ASCII documents, Gopher directories, image files, binary files, etc. The second type will find only Gopher directories whose titles contain the specified keywords. This search can be very useful for finding only major holdings of information that relate to your query. After Veronica finds the Gopher directories, you can open any of them to view the contents in more detail. This avoids generating an overwhelming list of search results.

Most Veronica servers will deliver only the first 200 items that match your query. For instance, if you use the Veronica server at the University of Cologne in Germany **gopher://veronica.uni-koeln.de: 2347/7** to search for the keyword 'engineering', you will be not only presented with first 200 items but also be told that there are altogether some 20 000 items found.

You can define the number of items by including the command '-mX' in your query, replacing. X with the number of items you wish to

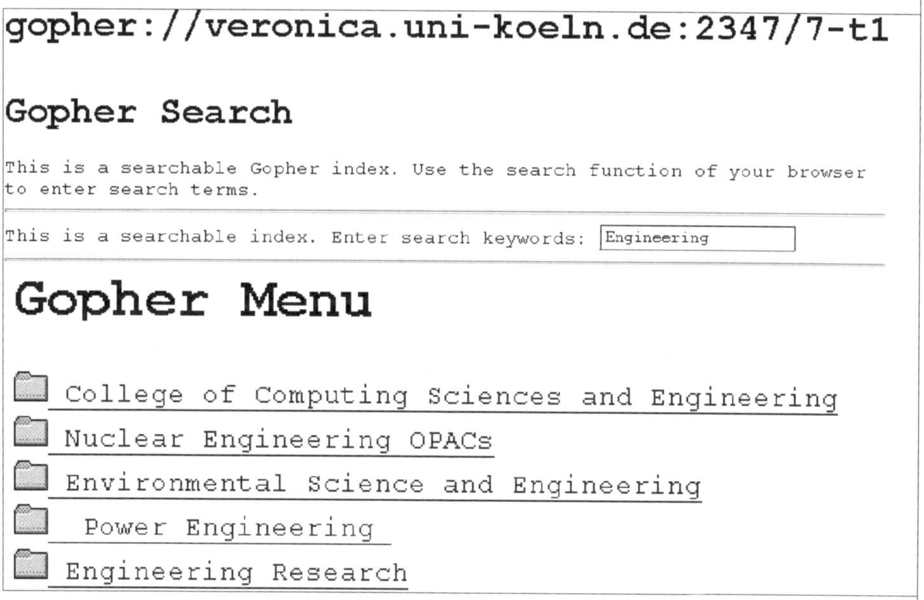

```
gopher://veronica.uni-koeln.de:2347/7-t1
```

Gopher Search

This is a searchable Gopher index. Use the search function of your browser to enter search terms.

This is a searchable index. Enter search keywords: `Engineering`

Gopher Menu

📁 College of Computing Sciences and Engineering
📁 Nuclear Engineering OPACs
📁 Environmental Science and Engineering
📁   Power Engineering
📁 Engineering Research

Figure 3.9 Search Results from Veronica server at the University of Cologne

retrieve. If you omit the number, there is no limit to the number of items delivered. When searching a common keyword, this may mean a long wait to see the outcome of your search.

An advanced type of Veronica search is to add the Gopher resource type in the search string. Gopherspace offers the resource types listed in Table 3-1 in the Gopher document. For instance, using the search string 'engineering -tgI' will produce images (both GIF and non-GIF formats) which have 'engineering' in their titles.

Code and resource type	
0 Text file	**e** Event
1 Directory	**g** GIF image (Graphics Interchange Format)
4 Mac HQX file	**h** HTML (HyperText Markup Language)
5 PC binary	**I** Image (other than GIF)
7 Full text index (Gopher)	**M** MIME (Multipurpose Internet Mail Extension)
9 Binary file	**s** Sound
c Calendar	**T** TN3270 session (emulates an IBM 3270 terminal)

Table 3-2 Gopher resource types

A Web document titled 'How to compose Veronica queues' is available at **gopher://gopher.scs.unr.edu:70/hh/veronica/About/ how-to-query-veronica(html)**. It is an excellent online document for Veronica beginners, and was written by one of its two inventors, Steven Foster.

Jughead is another Gopherspace searcher for retrieving menu information from various Gopher servers. The name is allegedly an acronym for 'Jonzy's Universal Gopher Hierarchy Excavation And

Display'. Like Veronica, Jughead can be easily accessed using Netscape. The Jughead server at Washington & Lee University, USA where Jughead was developed, resides at **gopher:// logic.uc.wlu.edu:3002/7**.

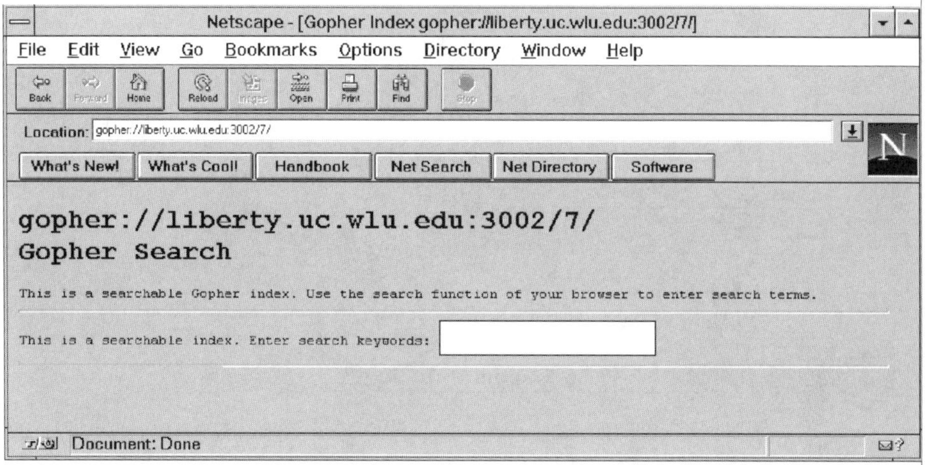

Figure 3.10 Jughead server at Washington & Lee University

There are many Jughead servers available on the Internet, and most of them can be located from the Gopher server. For instance, **gopher:// gopher.utah.edu:70/11/** will lead you to a good collection of Jughead servers. If one Jughead server is busy, choose another.

Like Veronica, Jughead searches Gopherspace. The difference is that its search is limited to directory entries and the top few levels of each Gopher. There are no text file links in Jughead, which means that it will produce a shorter list of search results than Veronica. However, once the search list is returned, you can further explore each directory by selecting its hyperlink. Jughead also supports Boolean operators in its search; moreover, you can use wildcard characters. For example, the search term 'VIBRAT' will result in a list of words beginning with 'vibrat'. The URL address for this search will be **gopher://logic.uc. wlu.edu:3002/7?vibrat**.

Jughead also supports some special commands, preceded by a question mark '?'. In Table 3-3, *xxx* stands for the string of characters you are searching for; *n* stands for a digit; and anything enclosed in square brackets is optional. All special commands must be preceded with '?'.

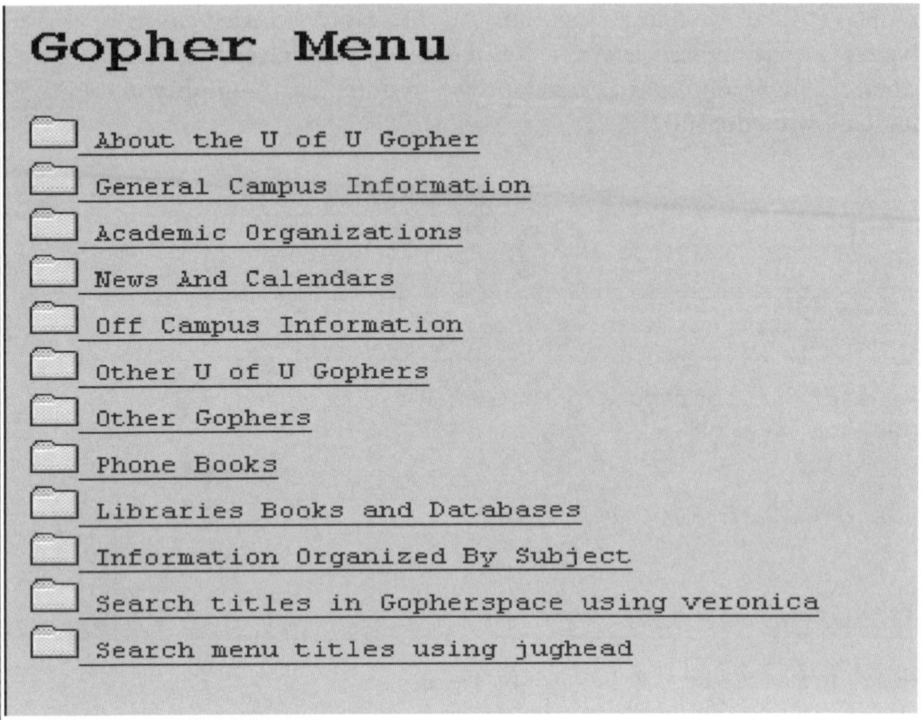

Gopher Menu

📁 About the U of U Gopher

📁 General Campus Information

📁 Academic Organizations

📁 News And Calendars

📁 Off Campus Information

📁 Other U of U Gophers

📁 Other Gophers

📁 Phone Books

📁 Libraries Books and Databases

📁 Information Organized By Subject

📁 Search titles in Gopherspace using veronica

📁 Search menu titles using jughead

Figure 3.11 Gopher server at Utah University

Commands and functions

?all xxx
Returns all the hits on the string *xxx*.

?help xxx
Provides documentation and any hits on the string *xxx*.

?limit=n xxx
Returns only *n* items on the string *xxx*.

?range=n1–n2
Returns items from *n1* through *n2*.

?version xxx
Tells you which version Jughead is being used and returns all hits on the string *xxx*.

Table 3-3 Jughead commands

Only one special command is supported per query, and if any syntax error is·encountered it is reported. For example, if you type '?help Jughead' you will receive a list of directories in Gopherspace related to Jughead online help.

Archie

Archie is a protocol for finding where files are located at anonymous FTP servers on the Internet, useful if you want to download a particular file, provided you know at least part of its name. Anonymous FTP archive sites offer software, data and other information that you can copy and use. For instance, you may want to find computer software for eigenvalue solutions. Using the keyword 'eigen', Archie will search and return you a list of computer programs whose file name or file descriptions contain the word 'eigen'. As Veronica is to Gopherspace, Archie is to FTP archives. The results of an Archie search are a list of file names that contain the search string, and their paths on the Internet.

The software for Archie was written by the Archie Group (Peter Deutsch, Alan Emtage, Bill Heelan, and Mike Parker) at McGill University in Montreal, Canada, who also maintain the Archie server's database at the University. Originally created to track the contents of anonymous FTP archive sites, the Archie service is now being expanded to include a variety of other online directories and resource listings. There are now numerous Archie servers on the Internet. An online technology company in the UK called Nexor UK has compiled a list of Archie servers which can be accessed from **http:// pubweb.nexor.co.uk/public/archie/servers.html**. Because Archie servers do not update their databases simultaneously, a search on different Archie servers often results in different search listings.

Like Gopher, Archie is available in three ways:

■ log-in to a remote Archie server: Telnet to the host **archie.mcgill.ca** and log in as user 'archie'
■ use a local Archie client program
■ use a WWW browser.

Logging in to a remote Archie server has become an outdated way to use it. A local client program usually provides a successful result. But the best way to use the Archie service is to use a Web browser.

Currently, Archie tracks the contents of over a thousand anonymous FTP archive sites containing several million files throughout the Internet. Collectively, these files represent well over 200 gigabytes of information, with more information being added daily. Using Archie, you can rapidly locate files that interest you. The Archie server automatically updates the listing information from each site regularly, ensuring that the information is always current. In addition to offering access to anonymous FTP listings, Archie also permits entry to the 'whatis' description database, a collection of names and brief synopses for over 3500 public domain software packages, datasets and informational documents available on the Internet.

The Archie search will return a list of files, some of which you may want to download to your computer. If you use Netscape Navigator,

Files to be retrieved as text (ASCII mode)

.asc Text file	**.shar** Packaged source files
.hqx Special MacIntosh format	**.txt** Text file
.ps PostScript file	

Files to be retrieved as binary

.arc DOS compressed	**.tar.Z** Unix archive and compressed
.exe DOS executable	**.tif** Graphics file
.gif Graphics file	**.Z** Unix compressed
.tar Unix archive	**.zip** DOS compressed
	.zoo Multi-platform compressed

Table 3-4 Archie file transfer—file name extensions

you can simply select a file on the screen and the hyperlink will activate the file transfer. If you use a client Archie program, it will connect you to an FTP client that enables file transfer. In this case, you may have to decide the mode of transfer: binary or ASCII text. Often, the file names should prompt you as to the type of file transfer you should use.

The downloaded files are usually compressed. To use them, you must uncompress them—you will find methods of uncompressing files in the Appendix.

Archie stores the names of files available for anonymous FTP and as a result, it searches the database using the name of the file. If you know the name of the file or program, then you can invoke an Archie search and obtain a list of relevant files with their geographical location. Often the file closest to you takes the least time to download. If you only know part of the filename, then Archie can still search for all files that contain that part in their names.

Archie also caters for case-sensitive searches. For instance, if you are searching for files related to TeX, then a case-sensitive search will return the files you want more rapidly. To ensure you get the latest files, Archie offers a search by date, where you specify a date and Archie returns only files created after that. A first-rate guide to Archie is provided by Suranet at **http://www.sura.net/archie/Archie-Usage. html#B2.0**.

ArchiePlex is the WWW gateway for Archie. It provides a form that you complete in order to call up a search. The form requires you to enter the search string and selections on the following items:

- type of search
- by host or by date
- impact on other users
- which Archie server to use.

In addition, you can restrict the results to a domain such as 'uk' and restrict the number of results. For a novice, many of these features are not immediately important. However, it is important to know that, for the same search string, different Archie servers may return different search results. Let's use Netscape Navigator to perform an Archie search on the term 'autocad'.

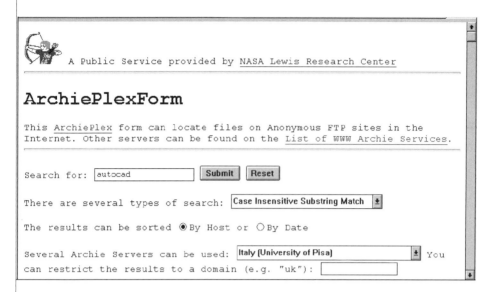

Figure 3.12 An Archie server accessed from Netscape Navigator

The ArchiePlex shown in Figure 3.13. is provided by the NASA Lewis Research Center at **http://www.lerc.nasa.gov/archieplex/doc/ form.html**. Our search uses the Archie server at the University of Pisa, Italy. It returns nearly 100 files with autocad on the file names; the first few are shown in Figure 3.13.

HyTelnet

We know that Telnet is a tool for linking a local computer to a remote one so that we can browse and retrieve information at the remote site. But how do we find the addresses of remote computers? HyTelnet was designed to act as the 'white pages' directory of the Telnet domain. HyTelnet is a tool created by Peter Scott at the University of Sasksatchewan, Canada, to assist users in reaching all of the Internet-accessible libraries, Free-nets, CWISs (Computer-Wide Information Systems), BBSs (Bulletin Board Systems) and other information sites connectable by Telnet. HyTelnet is available for IBM PC, Unix, VMS and Macintosh platforms. Some sites also make it available through their Gopher or WWW servers.

HyTelnet can be accessed by:

Figure 3.13 ArchiePlex at NASA'S Web page

- remote logging to a HyTelnet server (for example, go to access.usask.ca and log in as 'HyTelnet')
- running a local HyTelnet client program
- using a WWW HyTelnet server.

Using a WWW HyTelnet server is the recommended option. Table 3-2 lists some of the servers catering for Hytelnet searching on the WWW.

Using Netscape Navigator, we can link to the HyTelnet server at the University of Cambridge, shown in Figure 3.14.

If you select 'Search Hytelnet Data', this hyperlink leads to a HyTelnet search engine from where you can commence a HyTelnet search.

Name and Internet address

The server at Einet net
http://galaxy.einet.net/hytelnet/HYTELNET.html

The server at NOVA
http://www.nova.edu/Inter-Links/hytelnet/

The server at the University of Cambridge, UK
http://www.cam.ac.uk/Hytelnet/index.html

The server at the University of Saskatchewan, Canada
http://moondog.usask.ca:80/hytelnet/

Table 3-5 Some HyTelnet servers

Type in the keyword 'technology', and this HyTelnet server returns you some 50 sites containing the term 'technology' where HyTelnet service is offered—Figures 3.15 and 3.16.

On the list, click on 'Massachusetts Institute of Technology'. This leads you to the front page of the Telnet server at MIT—Figure 3.17.

From here, you can Telnet to the MIT library—Figure 3.18.

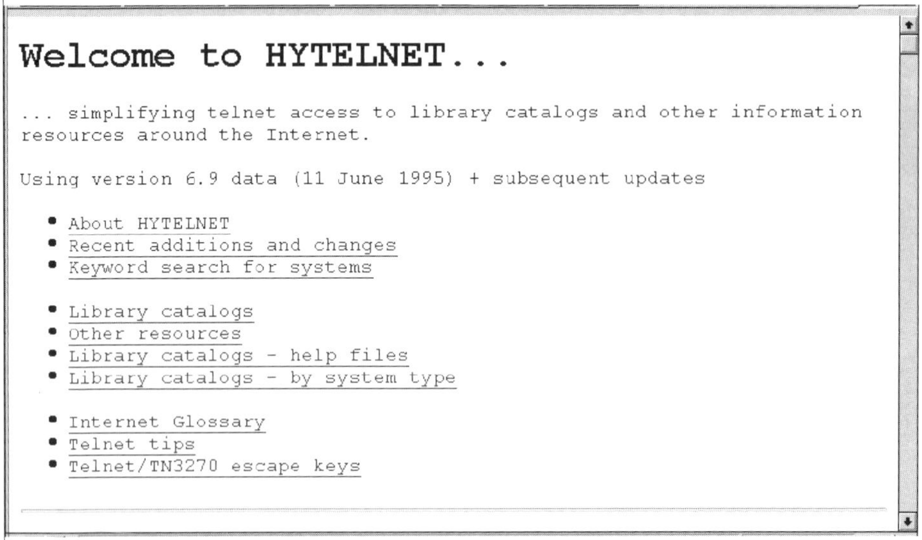

Welcome to HYTELNET...

```
... simplifying telnet access to library catalogs and other information
resources around the Internet.

Using version 6.9 data (11 June 1995) + subsequent updates

    • About HYTELNET
    • Recent additions and changes
    • Keyword search for systems

    • Library catalogs
    • Other resources
    • Library catalogs - help files
    • Library catalogs - by system type

    • Internet Glossary
    • Telnet tips
    • Telnet/TN3270 escape keys
```

Figure 3.14 HyTelnet server at the University of Cambridge

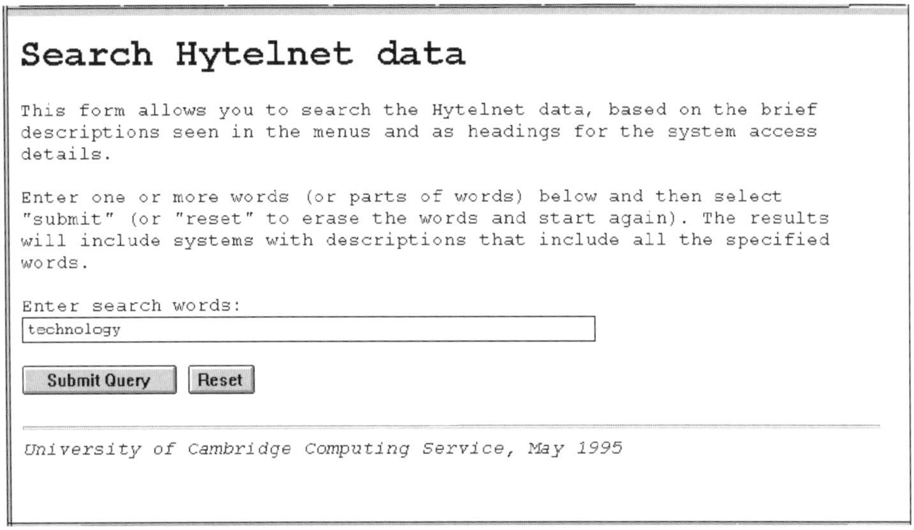

Search Hytelnet data

This form allows you to search the Hytelnet data, based on the brief
descriptions seen in the menus and as headings for the system access
details.

Enter one or more words (or parts of words) below and then select
"submit" (or "reset" to erase the words and start again). The results
will include systems with descriptions that include all the specified
words.

Enter search words:

`technology`

[Submit Query] [Reset]

University of Cambridge Computing Service, May 1995

Figure 3.15 A HyTelnet search form

Some Gopher servers also offer HyTelnet searches. An example is the
Gopher server at the University of Washington Lee at **gopher://
library.uc.wlu.edu:3004/7**.

Note that not all the Telnet sites you find through a HyTelnet search
offer public access. Usually, if a Telnet site is open for public access, it
will instruct you on how to log in.

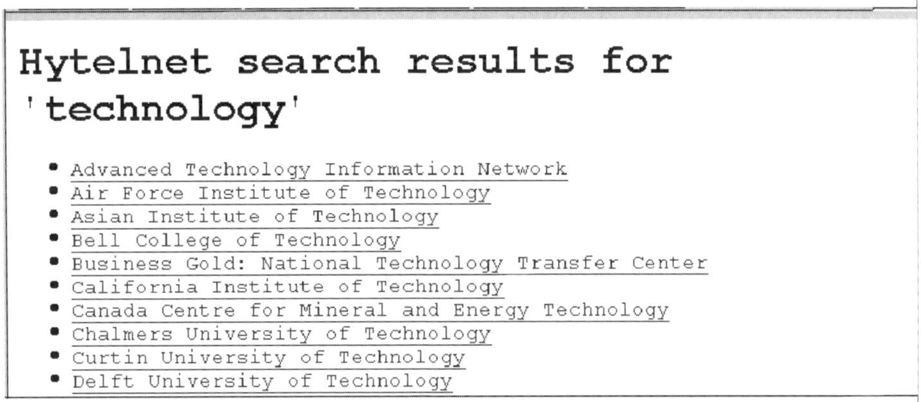

Hytelnet search results for 'technology'

- Advanced Technology Information Network
- Air Force Institute of Technology
- Asian Institute of Technology
- Bell College of Technology
- Business Gold: National Technology Transfer Center
- California Institute of Technology
- Canada Centre for Mineral and Energy Technology
- Chalmers University of Technology
- Curtin University of Technology
- Delft University of Technology

Figure 3.16 HyTelnet search results

Hytelnet - Massachusetts Institute of Technology

```
telnet library.mit.edu or 18.92.0.26
login: library
Password: PRESS RETURN

OPAC = GEAC Advance

To exit, select 4 on main menu
```

Figure 3.17 Telnet page at MIT

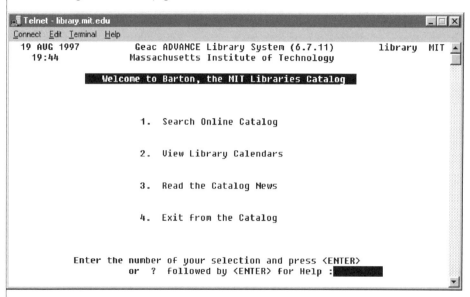

Figure 3.18 Telnet page of the Library at MIT

WAIS

WAIS (pronounced 'ways') stands for Wide Area Information Server. It is an Internet protocol that enables you to index and access different types of information from a single interface. WAIS servers are collections of databases containing mostly text-based documents and, to a much lesser degree, sound, pictures or video files. The databases may be organised in different ways, but you don't have to learn the query languages of the different databases. WAIS facilitates natural language queries to find relevant documents. It has databases on a wide range of topics.

WAIS was developed as a project of Thinking Machines, Apple Computer, and two stock brokerage firms: Dow Jones, and KPMG Peat Marwick. The original intention was to create a network protocol for speedy keyword access to frequently updated market information. This sounds like a scenario for many other applications on the Internet, but WAIS eventually grew to become much bigger than was originally envisioned. Thinking Machines no longer supports the publicly distributed WAIS; instead, support and development of the 'free' version of WAIS has been taken over by CNIDR (Clearinghouse for Networked Information Discovery and Retrieval) at **http://cnidr.org/**. Current CNIDR releases are called 'freeWAIS'. Commercial development and support of WAIS is now carried out by WAIS Inc., a company founded by many of the authors of WAIS.

Figure 3.19 WAIS server at Lund University in Sweden

There are many WAIS servers on the Internet. A 'directory-of-servers' database is available at several sites, which can be queried to determine databases available on a particular subject. Once you have identified which databases you require, the second step of a WAIS search locates relevant documents within those databases.

WAIS uses TCP/IP to connect client applications to information servers. Searches can be made by remote log-in to a WAIS server, by a local WAIS client program, or by using a WWW browser. Initially, you can try WAIS out by using a remote log-in. Among the WAIS servers you can use are **sunsite.unc.edu**, **wais.wais.com**, **quake.think.com** and **wais.com**. Although installing a local WAIS client program takes up a sizable amount of computer space, and the program needs continual updating, a WAIS client program usually provides more functions and flexibility. You can access WAIS servers using Netscape Navigator or other WWW browsers.

As an example of connecting to a WAIS server using Netscape Navigator, select the WAIS server at Lund University in Sweden at **http://www.ub2.lu.se/auto_new/UDC.html**—Figure 3.19.

From here, select the listed item 'Applied sciences, Medicine, Technology' and then 'Engineering. Technology in general'. A WAIS search form appears that contains list of WAIS databases—Figure 3.20.

Engineering. Technology in general

Select those **WAIS** databases you want to search.
┌ comp_techreports: Abstracts of technical reports worldwide
┌ dit-library: Library catalog of the Dept. of Comp.
Engineering, Lund Univ.
┌ ANU-Asian-Settlements:
┌ archie.au-ls-lRt: archie.au ftp archive (Australia)
┌ comp-acad-freedom:
┌ comp.robotics:
┌ comp.text.sgml: Standard Generalized Markup Language (SGML)
┌ ANU-Asian-Religions: Bibliographic references to selected
(mainly Buddhist) Asian religions
┌ comp.sys.mips:

Figure 3.20 A list of WAIS databases

```
ANU-CAUT-Academics
    S1 S1 The following database is not available:
    /wais/db/ANU-CAUT-Academics

The selected databases contain the following 40 items relevant to your
query.

TCD-CS-91-02     Crane, S. & Tangney, B. Failure and Recovery in an
Danilo Bruschi  (July) A Structural Overview of NP Optimization Problems
CSE-TR-35-89  Ajay J. Daga and William P. Birmingham  "Failure Recovery
CSE-TR-36-89  Ajay J. Daga and William P. Birmingham  "Failure Detection
CSE-TR-39-89  Ajay J. Daga  "Failure Handling in the MICON System", 1989,
[25]     A Design Space and Design Rules for User Interface Software Arch
tr-91-068.ps.Z          Construction of a pseudo-random generator from
[220]    Unit Testing and Analysis       SEI-CM-9-1.2, ADA236119      April
mln@blearg Re: Linear Static Structural Analysis and Vibration Analysis
No Title
Control in Functional Unification Grammars for
TITLE    = A Complete Proof System for Timed Observations    NUMBER    =
[29]     Studying Software Architecture Through Design Spaces and Rules
Pack.Heng@ Re: IRISA/INRIA-RENNES (LSP) Reports
```

Figure 3.21 WAIS database search results for 'structural failure'

If you use the search query 'structural failure', select a few databases on
the screen, the search on these WAIS databases will return with papers
related to structural failure—Figure 3.21.

A few other WAIS search forms or database forms can be accessed on
the WWW from the following addresses:

- **http://www.ub2.lu.se/auto_new/UDC.html**
- **http://techreports.larc.nasa.gov/cgi-bin/NTRS**
- **http://www.albany.net/allinone/all1gen.html**
- **http://129.69.70.62/search.html**
- **http://www.brunel.ac.uk/search.html**
- **http://163.121.10.41/www/**

Differences between WWW, Gopher and WAIS

Although WAIS, Gopher and WWW (via a Web browser) are all
client-server based information systems running over the Internet,
they differ in the ways in which they handle their data. In the WWW,
everything (document, menu, index etc.) is represented to the user as a
hypertext object. Two navigation operations are available to the user:
to follow a link or to send a query to a server. That's a simple model,
and brings about a simple user interface. The simplicity of the data

model for the WWW enables the accommodation of almost all other information systems. For instance, a WWW user can interrogate WAIS indexes and Gopherservers easily.

A WAIS database is a searchable document. The search list returned by a WAIS server is a hypertext document. Gopher menus on the WWW are also hypertext documents which link to other objects. In practice, this means that the WWW can accommodate both Gopher and WAIS data models. To be more precise, a Gopher menu is a list of links, but a Gopher document is a hypertext document without links (the search methods and Telnet sessions are the same for both); whereas a WAIS index is a searchable page that returns a document with no links. In the WWW, hyperlinks are used to WAIS, Gopher, FTP, Network News or other servers. In this regard you can view the WWW as a superset incorporating the FTP, WAIS, Gopher and HTTP spaces.

As an ordinary Internet user, you should always use the WWW whenever you can, and access Gopher, WAIS or other types of servers through the WWW. Only if you really need a local client program for, say, Gopher, should you embark on installing it.

Bibliography

Archie

Archie
http://www.state.lib.ut.us/archie.htm

Archie FAQs
http://www.intac.com//man/faq/archie_faq.txt

Archie Services by NEXOR
http://www.nexor.com/archie.html/

Guide to Network Resource Tools—Archie
http://www.cbpf.br/HelpOnArchie.html

SURANET's Archie Guide
http://www.sura.net/archie/Archie-Usage.html#B2.0

Browsers

A&S Training Materials
http://www.ipfw.indiana.edu/as/training/netscape/nsbrowser.htm

CWS AppList: Web Browsers
http://www.archi.tku.edu.tw/cwsapps/www.html

Dave's Utterly's Browser Poll
http://www.davesweb.com/davesweb/poll.htm

Internet Explorer: the Browser for Windows 95
http://wl8.windows.microsoft.com/windows/ie/ie.htm

Netscape
http://home.netscape.com/

Netscape Handbook
http://home.netscape.com/eng/mozilla/1.1/handbook/

Netscape Tutorials
http://ernie.bgsu.edu/departments/tcom/netscape.html

ThreeToad WWW Browser Comparison
http://www.threetoad.com/main/Browser.html

Web Browser Guide
http://www.industry.net/support/browser.htm

World Wide Web Browsers Statistics
http://www-iwi.unisg.ch/stats/ua.html

WWW Browsers
http://union.ncsa.uiuc.edu/HyperNews/get/www/browsers.html

WWW FAQ: Browsers Accessible by Telnet
http://fang.fa.gau.hu/www/faq/www-faq/telnet.html

Gopher

Gopher at University of Minnesota
gopher://gopher.micro.umn.edu:70/1

Gopher Jewels
http://galaxy.einet.net/GJ/

Gopher Menu
Gopher://gopher.tc.umn.edu:70/11/Other%20Gopher%20and%20Information%20Servers

Gopher Servers from A2Z
http://a2z.lycos.com/Internet/Indices,_Directories_and_How-To_Guides/Gopher_Servers/

Guide to Network Resources Tools - Gopher
http://www.acad.bg/beginner/gopher.html

How to Compose Veronica Queues
gopher://gopher.scs.unr.edu:70/hh/veronica/About/how-to-query-veronica(html)

HyTelnet

Browse HyTelnet Services
http://andromeda.einet.net/hytelnet/START.TXT.html

HyTelnet at University of Western Australia
http://www.library.uwa.edu.au/otherlibs/hytelnet/

HyTelnet Information Page
http://www.lights.com/hytelnet/

HyTelnet on the WorldWideWeb
http://library.usask.ca/hytelnet/

HyTelnet—Telnet Access to Library Catalogs
http://www.cam.ac.uk/Hytelnet/

Search All HyTelnet Entries
http://andromeda.einet.net/hytelnet/HYTELNET.html

WAIS

FreeWAIS
http://cnidr.org/welcome.html

Guide to Network Resources—WAIS
http://dawww.essex.ac.uk/wais.html

WAIS
http://www.paragon.co.uk/netuser/lssue_3/wais/wais.html

World Wide Web—FAQs
http://sunsite.unc.edu/boutell/faq/www_faq.html

World Wide Web

Chimera
http://www.unlv.edu/chimera/

Web Developer's Virtual Library
http://www.stars.com/

The World Wide Web Consortium
http://www.w3.org/

World Wide Web FAQ
http://www.unimelb.edu.au/public/www-faq/

World Wide Web Guide
http://www.inet.co.th/www/index.html

World Wide Web Servers—Summary
http://www.w3.org/hypertext/DataSources/WWW/Servers.html

General

Internet: Indices, Directories & How-To Guides
http://a2z.lycos.com/Internet/Indices,_Directories_and_How-To_Guides/

Internet Life Surf School
http://www.zdnet.com/yil/filters/surfjump.html

Yahoo! How-to
http://howto.yahoo.com/

CHAPTER

4

WWW Search Engines and Internet Directories

Main WWW search engines

Multi-threaded search engines

Which WWW search engines to use?

Internet directories

Don't overlook hotlists

Other search engines

Tips for using search engines

Further reading on search engines

The rapid growth of the Internet has been accompanied by the increasingly daunting task of locating information. The Internet is like a huge library with vast resources of information available. It is impossible to keep track of all the numerous services it provides as well as account for frequent changes. Without a feasible means of searching, and, better still, of cataloguing and indexing, finding information on the Internet is like looking for a needle in a haystack.

The development of the World Wide Web has made the idea of an Internet search easier for people with few computer skills yet who are 'serious' Internet users, who account for the majority of Internet users. Hypermedia, upon which WWW is built, provides convenient and transparent links to various sites and services in Webspace which has made the task of searching information simple and transparent. In Webspace, WWW clients or users search for information provided by various servers. The process of finding information may be partially automated, but, like most computer software or applications, human operation is vital. This human operation involves initiating a search, browsing through the search results and making an intelligent analysis and judgment on the information retrieved.

In order to search in Webspace, we need Web search engines. As described in Chapter 1, a Web search engine is a computer program that helps us find information on thousands of information servers and databases in Webspace. The front end of a Web search engine is a hypertext page which allows you to enter keywords that relate to the topic of interest, and generates a list of pages that relate to those keywords. It guides us through the maze of servers and databases. Some of these engines can occasionally be difficult to access due to heavy usage, particularly during peak Web usage hours. However, since the Internet service is global, those peak hours are not necessarily your local working hours.

Both the terms 'search engines' and 'Internet directories' (sometimes called 'Web indexes') are in common use. There is a fine difference between a Web search engine and a Web index. A Web search engine collects information scattered through Webspace by combing through the Web documents, identifying text that is suitable as the basis for keyword searching, and returning useful information which is then sorted, indexed, and categorised for its database—all automatically. Each search engine works differently: some scan for information in the title or header of the document; others look at the bold 'headings' on the page for their information. As a result, search engines gather information differently and consequently may yield different results for an identical search query. Therefore, it is not surprising that some search engine names themselves are revealing, such as Lycos, Sleuth and Webcrawler. Once you submit a search query, the search engine searches through its database and identifies records that 'match' your query and returns these records to you.

The Web index, however, has a different emphasis. It categorises Internet resources in a subject-oriented, alphabetical, or chronological manner for the user to browse through. Since this involves laborious work in collecting, indexing, and annotating resources, many Web indexes also allow searches. The gap between the search index and the Web index is narrowing and the difference can be obscure. Some of the main search engines nowadays are linked to Web indexes, facilitating both searching and browsing. However, searching in a Web index can return 'categorised' information, which may not be as complete as the results (albeit unorganised) returned by a search engine.

In order to conduct a thorough search on a selected topic through available Internet resources, we need to use different search techniques covering different parts of the Internet. For example, the information you are looking for may reside on an Archie server, a WAIS server, a WWW server, a Gopher server, or elsewhere. Fortunately, since most of these servers have now been made accessible on the Web, we only need to learn the one set of search techniques. As the data available on one server may be more up-to-date and complete than that on another, in general we have to search a number of different databases or servers in order to obtain the most complete results. There have been concerted efforts on the Internet to develop integrated search techniques which enable users to dispatch one search request and have the work carried out over several databases or servers. Another significant development is the advent of an increasing number of subject-oriented guides and directories offering access to databases that have already been searched, categorised and packaged for potential users.

Search engines appear to be easy to use . Simply type in the words you are searching for (or 'keywords'), and the engine returns to you a list of pointers, titles or hyperlinks. The items in the list are usually rated according to their relevance to the query words you used for your search, and are provided with a hyperlink to more specific topical information. In reality, a Web search is more than this mechanical process. An important issue is knowing which search engine or engines to use, since different engines produce different results. Then there is the matter of choosing keywords and using them wisely. Up-to-date information requires a diligent search through the Internet. All in all, skills and craftsmanship in searching the Web are essential for satisfactory results.

Main WWW search engines

Single search engines

There are hundreds of search engines currently available on the WWW, and it appears that the craze for inventing more may not have stopped yet. To compound the problem, search pages or sites created by individuals have mushroomed. These sites are not themselves search engines; they merely provide tailor-made search forms or search links so that the user can visit one site and be exposed or connected to a few search engines which do the actual search work. This type of service may be helpful in that hunting for a particular type of information (for instance electronic journals) becomes easier, but there is a possibility of being 'guided' to certain search engines and ignoring others.

Some search engines are specialised for particular tasks. There are search engines for the WWW, some for Usenet, for email addresses, for mailing lists to email discussion groups, for sound or picture files, for software, and so on. Except those for the WWW, search engines with a single function are not numerous, so it is relatively easy to select the appropriate one for a specific search. However, a number of large search engines are actually becoming multi-functional, so that using a single engine you may elect to search WWW resources, mailing list, e-mail address, and so on.

In the following pages, you will be introduced to some commonly used WWW search engines, their Web addresses and their characteristics, listed in alphabetical order. Like many things in

Webspace, these addresses are subject to change. Later, we will briefly compare these engines and suggest certain ones for major consideration in the search for engineering-related information. This book does not intend to 'guide' you to use some of the search engines rather than others. You should always listen to advice, experiment, and identify those search engines which you find most useful for your own information searching.

AltaVista

http://www.altavista.digital.com/

AltaVista is the result of a research project started in the summer of 1995 at Digital's Research Laboratories in Palo Alto, California. It was launched in December 1995 and soon became one of the major WWW search engines on the Internet. AltaVista has a practically unmatchable Web index with over 30 million Web pages and several million Usenet articles. It allows access to nearly 11 billion words found in a near 30-gigabyte Web index. The database is updated daily. It contains full texts of Web pages, which enables it to attach to each URL it retrieves the header of each document it finds, providing a useful description for each search item. AltaVista also contains a full-text index of over 14 000 news groups and offers the full text of articles it finds. AltaVista's advanced query supports Boolean search.

AltaVista ranks returned pages and presents scores. Documents that contain the query words or phrases in the first few words are given high scores. Query words or phrases found close to one another in the

Figure 4.1 AltaVista home page

document or appear frequently also attract high scores. The results are displayed using standard, compact or detailed formats, as you select.

AltaVista is 'mirrored' (i.e. there are exact copies in other locations) in Europe and Australia, where users have a 'local' AltaVista site for speedy access. AltaVista currently powers a number of search sites such as Yahoo! and Internet Sleuth. In terms of size, speed, information and search power, AltaVista should be a favourite search engine for Web users.

DejaNews

http://www.dejanews.com/

DejaNews is a search engine for Usenet, designed to search the online archive of all Usenet newsgroups. It returns a list of titles of Usenet news articles with their hyperlinks. According to its host Deja News Inc, more than 500 megabytes of information is posted daily to Usenet—this is equivalent to about 50 ordinary-sized books. Deja News has indexed every word of more than 120 gigabytes of postings on the Usenet—the equivalent of a 10–15 000 book library! You can search using any topical keywords. DejaNews allows you to filter queries by date, Usenet group, author, subject, or the presence of keywords. It also provides hyperlinks to authors that let you track down other records made by the same author. DejaNews boasts a searchable archive of several thousand Usenet newsgroups, some dating back two years, and the company plans to extend its archive to date back many years. It includes detailed discussion threads, as recent as yesterday, on thousands of topics. This is undoubtedly a quite unique information source.

Figure 4.2 DejaNews home page

The DejaNews search form not only accepts query terms for general searches, but also accommodates a separate search option to find the newsgroups that are of relevance to the topic.

Excite

http://www.excite.com/

Excite is also a relative newcomer to the myriad Internet search tools. It provides searches on the World Wide Web, Usenet, Usenet classifieds, and Excite's own database of Web site reviews. It has one of the larger database pools. One unique feature of Excite is its ability to produce a list of documents matching the keywords used in search to a document already retrieved by a search (also referred to as 'Query by Example'). This is carried out by a hyperlink option called 'More Like This' attached to each returned Web site from a search. This feature accelerates the search to locate relevant Web sites without resorting to a new search query. Excite has a directory with 14 subdirectories (called 'channels'). It also holds a large collections of reviews of Web sites written by professionals.

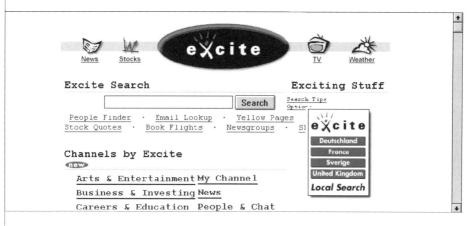

Figure 4.3 Excite home page

HotBot

http://www.HotBot.com/

HotBot is a newcomer in the search engine field. However, it has already established a very sizeable database (indexed to over 54 million Web pages with promises to index 100% of the Web and Usenet news and mailing lists). HotBot offers the ability to search by date, resource and location. It supports Boolean operators 'and', 'or' and 'not' and phrase searching. HotBot also has a 'modify' option which allows you to add additional filters on search terms. The 'date' option allows you to specify information published before or after a specific date. The 'location' option allows a search for results from a specified geographical location. The 'media type' option offers a selection of media types such as image, audio, video, Java (a network-oriented programming language) or VRML (Virtual Reality Modeling Language). It also permits the choice of file extension such as '.gif' and '.txt'. In brief, HotBot allows you to customise your search, a feature not generally shared by other search engines.

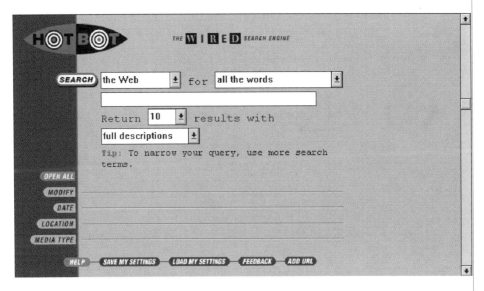

Figure 4.4 HotBot home page

Infoseek

http://www.infoseek.com/

Infoseek Corporation, based in Santa Clara, California, was founded in January of 1994 by Steven Kirsch (founder of Frame Technology and Mouse Systems) and an experienced team of professionals. Infoseek database owns over 80 million URL addresses and 50 million indexed documents, making it one of the largest databases available. It covers the WWW, Gopher and FTP. Searches can be limited to either the Web, Usenet newsgroups, newswires, business, email addresses, company profiles, Web 'FAQs' (Frequently Asked Questions) or other categories.

Infoseek ranks the search results from a highest score of 100. A high score is assigned if the query terms (words or phrases) are found near the start of the document or in the title, or they appear frequently in a document. High scores are also given if a document contains query terms which are relatively uncommon and therefore possess high weighting. Infoseek also provides a large directory.

Through its Ultraseek search page, Infoseek also offers some unique search functions. For example, its 'imageseek' search lets you a search for pictures related to the query words. 'Sitesearch' activates searches for pages from a particular Web site. And 'linksearch' counts and lists the pages that have links to a particular URL.

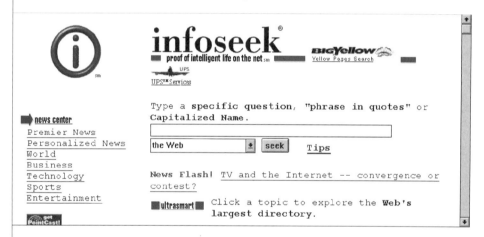

Figure 4.5 Infoseek home page

Inktomi
http://www.inktomi.com/

Inktomi is a search engine from the University of California at Berkeley. It hosts a very large database and is a very fast Web indexer. The name Inktomi could be read as 'ink to me', but it is also the name of a mythological spider of the Plains Indians, which was known for bringing culture to the people and was considered to be a representative of the underdog. Nowadays, Inktomi powers a number of search engines, including HotBot, Goo in Japan and Anzwers in Australia (you can find the URL addresses of the last two by using a search engine).

Lycos

http://www.lycos.com/

Lycos originated at Carnegie Mellon University and was acquired by CMG Information Services, Inc. in June 1995. It is now operated by Lycos Inc., Pittsburgh, Pennsylvania, USA. It allows you to search document titles and contents. The index searches on document titles, headings, links and texts it locates in these documents. It is one of the largest Web indexes and its database is updated frequently. Lycos allows searches for sound or picture records. Its advanced search function, called Lycos Pro, applies a Boolean search. Lycos ranks the researched sites from a highest score of 1000 and assigns numbers based on how much or how little they match your search query. The ranking is done differently from many other search engines—Lycos assigns higher scores to pages that contain the words in the search query. It also assigns higher scores to documents that mention these query words earlier rather than later. In addition, in its ranking process Lycos favours those sites that are linked by many other sites. The new

Figure 4.6 Lycos home page

CHAPTER

4

Lycos search page has interfaces to bookshops, news, software and other features. The search page may appear to be complicated initially, but with the right keywords, you can find just about anything.

In addition to its searching capacity, Lycos hosts an exceptionally comprehensive directory called A2Z, which constitutes an enormous Internet resource list with 16 categories. A2Z also allows searching within its directory. Under its Science and Technology category, A2Z maintains a subdirectory titled 'Engineering' with an extensive collection of Internet resources on engineering. It can be accessed from **http://a2z.lycos.Com/Science_and_Technology/Engineering/**.
The other directory hosted by Lycos is Lycos Top 5% (known as the Point Top 5% before it was acquired by Lycos). This directory only includes those Web sites evaluated by Lycos for its contents, presentation and experience and awarded the 'Lycos Top 5%' logo. Each Web site in the Lycos Top 5% database belongs to a category from which the user can proceed to other Lycos Top 5% sites on similar topics.

WebCrawler

http://www.webcrawler.com

WebCrawler was a part of the WebCrawler Project managed by Brian Pinkerton at the University of Washington in Seattle before being acquired by America Online in April 1995. It is now operated by the WebCrawler Inc. WebCrawler allows keyword searches of the titles and full contents of documents available on the World Wide Web. Its advanced search facility supports Boolean queries. It searches a database generated by a special program that automatically looks throughout the WWW. The database is updated at least monthly. WebCrawler builds an impressively complete index. On the other hand, since it indexes the contents of documents, it may find many links that are less than accurate. However, WebCrawler sorts the documents it finds according to how closely they match your search. The ranking is done by examining the frequency of keywords in a document, and the returned items are ranked and presented in order. You can choose the number and format of displays after the search. Results can be displayed in two formats: the short format gives you a list of titles of Web resources that match your query; and the detailed format provides titles plus summaries, URLs, numerical relevancy scores and the option of viewing similar pages for each result returned. WebCrawler is not the largest Web index, but it is less busy than others and fast. It is an excellent choice for a general search.

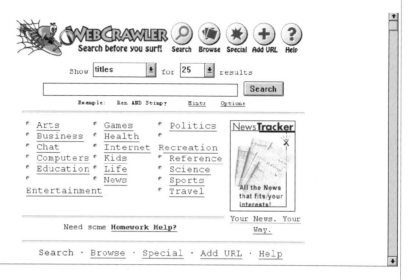

Figure 4.7 WebCrawler home page

Yahoo!

http://www.yahoo.com/

Yahoo! was developed in 1994 at Stanford University, Palo Alto, California by two graduate students, David Filo and Jerry Yang, before it was converted to a public company. Yahoo! is probably the most complete hierarchical, topical index of all Web sites, and features a sophisticated search facility. It builds up its index databases by collating URL addresses submitted by users, automated searches through Webspace and indexing. Yahoo! supports Boolean searches.

Figure 4.8 Yahoo! search form

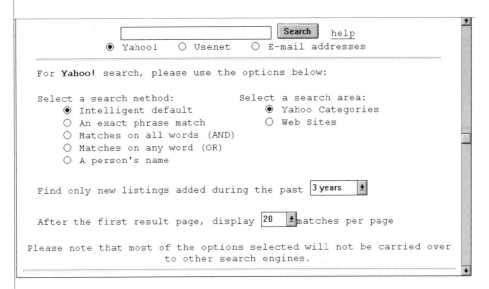

Figure 4.9 Advanced Yahoo! search form

Yahoo! organises its database into 'categories'; a search results in a display of the categories that match the search keywords and the corresponding URL addresses. This may appear confusing for the first-time user, but the results are quite informative. When you know what you are looking for, this is often a very handy place to start searching. Yahoo! is now powered by AltaVista engine. At present, Yahoo! provides jump points to other search engines, enabling you to conveniently search other engines with the same search query without having to exit from Yahoo!

Yahoo! also provides many useful search options not well known by all Yahoo! users. These options, when used wisely, can greatly enhance the search performance and yield more accurate information from the database.

Multi-threaded search engines

All the search engines mentioned so far are single-search engines. To conduct a thorough search for a topic, it is often necessary to activate several of them separately. To achieve this, search engines have been developed which carry out topical searches using databases comprising several single search engines. By tapping into these databases, you only need do one search to retrieve items from all of them. These search engines are called 'multi-threaded search engines' (otherwise known as 'parallel Internet query engines'). Typically, they differ from other search engines in that they do not maintain a local database. Rather, they rely on the databases of various Web-based sources. They send your queries to individual Web search engines on their search lists, organize the search results into a uniform format, rank them by relevance, and return them to the user. In effect, they are like employment agencies that delegate your job enquiries to a number of companies. This means that these multi-threaded search engines do not measure up to single search engines in speed. However, coverage and accuracy are the benefits. Several multi-threaded engines are listed below, in alphabetical order.

Dogpile

http://www.dogpile.com/

Dogpile is a new multi-threaded search engine developed by Aaron Flin, designed to obtain more focused results than other multi-threaded search engines by using several search engines. It searches the Web, FTP, Usenet and newswire services. For a Web search, Dogpile links to all major search engines, including Yahoo!,

Figure 4.10 Dogpile home page

Lycos (including A2Z), Excite, WebCrawler, InfoSeek, AltaVista and HotBot.

InfoMarket

http://www.infomkt.ibm.com/

The InfoMarket Search service was launched by IBM in 1995, with the aim of becoming a major information search tool on the Internet. It allows simultaneous searches on multiple databases on the Internet for documents, news and references, and generates a single, relevancy-ranked list of results. The search engine acts as a type of bridge between Internet browsers and online databases. It can translate a single search command into computer language that can be understood by a variety of database systems. It uses an easy interface that provides a simple and consistent way to access text, graphics, video, and sound. InfoMarket Web sources includes MagallanInternet Directory, OpenText index, Usenet News, and Yahoo! Its commercial sources include 75 newswires, 300 newspapers, 819 newsletters, 6882 journals and 11 million companies. You can purchase information on a per document basis using IBM's Cryptolope technology, a technology which enables users to buy and sell content securely over the Internet.

The Internet Sleuth

http://www.isleuth.com/

The Internet Sleuth maintains an extensive search form that contains many databases. This enables you to select a database or databases that you want the search to be carried out in before it actually begins. The Sleuth offers several categories:

- Web search engines
- news
- business and finance
- sports
- software
- Usenet

Each category embraces several databases. One or more databases from each category can be selected for each search. For instance, under 'Web search engines', the Sleuth allows you to select up to six databases from A2Z (hosted by Lycos), AltaVista, Excite–Documents, Excite–Reviews, HotBot, Infoseek, Lycos, OpenText, WebCrawler and Yahoo!. The search is performed sequentially from the selected databases and results returned in a combined and itemised list.

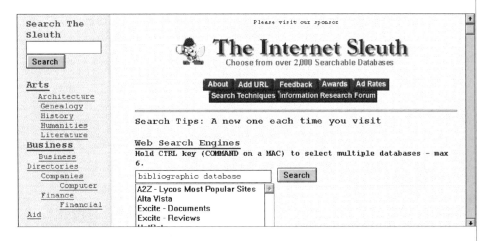

Figure 4.11 The Internet Sleuth home page

MetaCrawler

http://www.metacrawler.com /

Originated and developed by Erik Selberg, Oren Etzioni and Greg Lauckhart at the University of Washington, MetaCrawler was first released to the Internet in June 1995, but later acquired by the Internet company go2net Inc. When you submit a search, MetaCrawler queries a number of existing search engines, organises the results into a uniform format, and displays them. If you use a specially defined syntax, it loads all documents returned by the various engines in parallel and processes them to ensure they contain valid data. Among search engines MetaCrawler currently accesses are Lycos, WebCrawler, Excite, Hotbot, InfoSeek, Inktomi, AltaVista, and Yahoo! MetaCrawler also allows you to sort the hits in a number of ways such as locality, region and organisation.

MetaCrawler offers the search query in three different options:

- as all of the words
- as any of the words

■ as a phrase.

Searches using the first two options return results that contain either all of the query keywords or any of them. The final option ensures that results contain query words as a phrase. This will require additional verification of the search results by the search engine. When the search is finished, MetaCrawler combines the ranking scores from each search engine and formulates its own ranking from the highest 1000 to the lowest 100.

The MetaCrawler search form is shown in Figure 4.12.

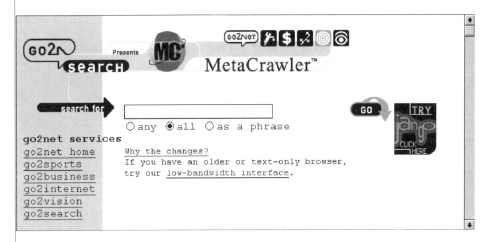

Figure 4.12 MetaCrawler home page

Mother Load

http://www.cosmix.com/
motherload/

Mother Load is another multi-threaded search engine. It provides two tiers of search, 'The Insane Search' and 'The Web Search'. The former is a thorough search allowing you to determine what combination of search engines to activate or what online magazines to link to in the search. In addition, Mother Load maintains its own directory, which can also be searched.

Figure 4.13 Mother Load home page

ProFusion

http://www.designlab.ukans.edu/
profusion/

ProFusion is was developed at the University of Kansas, USA, and
allows you to customise your selection of search engines for individual

Figure 4.14 ProFusion home page

queries. ProFusion connects to search engines such as AltaVista, Excite, Infoseek, OpenText, Lycos and WebCrawler. It also permits you to rerun search queries: you first run a search, then enter your name and a new password, and ProFusion reruns the search query for you periodically and tells you when there are new results.

SavvySearch

http://www.cs.colostate.edu/
~dreiling/smartform.html

SavvySearch is the work of Daniel Dreilinger, a former student at the Department of Computer Science at Colorado State University. It is a unique and innovative Web search engine, because it was one of the earliest parallel Internet query engines available. When you type in a keyword query, SavvySearch initiates a number of major Internet search engines, including AltaVista, Excite, Infoseek, Lycos, OpenText, WebCrawler, HotBot, and DejaNews, gathers information from each source, and then returns the linked results displayed in a homogeneous format, identifying the source search engine for each. SavvySearch also offers a menu for restricting searches to particular types of information, e.g., WWW resources, software, reference, technical reports and academic papers. One of the unique features of SavvySearch is that its search form is available in several languages.

SavvySearch permits three query options, providing additional flexibility:

- all query terms
- any query terms
- query terms as a phrase.

It retrieves up to 50 hits from each search engine it interfaces, with unless there are other limitations from the individual engines.

SavvySearch offers elastic display options for the search results. There are three different formats for display:

- 'Brief' format typically displays a result with a title and hypertext link to the retrieved item, the search engine that returned it, and links to all of the search engines used in your search.

- 'Normal' format unveils most of the available information displayed. This includes information on the 'Size', 'Length', 'Score', 'Date', 'Type' author and location, together with descriptive information such as 'Abstract', 'Description', 'Excerpt', and 'Keywords'.
- The 'Verbose' display adds fields that don't fit into either of the above categories or have not yet been classified, in addition to a textual quote of the search result's URL. Timing and other search engine statistics are also included in this display.

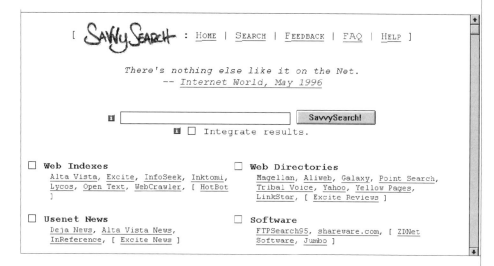

Figure 4.15 SavvySearch home page

SuperSearch

http://www.robtex.com/search.htm

SuperSearch is another mega-search engine. It connects to a number of major single search engines, among them are Infoseek, Lycos, WebCrawler, AltaVista, Excite, Inktomi, Magellan, OpenText and HotBot. SuperSearch provides categories like 'Crawlers', 'Indices', 'Usenet', 'People', 'Articles', 'Software' and 'Unsorted'. A search query can fall into one of these categories.

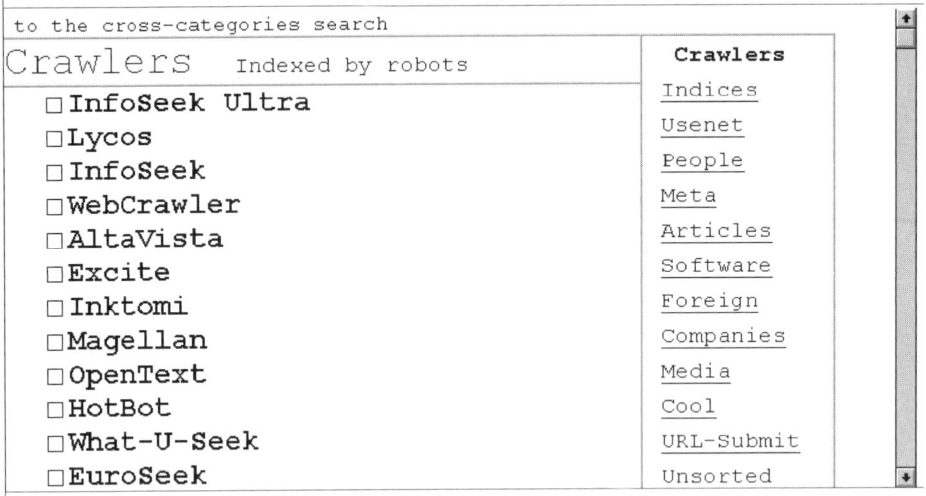

Internet Resources for Engineers

```
to the cross-categories search
Crawlers     Indexed by robots        Crawlers
□ InfoSeek Ultra                        Indices
□ Lycos                                 Usenet
□ InfoSeek                              People
□ WebCrawler                            Meta
□ AltaVista                             Articles
□ Excite                                Software
□ Inktomi                               Foreign
□ Magellan                              Companies
□ OpenText                              Media
□ HotBot                                Cool
□ What-U-Seek                           URL-Submit
□ EuroSeek                              Unsorted
```

Figure 4.16 SuperSeach home page

Summary

All Web search engines allow you to search Webspace using keywords or other types of search criteria. However, they operate differently. Some of them cruise around the WWW constantly building up their databases and indexes, enabling them to provide hyperlinks to Web sites containing information matching the keywords. Engines such as AltaVista, WebCrawler, Infoseek and Lycos are of this type. They are sometimes called 'keyword indexes'.

Another type of search engine collates Web pages submitted and categorises them in their databases. When you enter a search term, they provide a category structure as well as individual hyperlinks to Web sites allied to the search keywords. Yahoo! exemplifies this engine type, also called 'subject-oriented guides', 'subject directories' or 'Internet directories'.

Which WWW search engines to use?

A good question—but one that has no 'correct' answer. A sloppy 'solution' for some users is to cling to the one search engine they started using in the beginning—a 'stick-with-the-devil-you-know' mentality. This approach may by convenient or easy to use, but does not reconcile the fact that no search engine is thorough over all topics.

A good search engine has three main features: speed, comprehensiveness and accuracy. For the user, the first obvious measure of a good search engine is the speed (though a good search engine can be crowded and this slows it down). With the increasing capabilities of computer hardware, speed is becoming less a real impediment when searching non-multimedia data. The quality of search results then becomes a real measure of a search engine. For a particular subject, you need to choose appropriate engines. The sheer number of items retrieved from a search does not naturally reflect the search's comprehensiveness. Accuracy is another important factor. The items retrieved should generically be related closely to the topic you are searching. A long list of dubious items means that either you entered inappropriate words for searching or that you chose the 'wrong' engine for that topic. Flexible search options are also a feature of a good search engine. In addition, informative descriptions of the links displayed are desirable.

Obviously, the comfortable approach of sticking with one search engine and disregarding others outright is not recommended. From known performance to date, it's possible to make an informed assessment of the existing single-search engines and select those which are valuable for searching for information on your particular engineering and technology interests.

At the end of this Chapter, some online reading materials are suggested that will help you to select search engines. However, for engineering information it is advisable to try at least the well-known single-search engines such as WebCrawler, Infoseek, Lycos, Yahoo! and AltaVista.

Search engines operate differently. To unravel the puzzling variety of search engines, there are now so-called 'search metapages' on the Web, which allow you to access a number of different search engines individually from one site, thus eliminating the hassle of hopping between them. CUSI (Configurable Unified Search Engine) at **http://web.nexor.co.uk/public/cusi/** is such a metapage.

Multi-threaded search engines not only permit searches across a variety of engines simultaneously, but also give you the freedom to specify which engines to use. When you enter the keywords, such search engines summon individual search engines to work, and collate the results and present them in a homogeneous format. This is definitely a more thorough search for the time spent. Whenever you suspect that the comprehensiveness of information outweighs the time taken to search, it's time to seriously consider multi-threaded search engines. The time saved is often the time you need to spend sifting through the huge list of retrieved items, rather than the time actually taken by the computer to run the search.

An intriguing question arises naturally from using Web search engines: if we are all interested in an area or a subject, say, manufacturing engineering, then why can't some concerted search be done so that people with common interests can share the results? The answer is: it already has been—it's called 'subject-oriented Web searches'. The result of such searches are the many 'subject-oriented guides'—now often referred to as 'Internet directories').

Internet directories

Historically, a subject-oriented guide, or an Internet directory, can evolve from lengthy and disorganised 'hotlists' (collections made by individuals). More directories, however, are accomplished by intensive Web searching carried out by search engines followed by laborious human indexing endeavour. Many Web search engines are providing Internet directories which are the results of such intensive subject-oriented searches and indexing, and more are likely to follow. Among the major Internet directories are those provided by Yahoo!, Lycos, WebCrawler and Infoseek. Yahoo! is undoubtedly the pioneer and champion in this relation. These engines provide directories that normally include topics like engineering, technology or science.

They are special because the directories they offer are produced by people conversant with the methods of carrying out an effective Internet search and, at the same time, knowledgeable in engineering and technology. They represent the experts' work of evaluating and organising information which cannot be paralleled by perfunctory keyword search by individuals using Web search engines. These Internet directories are not only an information reservoir for advanced topical resources, but also perfect starting points for beginners to browse through and to experience the information resources for a particular topic.

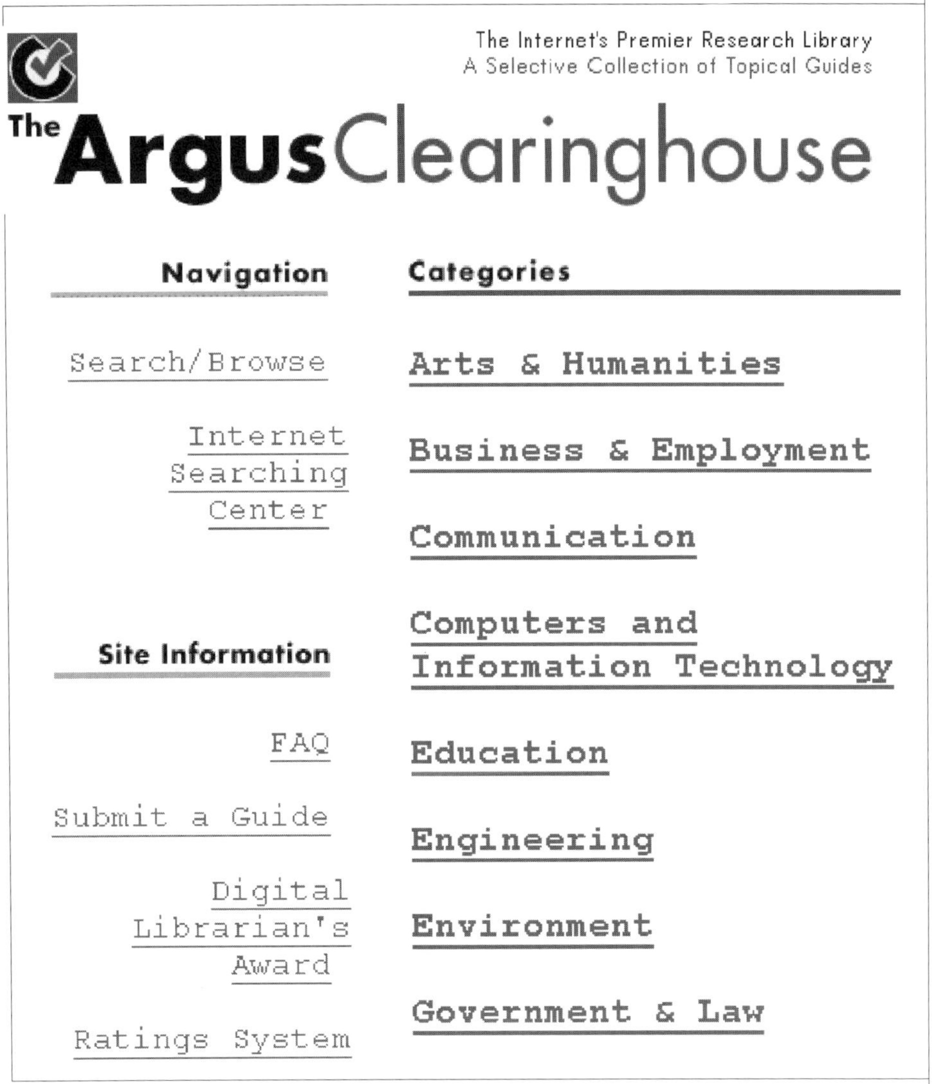

The Internet's Premier Research Library
A Selective Collection of Topical Guides

The**Argus**Clearinghouse

Navigation	Categories
Search/Browse	Arts & Humanities
Internet Searching Center	Business & Employment
	Communication
	Computers and Information Technology
Site Information	Education
FAQ	Engineering
Submit a Guide	Environment
Digital Librarian's Award	Government & Law
Ratings System	

Figure 4.17 The Clearinghouse for Subject-Oriented Internet Resource Guides

Having organised the subject hierarchy, an Internet directory can also offer search capability. This usually requires you to devise a query containing the most likely search parameters for the topic you are interested in, since searches within a WWW directory do not use keywords—this is obvious, for example, in Yahoo!. Before attempting to use any other directories, you should explore Yahoo! and the directories affiliated with the major WWW search engines; you can be amazed by the information you can get from them.

As an example of a WWW directory, let's visit the Clearinghouse for Subject Oriented Internet Resource Guides, a resource compiled by the University of Michigan in the USA, at **http://www. clearinghouse.net/**. The home page lists a number of subjects, shown in Figure 4.17.

Clicking the subject 'Engineering' leads to a comprehensive subject list for engineering.

Another good example of an Internet directory is Yahoo! Yahoo! contains 14 major subjects, shown in Figure 4.18.

Each subject has sub-listings. For instance, 'Science' contains over 50 sub-listing titles, including engineering, acoustics, energy, mathematics, etc. These titles and subjects represent the richness of Internet connections which have been gathered through intensive Internet searches.

Within an Internet directory like Yahoo!, we can also initiate a search. Such a search sifts through the database of the directory which has already been categorised and indexed. For instance, if we search in

Figure 4.18 Subject directories at Yahoo!

Yahoo! for the term 'materials', the output will point to nearly 400 Web sites. The bonus of using Yahoo! is that it provides the subject and sub-listing title for each item found, as well as its Web connection. Many items retrieved by this search are arts- or business-related which may not be of relevance to engineering and technology. However, by refining our search by adding extra terms like 'engineering materials', we are rewarded with a plentiful list of engineering-relevant Web pages.

This quality is shared by many other Internet directories which have search capacities. Using appropriate keywords to search is essential for successful information retrieval from the Internet. In addition, databases behind Internet directories are usually updated frequently, so a search repeated at a later date may not retrieve the same results as the original search.

At present there are ample numbers of directories available on the Internet, some of them also offering searching capabilities. Undoubtedly, this number will swell. The first types of directories are those offered by the main Web search engines. Many of them began purely as a search engine, but the production of a directory is a natural

Name and Internet address

AltaVista
http://www.altavista.digital.com/

Infoseek
http://www.infoseek.com/

Lycos Top 5% Web Sites
http://point.lycos.com/categories/index.html

Starting Point
http://www.stpt.com/

WebCrawler
http://www.webcrawler.com/

Yahoo! Guides
http://www.yahoo.com/

Table 4-1 Internet directories from search engines

Name and Internet address

American Society for Engineering Education
http://www.asee.org/

Argus Clearinghouse
http://www.clearinghouse.net

Awesome Lists
http://www.clark.net/pub/journa lism/awesome.html

CMC Information Sources
http://www.december.com/cmc/info/

Galaxy
http://galaxy.einet.net/

ICE—Internet Connections for Engineering
http://www.englib.cornell.edu/ice/ice-index.html

I-Explorer
http://www.i-explorer.com/

Info Access
http://sunsite.nus.sg/bibdb/bibdb.html

Internet Resources—Internet Lists
http://www.brandonu.ca/~ennsnr/Resources/lists.html

Internet Subject Directories
http://www.albany.edu/library/internet/subject.html

InterNIC Directory of Directories
http://ds.internic.net/cgi-bin/tochtml/0intro.dirofdirs/

IntIndex: an Internet Index
http://www.silverplatter.com/intindex/intro.htm

Magellan
http://www.mckinley.com/

National Internet Resources by Subjects
http://www.leidenuniv.nl/pun/ubhtm/marten/national.htm

Nerd World
http://www.nerdworld.com/

Subject Lists
http://www.apl.org/pages/subject.html

WWW Virtual Library
http://www.w3.org/hypertext/DataSources/ bySubject/Overview.html

Yanoff's Internet Services List
http://www.spectracom.com/islist/

YellowPages
http://theyellowpages.com/YellowPagespage.htm

Table 4-2 Some useful Internet directories

extension of the laborious work of creating a huge database. Table 4-1 lists a few of these directories.

It is sometimes difficult to distinguish clearly between a search engine and an Internet directory with a search function. The criterion used here is that if one was designed as a search engine first and acquired a directory later, for example WebCrawler, then it is a search engine with a directory. On the other hand, if it originated as a directory with or without a search function, then it is an Internet directory. More and more engineering-related directories are being created by various institutions. Table 4-2 offers a current summary of some prominent ones, some of which are described in detail below. Needless to say these directories are not the only ones on the Internet.

CMC Information Sources

http://www.december.com/cmc/ info/

This is a directory of information sources produced by John December since 1992. Initially known as 'The December List', it resides at Renesselar Polytechnic Institute, New York. The Source has a comparatively small section for 'Technology'. However, its 'Bibliography' section is particularly extensive, and provides engineering-oriented users with a useful collection of bibliographic resources, electronic publishing and online literature.

Galaxy

http://galaxy.einet.net/

Galaxy is one of the oldest Web directories on the Internet. In the present fast-changing environment, the age of the directory may be greeted with apprehension, but actually Galaxy has been evolving and improving to earn its place on the Internet. It compiles information not only for the Web but also for Gopher and Telnet protocols. Galaxy's index contains only those pages submitted to it. Its strength is in classifying, compiling and indexing information. Its 'Engineering and Technology' Web page has an extensive list of resources. Galaxy also provides a search form for searching through its resource database.

Internet Connections for Engineering

http://www.englib.cornell.edu/
ice/ice-index.html

Internet Connections for Engineering (ICE) is a project embarked on by the Engineering Library at Cornell University. It has become an extensive resource for chemistry, engineering, math, physics, and other 'hard' sciences. The Web site also offers a search form for the resource database. Searches on ICE usually return with a large number of sites, some of which may not be directly relevant to the search query.

Magellan

http://www.mckinley.com/

Magellan, from the McKinley Group, Inc., a subsidiary of Excite, Inc., is one of the new online directories of described, rated and reviewed Internet resources. It offers 15 categories, but engineering- and technology-related Web sites are scattered over several categories. The Magellan Internet directory presents both star ratings and detailed previews of descriptions right at the first level of searching. Magellan's comprehensiveness is not comparable to Yahoo!, but its star rating system is a useful Internet service. Its search engine offers concept search as well as keyword search, so can look for sites closely linked to the words in the search query.

The WWW Virtual Library

http://www.w3.org/hypertext/
DataSources/bySubject/Overview.
html

The WWW Virtual Library Project was started in 1991 at CERN, at **http://www.cern.ch/**, the European Laboratory for Particle Physics and the origin of the WWW. It has developed to be one of the major Web resources available on the Internet. The project is now distributed to many academic, government or industrial institutions, but is still centrally coordinated at the WWW Consortium **http://www.w3.org/pub/WWW/**. The Engineering Virtual Library is administered by NASA, at **http://arioch.gsfc.nasa.gov/wwwvl/ engineering.html**. The site contains comprehensive lists of hyperlinked engineering subjects, as well as 'Information Resources Applicable Across Engineering Domains' and 'Engineering Standards Organizations and Activities'. This is a primary location for anyone looking for online engineering resources.

Yanoff's Internet Services List

http://www.spectracom.com/
islist/

Few one-man crusades on the Internet have gained similar recognition as Scott Yanoff did with his Internet Services List. Previously known as Special Internet Connections, the list is the outcome of the author's consistent work since 1991. It is particularly extensive, covering numerous areas of the disciplines and subjects. The list includes pages predominantly from the Web, but also from Gopher and other protocols. The List does not specifically itemise 'Engineering' or 'Technology' but information has proliferated under headings such as 'Automotive', 'IEEE', 'Chemistry' and 'Science'.

Summary

Most of the Internet directories reside on Web servers. Some of them are Gopher servers, but they can also be accessed from the Web. Many of these directories are experimental and you will find great disparity in content and organisational methods. It is wise to experiment and identify sites preferable for your own engineering interests. Sites built by librarians or by engineers may have different emphasis. In any case, you can save significant time and effort by tapping into these information pools created by experienced searchers. A word of caution: search engines *complement* Internet directories, one being systematic and rigorous, and the other up-to-date and possibly thorough. They should not be seen as *exclusive* of each other.

Tables 4-1 and 4-2 contain only Internet directories from non-academic institutions, although some of them were originally created in universities.

Name and Internet address

Holicom's Engineering Hotlist Links
http://www.holli.com/hotlist/engin eering.html

Hotlist on Architecture, Engineering and Construction
http://www.ics.uci.edu/~jgong/hotlist.html

INCOSE Hotlist
http://internet-plaza.net/incose/hotlist.html

Jaimi's Hotlist
http://holgate.jsc.nasa.gov/~jjf/hotlist.html

Materials Science and Engineering Hotlist
http://www2.nas.edu/nmab/2176.ht ml

Michael Louis Scott's Hotlist
http://sprawl.sensemedia.net:8080/people/scott/ scotlist.htm

Software Engineering Hotlist
http://www.cs.umd.edu/projects/So ftEng/tame/hotlist.html

Software Engineering Hotlist at Georgia Technical University
http://www.cc.gatech.edu/computing/SW_Eng/hotlist.html

Thermal Engineering Hotlist
http://stecwww.fpms.ac.be/htmls/HotList/hlmain.html

Tom Duffey's Hotlist
http://www.stx.com/~tduffey/

Table 4-3 Some Internet hotlists for engineering

Another important source of Internet directories is university or public libraries worldwide. The arrival of the Internet has transformed the service landscape of libraries. As information providers, libraries are expeditious in adapting and providing new services, one being the compilation of the Internet directories. A list of Internet directories created by libraries world wide is presented in Chapter 5.

Don't overlook hotlists

In addition to the many Internet directories, there are numerous 'hotlists' on the Internet. A hotlist is usually a compendium of URLs for Internet documents of particular interest. There is no fundamental difference between Internet directories and hotlists, except that many hotlists are specifically targeted and authored by individuals working on hobbies or driven by academic interest. Internet directories are usually products of concerted institutional effort. Hotlists can be unglamorous, specific to a particular topical interest, lacking online assistance and seasonal.

Some hotlist authors are researchers in their own fields, whose research work has triggered the urge to create a hotlist. This does not preclude hotlists which grew primarily out of pastime activities. Currency, as a distinct feature of hotlists, reflects the character of the Internet: up-to-date and swift information. Though there are not as many hotlists of direct engineering relevance as there are for other disciplines, there are still some really informative ones in Webspace which are worth a visit. In the following, a few examples of hotlists are provided. Don't be surprised if some of them have become obsolete or unavailable by the time you try to link to them.

Other search engines

It's practically impossible to keep up with the list of search engines on the Internet. Some of them are WWW search engines while others are engines for Gopher, Telnet, Archie or other protocols. For the majority of Internet users, only a few prominent search engines matter. However, occasionally you may want to use other search engines, especially those specialising in particular types of information search. Some of the Web or non-Web search engines below are listed as additions to those introduced earlier in this Chapter.

ALIWEB

http://web.nexor.com.uk/aliweb/

This Archie-Like Indexing for the Web is a public service provided by Nexor in the United Kingdom. Its database is a collection of document summaries written by their publishers and regularly collected by ALIWEB. The search page provides exceptional flexibility, allowing you to select search fields through the title, description, keywords or URLs. It permits domain restriction, for searching sites in a particular country. The display of the returned items can also be controlled by the user. ALIWEB has a number of mirror sites.

CAIN Europe Server

http://www.can.nl/index.html

Computer Algebra Information Network is a server providing all kinds of information about symbolic and algebraic computation. Its search engine looks up software, applications of computer algebra, literature and more.

CompuServeFind

http://csifind.csi.com/

CSI, CompuServe Interactive, is a search engine run by CompuServe, one of the world's largest providers of Internet and online services.

CyberHound Online

http://www.thomson.com/
cyberhound/

CyberHound Online is affiliated with International Thomson Publishing. It establishes its own index by rating and reviewing individual Web sites.

Electric Library

http://www.elibrary.com/

Electric Library is designed to be an integrated database for Internet resources. It searches images and text from brand-name publishers, newspapers and newswires, magazines and journals, reference works, and more.

EuroSeek

http://www.euroseek.net/

EuroSeek is a new search engine. It caters for an impressive list of languages and hosts its own Web directory.

eZines

http://www.DOMINIS.com/Zines/

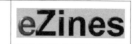

This is a Web site for a database of online magazines. It provides a form for users to search for a given magazine name among its collection of hundreds of online magazines.

Galaxy (TradeWave)

http://www.einet.net/

EINet's Galaxy is a good overall index that covers the Web, Gopher documents (huge archives of plain text documents), and EINet's own Web pages. Galaxy was acquired by SunRiver Corporation in April 1995. The search engine is now called TradeWave. Galaxy rates the search items out of 1000 scores. Its advanced search allows selection of output length and search domains such as Gopher and Telnet.

Harvest

http://harvest.transarc.com/

Harvest is an integrated set of tools for gathering, extracting, organising, searching, caching and replicating relevant information across the Internet. Originally started at the University of Colorado at Boulder, Harvest is now a company separate from the university. With modest effort, you can tailor Harvest to display information in many different formats, and it offers custom search services on the Internet.

InterCat

http://orc.rsch.oclc.org:6990/

InterCat is a searchable database which contains bibliographic records for Internet resources that have been selected and catalogued by libraries worldwide. Each descriptive record provides Internet access information, and you can access many resources just by clicking the underlined portion of the 'Electronic Access' field.

Inter-Link

http://www.nova.edu/Inter-Links/
search/search.html

Inter-Link Search at Nova Northeastern University offers this search form for searching for people on the Internet, searching Gopherspace, Webspace, Telnet sites, discussion groups and software.

Internet Yellow Pages

http://www.superpages.com/

This is probably the best of the general Internet yellow pages, with a tidy interface that makes for uncomplicated searching. The pages can be searched by company name or category. There is also a 'Category List' for browsers. A new feature of Super Yellow Page called 'Search By Distance' allows you to refine the search results based on the distance from a specified location.

LinkStar

http://www.linkstar.com/

LinkStar is a search engine that executes searches for names, companies, cities, countries, states, provinces, postal codes, subject categories, keywords, or combinations of these criteria, by direct input into an entry screen, without the need for Boolean logical commands. LinkStar maintains its own directory, which can be browsed.

NetFind

http://nearnet.gnn.com/

The Global Network Navigators Inc (GNN) catalogue is now hosted by America On Line (AOL). Its search engine NetFind has an impressive selection of search functions at the same Web site. Apart from searching Webspace, NetFind allows you to search for persons, businesses and newsgroups. NetFind also hosts an extensive directory for browsing.

Nordic Web Index

http://nwi.ub2.lu.se/

Nordic Web Index is designed to cater for Scandinavian countries. Its search engine searches the computer servers in a selected country. It facilitates searches in different local languages.

OpenText

http://www.opentext.com/

OpenText is a robust Web searching facility made by Open Text Corporation based in Waterloo, Ontario, Canada; the technology was created by the University of Waterloo. OpenText enables full-text indexing, search, retrieval and display of text. The software is designed for search and retrieval on very large databases. Apart from its Web searching service, the company is in the business of developing and supplying Intranet software products to major corporations and government organisations.

Starting Point

http://www.stpt.com/

This is literally a starting point for new users. It offers keyword search and categorised directories.

UK INDEX

http://www.ukindex.co.uk/
uksearch.html

UK INDEX is a manually maintained index of resources in the UK that provides search service on the index.

Web411

http://www.sserv.com/web411/

Formerly known as Spectra Searcher, Web411 at Santa Cruz, California is a Web URL directory that offers a search service.

WebFinder

http://ds.internic.net/ds/
webfinder/WebFinder.html

WebFinder, provided by The InterNIC, is an engine that searches for organisation's web servers. This distinguishes WebFinder from other Web search engines.

Web-search

http://www.web-search.com/

Web-search offers several different options for Web search. It ranges from simple searches to simultaneous searches on several search engines.

What-U-Seek

http://www.whatuseek.com/

What-U-Seek is a relatively new search engine. It offers some unique features that most other search engines do not have. In the research results, it can highlight the keywords used in the search query. Each hyperlink can lead to more similar links without further searches.

ZDNet

http://www5.zdnet.com/findit/
search.html

ZDNet is a search engine hosted by ZDNet.com that was initially developed to search the contents of a number of electronic magazines published on the Internet. Among those magazines are *Computer Life, Computer Shopper, Family PC, MacWeek, PC Magazine, MacUser, PC Week* and *PC Computing*. It returns a list of article titles with hyperlinks to full articles. This search engine also uses logical or Boolean operators. ZDNet now allows searches for PC or Mac-based shareware and companies.

Tips for using search engines

The challenge of drawing maximum benefit from the Internet arises from its ability to sift through vast resources efficiently to find relevant information. For searching for information on a particular engineering subject, a few good subject-oriented guides serve well as starting points, such as Clearinghouse, Engineering Index at Cornell University, WWW Engineering Virtual Library and ICE Engineering Index. These guides provide links to well-endowed Web sites which enable the search to sprout outwards. Subject guides at Galaxy, Yahoo!, Lycos, etc. are not only searchable indexes, but also provide hierarchical menus so that you can browse through.

When using individual search engines, selection of keywords may dictate the outcome of the search. For instance, entering the freetext term 'rollover' will produce a list almost full of superannuation rollover matters. However, 'truck rollover' will generate mostly engineering-related sites. Take advantage of the Boolean operators offered by many search engines. You can speed up your search and ensure accurate returns by combining your terms using the Boolean operator 'AND'. A Lycos search for 'logic' will result in over 10 000 items, while a search for 'logic AND fuzzy' will return some 200 pertinent items.

To be able to use a search engine effectively, you have to know the format of the query terms it can accept. There are several important aspects of formulating effective query terms: namely specifying whether the engine is to search for any words, all words, a phrase, Boolean operators, truncated word, and word proximity.

A thorough information search should reach to all Internet resources available, rather than to rely solely on the Web resources. For example, the information sought may reside on an Archie server, a WAIS server, a WWW server, or a Gopher server. The data available on one server may be more current and complete than that on others. So be prepared to search different resources. All types of resources now have gateways to the Web, and the search can be performed by the same Web browser. If you are an avid information hunter on the Internet, try to make your own 'bookmarks' or 'hotlist' for useful sites. Usually, your Web browser should allow you to store useful links into a 'bookmark' or 'favourites' file which you can recall later to link to those sites.

Competition among the Web search engines is inexorable. Not only are there new search engines continuously emerging (many are specialised in a particular type of information or in geographically localised information), but established search engines have to look at ways of expanding their services and distinguishing themselves from their competitors. In recent years, the most notable improvement large search engines embarked on is to offer subject directories of Internet resources as well as Web indexing. Lycos, Infoseek, WebCrawler, Excite and Magellan have all established their subject directories in varying forms. When using these search engines, take advantage of their dual functions of searching and offering directories.

Further reading on search engines

There are many Web sites on the Internet that contain excellent introductory, review, discussion and comparison articles on WWW search engines. Being often more current than print publications, these sites constitute the most appropriate further readings for the search engine users. For instance, Carleton College Library maintains a guide for Web search resources at **http://www.library.carleton.edu/websearch/welcome.html**. It is an extensive resource for learning more about Web search engines and directories and how they function. CNET.COM conducted a test on 19 major search engines, and evaluated their ease of use, their power, and the accuracy of their results. It hosts a page with a comparative review of these search engines at **http://www.cnet.com/Content/Reviews/Compare/ Search/**. The Bush Library at Hamline University, USA maintains a Web site at **http://www.hamline.edu/library/bush/handouts/ comparisons.html** that hosts a series articles about search engines. All are fine reading for the user.

The Lund University Library has produced a detailed guide for searching and browsing the Internet resources at **http://www.ub2.lu. se/nav_menu.html**. For those who are more curious on the technical aspects of search engines such as their database size, harvesting software, robot type, indexer, search software, etc., that site leads to **http://www.ub2.lu.se/tk/websearch_systemat.html**, where you can connect to the Tampere City Library in Finland for technical descriptions of major search engines. There is a collection of printed articles, many available online, on search tools at Carleton College Library, **http://www.library.carleton.edu/websearch/bibpaper. html**. The University of Victoria in Canada also maintains a Web page at **http://burns.library.uvic.ca/searchengineanalysis. html**, with a comprehensive chronologically arranged list of articles on search engine analysis. Most of the them are online and many of them provide insights into how search engines work. A similar list titled 'Which Search Engines?' at **http://www.luton.ac.uk/LR/wse.htm**, hosted by Luton University in the UK, has a series of revealing online articles.

If you are interested in learning more about search engines, you could also visit some online electronic journals and magazines for later updates on Web search engines, one notable choice being *Online* magazine published by onlineinc.com at **http://www.onlineinc. com/onlinemag/index.html**.

Bibliography

General Indices & Search Engines from A2Z
http://a2z.lycos.com/Internet/Indices__Directories_and_How-To_Guides/

Global Internet Resources by Subjects
http://www.leidenuniv.nl/pun/ubhtm/marten/sources.htm

Guide to Internet Search
http://www.mnsfld.edu/%7Elibrary/helpsearch.html

The Inquirer
http://www.mcs.net/~bratton/www/search.html

Literature Search Practicum
http://www.welch.jhu.edu/classes/tut/lit-srch/

Looksmart
http://www.looksmart.com/

Michael Louis Scott's hotlist
http://sprawl.sensemedia.net:8080/people/scott/scotlist.htm

Nerd World Media Subject Index
http://www.nerdworld.com/index.cgi

Robots in the Web: Threat or Treat?
http://info.webcrawler.com/mak/projects/robots/threat-or-treat.html

Search Engine Watch
http://searchenginewatch.com/

Search for Information by Keywords
http://www.leidenuniv.nl/pun/ubhtm/marten/findtool.htm

Searching Elsewhere
http://andromeda.einet.net/search-other.html

Searching the Web
http://www.larc.nasa.gov/facts/search.html

Searching the Web from Yahoo!
http://www.yahoo.com/Computers_and_Internet/Internet/World_Wide_Web/Searching_the_Web/

Steve's Search Bookmarks
http://www.aea11.k12.ia.us/search.html

Systematic Overview over Indices
http://www.ub2.lu.se/tk/websearch_systemat.html

World-Wide Web Search Engines
http://www.amdahl.com/internet/meta-index.html

Don't forget to visit us at
http://dingo.vut.edu.au/~jimin/book.html

CHAPTER

4

CHAPTER

5

Access to Libraries Worldwide

WWW access to libraries

Libraries accessible on the WWW

Online public access catalogues (OPACs)

Library Internet resources

Internet projects by libraries worldwide

Improved library services using the Internet

Further reading

WWW access to libraries

A library is traditionally an information provider. In the Internet age, libraries have become pioneers in recognising the Internet's potential and maximising its application to the services they offer. Developed as a multimedia information distribution and retrieval system, the World Wide Web has provided libraries with an excellent basis for creating a unified information infrastructure for users. The first challenge was to implement a library's catalogue on the Web, to enable users to search library collections using just a Web browser, thus circumventing the need to negotiate different Internet protocols such as Telnet, Gopher or HTTP. The use of the WWW also offers an opportunity to exploit an online database's hypertext. Integration with other networked resources and services is much more realistic and practical within the WWW environment than ever before.

A growing number of libraries have established their own World Wide Web interfaces. Remote access to libraries is one of the Internet's greatest accomplishments. Initially, Internet access to libraries was limited to merely remote Telnet connection; this allowed access only to the library's own catalogue for materials stored on site. Telnet delivered plain text and local contents but no images, sound or other multimedia documents. It usually failed to display a wide range of characters, fonts or colours, to support many terminal types, and to provide direct download and printing options. It was also impossible to link the user from one library to another. The Web interface has overcome these shortcomings: a library is now able to offer users a variety of services such as academic and scholarly information, subject indexes, links to organisations for specific disciplines and scholarly societies, as well as online catalogues. Nevertheless, many Telnet connections still exist in parallel with Web connections.

The majority of libraries that provide Web access are from educational institutions. An increasing number of universities world-wide have linked their libraries to the Web. To help the user, some libraries have made concerted efforts in the collection, organisation, classification, and dissemination of Internet resources. Some provide significant online assistance for using the Web and the Internet effectively. It's a good idea to spend time browsing through these libraries on the Web. There are also public and private libraries which have extended their services into the Web, such as the Library of Congress, which also provide a diversity of services inconceivable in the pre-Internet age.

Nevertheless, libraries with a Web connection do not always make their services completely accessible to public. There are reasons for this. A library's primary customers are its constituent or local users. For a university, these are students and staff members—it must extend its services first and foremost to them. When the network resource has difficulty coping with growing demands, restrictions have to be imposed on remote users of the library. Sometimes, a library may be engaged in some information exchange projects with other institutions, whose outcome may be available only to local users. Of course, there are also facilities such as research databases and CD-ROMs for which a library has incurred financial cost in acquiring for its own patrons. These facilities will usually be inaccessible to remote Web users without authorisation. In addition, software licenses, copyright restrictions and other contractual agreements may require that access to certain library services be restricted to authorised users only. A convenient mechanism for authorising users on the Web is to impose passwords.

Once you have access to a library on the WWW, you are able to use its services. A common service is of course the ability to search the library's catalogue for its on-site collections. Searching a library's catalogue via Web access is on its own a momentous development for the library user. However, this is just one of many benefits the Web has to offer. Libraries accessible on the Web often provide useful links to other libraries or locations where you can find more information. Other new library services associated with the Internet will be covered later in this Chapter.

Once you are connected to a library via the WWW interface, you may be directed to a Telnet address where you log in like a local user (if log-in is permitted) and start using the library's online catalogues. However, a library may also provide other protocols for a remote user. For instance, many libraries use Z39.50 protocol for information searching and retrieval. Z39.50 is a national standard from the National Information Standards Organisation (NISO), a committee of the American National Standards Institute (ANSI), and approved by NISO in 1988. It defines a protocol for computer-to-computer information retrieval, and makes it possible for a user in one system to search and retrieve information from other computer systems (that have also implemented Z39.50) without knowing the search syntax used by those other systems. For example, the Library of Congress provides the Z39.50 gateway and a list of Z39.50 servers. Z39.50 databases or catalogues on the Web are often accompanied by HTTP to Z39.50 gateway software; as a result, they can be directly accessed by common Web browsers. More information on Z39.50 can be found at **http://ds.internic.net/z3950/z3950.html**.

Libraries of some universities and institutions have established their own search engines for the library's resources on their own Web server. An example is the search engine at the Northwestern University, **http://www.library.nwu.edu/search/**. These tailor-made search engines are generally less sophisticated than Web search engines and the associated databases are limited or have a specific focus. For instance, the search engine for the discipline resources at the Library of University of Waterloo in Canada (**http://www.lib.uwaterloo.ca/ discipline/discip.html**) searches keywords in specified discipline areas only (Figure 5.1). Nevertheless, the resources provided by this library are impressive.

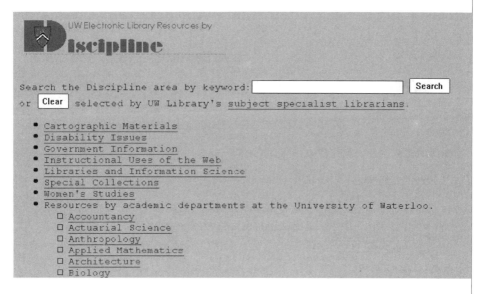

Figure 5.1 Library of University of Waterloo search form

Libraries accessible on the WWW

A library can offer its Internet link in different protocols. Traditional protocol Telnet has now been marginalised by the Web and Gopher interfaces. To find out the libraries in Australia which have established Web interfaces, you can visit **http://info.anu.edu.au/ozlib/ozlib. html**. This Web site at the Australian National University indexes all Australian public and university libraries and their Web interfaces. You'll find a broader index for libraries accessible world-wide on the Internet at University of Califormia, Berkeley, **http://sunsite. berkeley.edu/Libweb/** (Figure 5.2).

This index includes libraries in over 60 countries. Linda Hall Library also hosts an updated list for online catalogues with 'webbed' interfaces at **http://www.lib.ncsu.edu/staff/morgan/alcuin/wwwed-catalogs.html**.

However, such lists, albeit broad, are rarely complete. They are usually intended as an informal research tool for librarians and interested users

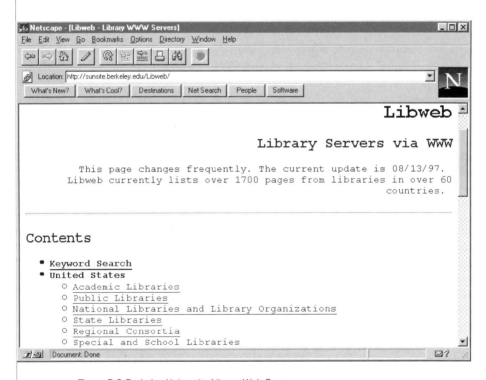

Figure 5.2 Berkeley University Library Web Page

Name and Internet address

All Australian Libraries
http://info.anu.edu.au/ozlib/ozlib.html

Gabriel—Gateway to Europe's National Libraries
http://portico.bl.uk/gabriel/en/welcome.html

IPL Libraries Using Internet
http://ipl.sils.umich.edu/svcs/libtech/librariesusinginternet.html

Libraries on the Web
http://sprawl.sensemedia.net:8080/people/scott/034.htm

Libraries on the World-Wide Web
http://www.freenet.victoria.bc.ca/libraries.html

Library Catalogs
http://ds.internic.net/cgi-bin/tochtml/library/0intro.library

Library WWW servers
http://sunsite.berkeley.edu/Libweb/

Library of Congress
http://lcweb.loc.gov/

Online Catalogs with 'Webbed' Interfaces
http://www.lib.ncsu.edu/staff/morgan/alcuin/wwwed-catalogs.html

Online Library Catalogs from Galaxy
http://galaxy.einet.net/hytelnet/SITES1.html

Portico—The British Library
http://portico.bl.uk/

UK Public Libraries Page
http://dspace.dial.pipex.com/town/square/ac940/ukpublib.html

UK University and College Library Map
http://www.scit.wlv.ac.uk/ukinfo/uk.map.html

United States Public Libraries
http://galaxy.einet.net/hytelnet/US000PUB.html

Yahoo—References: Libraries
http://www.yahoo.com/Reference/Libraries/Indices/

Table 5-1 Web sites for libraries accessible on the Internet

to access online library catalogues and to explore the possibilities of creating World Wide Web browser-accessible online public catalogues. Table 5-1 lists a number of useful sites which index the libraries available on the Internet.

A number of libraries have provided Internet access to the catalogues of their collections, which help you find books, audio and video materials and other documents not available at local libraries. Once you have located what you are looking for, it may be possible to borrow it at your local library via the Inter-library Loan scheme. A list of a few accessible library catalogues can be found at **http:// ds.internic.net/cgi-bin/tochtml/library/0intro.library**.

Online public access catalogues (OPACs)

Over a thousand academic and public libraries throughout the world with WWW access now make their catalogues and other bibliographic databases available for Internet users to search. Before the Internet age, these resources were only available through physical access to the libraries, but now this wealth of information is at every Internet user's fingertips. These catalogues are called 'online public access catalogues' or often referred to simply as OPACs. (With so many catalogues online, it is not surprising to see names like LIBCAT, MADCAT, WATCAT, etc.) Online catalogues are the most important tool for plugging into a library's information resources. The Internet provides an excellent platform for numerous libraries to offer public access to their catalogues. Although the software and hardware used for each OPAC may differ, to the user any OPACs are simply catalogues. Because of remote access and the lack of on-site help, OPACs often provide tips for the use of the catalogues and other online help.

Online public access catalogues are nowadays usually made accessible through a library's Web homepage. The interface with these catalogues used to be Telnet. They either do not require an authorised log-in, or the log-in name is presented on the computer screen. Now, more libraries have made their OPACs available in Webspace, thus bringing considerable benefit to local or remote users. By using OPACs, you can, for instance, connect to a library on a different continent and search its catalogues.

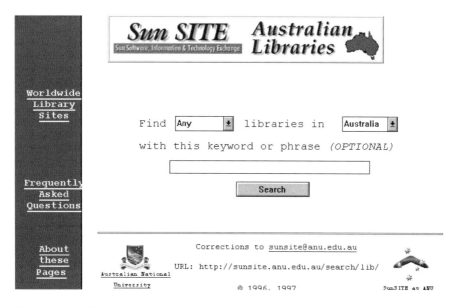

Figure 5.3 Australian National University Web page

As an example, let's visit the Web site for libraries in Victoria, Australia at **http://info.anu.edu.au/ozlib/vic.html**. Figure 5.3 shows a Web page of the Australian National University in Canberra.

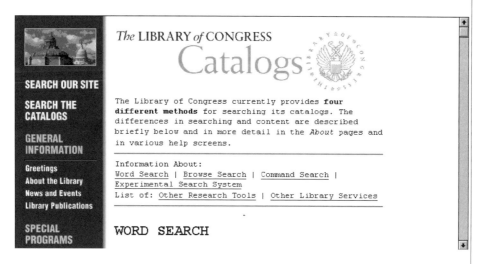

Figure 5.4 The Library of Congress

All the libraries in this Web page allow public Telnet access to their online catalogues. Some have also developed Web interfaces for online access.

More and more libraries have now abandoned the Telnet protocol for their OPACs and have turned to a Web interface instead. Some keep the Telnet connection in parallel with their Web connection. The benefit of using the Web interface over Telnet is obvious when you try using both connections to the same OPAC. As one of the most prominent public libraries in the world, the Library of Congress at **http://lcweb.loc.gov/** has developed its OPAC on the Web (Figure 5.4).

From here, users all over the world can access the catalogue and search online. In addition, the Library has developed a search tool called 'Experimental Search System' (ESS) (Figure 5.5). It not only facilitates relevancy-ranked searching of catalogue records in the Library, but also performs sorts and emails search results. ESS can also analyse search results by subject heading and 'browse' the shelf for items with similar Library of Congress call numbers.

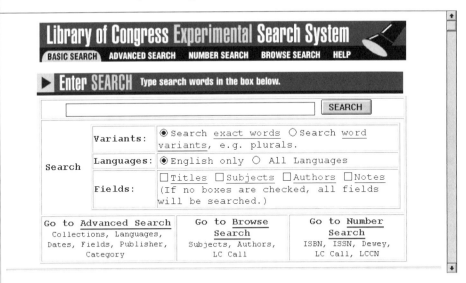

Figure 5.5 Library of Congress ESS search

The Library of Congress has also created a Z39.50 gateway (Figure 5.6) at **http://lcweb.loc.gov/z3950/**. Z39.50 is an ANSI (American

National Standards Institute) standard for electronic data protocols. The gateway uses the Z39.50 communication tool from the Center for Networked Information Discovery and Retrieval CNIDR (**http://www.cnidr.org/ir/isite.html**) that links to an impressive list of OPACs of academic institutions or public libraries world-wide. The same communication tool has been adopted by many other libraries.

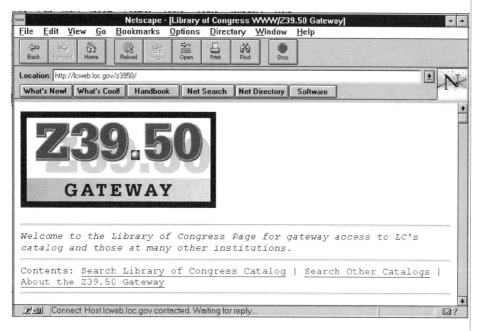

Figure 5.6 Z39.50 Gateway at Library of Congress

From this gateway, you can link to all the listed major US libraries and search their databases or catalogues. The gateway also offers sequential searching on the Library's own catalogues or cooperatives of catalogues. (A 'sequential' search consists of an algorithm for searching through a list or file of items which may or may not be in some order. The search proceeds from the beginning of the list or file until the desired item is located.) Figure 5.7 shows a typical Z39.50 search form at the Library of Congress, where you can enter the search terms and select search types by clicking the options on the screen.

Finding documents or other publications from a library online catalogue is not just a mechanical activity. It is a dynamic, interactive decision-making process. It requires from the user careful consideration not only of the information to be provided for the

First Record to View: 1   Maximum Records to Retrieve: 10

Enter Search Term(s)

```
Submit Query    Clear Form
```

Check Search Type to be Executed

● KEYWORD -- keywords may appear in titles, contents notes, etc.

○ AUTHOR -- enter last name first (e.g, Heim, Pat) or name of an organization (beginning with the first word).

○ TITLE -- enter as much or as little of the title as you want (beginning with the first significant word).

○ SUBJECT -- enter as much or as little of the subject as you want.

○ ISBN -- International Standard Book Number search (omit hyphens).

Figure 5.7 Library of Congress Z39.50 search form

search, but also of the manner in which that information is presented. Thus, a major goal of an information system design is to develop a user interface that takes into account the diverse levels of comprehension and decision-making on the part of users. The World Wide Web has provided an ideal environment for this.

Service Provided by Michigan State University

You may either select a specific catalog from the list below, or you can create a smaller list of catalogs by entering a search phrase. For instance, you can create a list of catalogs in Michigan by entering michigan as a search term.

Many libraries are accessible directly over the internet. For location specific capabilities, you may want to connect to these sites directly.

```
Africana Literature
Alex Database
AT&T Customer Information Database
AT&T Book Catalog Sampling
Auburn University
Colorado School of Mines
Denver Public Library
Education Resources Information Center (ERIC)
```

Figure 5.8 Zweb at Michigan State University

Many more libraries have now installed their Web interfaces with a Z39.50 gateway. Such a gateway bridges the Hyper-Text Transfer Protocol (HTTP) used on the WWW and the Z39.50 search and retrieval protocol, making vast library information resources readily available. Michigan State University has provided a useful Web service called 'ZWeb' (Figure 5.8): a form for accessing online public access catalogues which lists existing Z39.50 servers offered by various universities. By selecting one of the servers, you can search the remote Z39.50 database as if you were a local user. You can access 'ZWeb' at **http://zweb.cl.msu.edu/**.

Let's try it out. From the list of catalogues, select the University of Wisconsin-Madison. We will be connected to the Z39.50 database at that university, **http://zweb.cl.msu.edu/zweb/DB/wisc.html** (Figure 5.9).

We'll conduct a key-word search using the term 'modal analysis'. When you have typed the words in the space and clicked the 'Submit' button, you get a screen that looks like Figure 5.10.

This screen shows a summary of the first 10 items containing the keywords 'modal analysis'. Each individual item is also listed with more detailed information. For instance, item 16 is titled

University of Wisconsin-Madison

Note: if your browser doesn't support tables, you will probably want to check plain response format. standard format uses tables, but eliminates backgrounds and special colors.

Select Submit to submit your search, or clear to start over.

Response format ● fancy ○ standard ○ plain

Subject
Execute ●word or ○phrase subject term matching.
Title
Execute ●word or ○phrase title term matching.
Author
Execute ●word or ○phrase author term matching.
Keyword

Term truncation ●right ○left ○left and right ○none

Figure 5.9 Zweb search form

CHAPTER 5

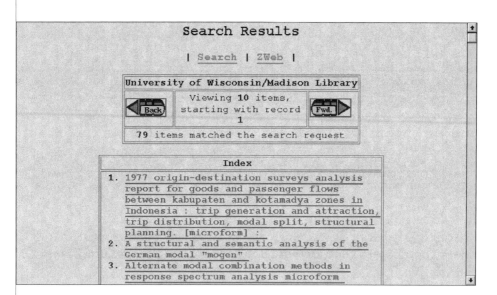

Figure 5.10 Zweb search results

- **Author:** Camarda, Charles J.
- **Other Authors:**
  1. Langley Research Center.
- **Title:** Development of advanced modal methods for calculating transient thermal and structural response microform Charles J. Camarda.
- **Subjects:**
  1. Structural analysis (Engineering) Approximation methods.
- **Series:** NASA technical memorandum ;104102
- **Published:** Hampton, Va. : [Springfield, Va.? : National Aeronautics and Space Administration, Langley Research Center ; National Technical Information Service [distributor] 1991]
- **Physical Description:** 1 v.
- **Notes:** Distributed to depository libraries in microfiche.
- **Call Number:**

Figure 5.11 Zweb search results (details)

'Development of advanced modal methods for calculating transient thermal and structural response microform'. Click on the underlined text, and you get further details of this title (Figure 5.11).

This list provides not only the bibliographic information for the article, but also a hyperlink to the author's Web page if one is available. In addition, the list offers hyperlinks to subjects: clicking on these takes you to lists of papers on the same subjects as the one you have retrieved. This further enhances your ability to pin down the most relevant papers.

Apart from the online OPACs at academic, public and private libraries, there are catalogues from other sources such as publishers. In the past, publishers relied on postal delivery to supply information on their publications. With the Internet, they can now set up their online catalogues for anyone interested in their publications arsenal on a particular discipline. These catalogues can even announce upcoming publications. A good example of an online catalogue is at the Elsevier Science Web site at **http://www.elsevier.nl/**. Its 'Engineering, Energy and Technology' publishing programme provides an extensive collection of relevant publications from Elsevier Science (Figure 5.12). The Elsevier Science Catologue can be searched like other OPACs. The search form allows you to select one or more scientific fields itemised by Elsevier Science.

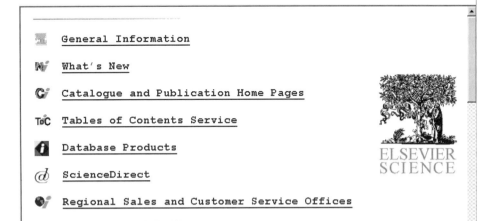

Figure 5.12 Elsevier Science Web page

Engineering professional societies are another sources of OPACs. For example, the Library of the Institution of Civil Engineers in UK at **http://www.ice.org.uk/ice/library/libindex.html** has an extensive collection of civil engineering-related books, periodicals, audio-visual materials and civil engineering archives. The library allows remote users to search its collection using a Web browser.

In addition to the OPAC list at the Library of Congress, there are other lists on the Web that compile OPACs world-wide. One of these lists is hosted by the Gopher server at the University of California, Irvine at **gopher://peg.cwis.uci.edu:7000/11/gopher.welcome/peg/ LIBRARIES**. Many OPACs on the list cater for Telnet protocol, though the Web interface counterparts may also be available separately.

Another comprehensive list of OPACs is currently maintained at **http://www.niss.ac.uk/reference/opacs.html**, which lists the OPACs of higher education and research library catalogues in the United Kingdom, and provides links to the libraries in universities and colleges all over the UK. It lists both Telnet and Web protocols. A similar list for OPACs in the USA is maintained at **http://www. metronet.lib.mn.us/lc/lca.html**.

As mentioned in Chapter 3, HyTelnet is a tool for Telnet domains around the world. It is ideal for accessing online library systems that still use the Telnet interface protocol. The birthplace of HyTelnet, the University of Saskatchewan, hosts an extensive list of library catalogues around the world at **http://library.usask.ca/hytelnet/**. A more recent site for 'WebCats' has been created at **http://library.usask.ca/ hywebcat/**, and you can find a similar list at the University of Kansas at **http://www.cc.ukans.edu/hytelnet_html/START.TXT.html**. Both sites provide comprehensive listings of library catalogues throughout the world.

Now that over a thousand library catalogues are available on the Internet, which are the best ones to search for a particular topic or subject? Unfortunately, there is no general answer. A library from a prominent university with huge collections obviously would be worth searching. You would already be aware of which institutions are foremost in your particular field, so their library catalogues are another obvious place to begin. Gopher is a distributed document delivery service for searching for and retrieving materials from local sources and remote sites alike. Use the Gopher searcher Veronica to search the topic keywords (see Chapter 3); likewise WWW search engines can reveal those library sites which may have topical collections.

Library Internet resources

Like the subject-oriented guides or Internet directories introduced in Chapter 4, many libraries with a Web interface compile their own Internet directories, known sometimes as 'library Internet resources' or 'subject trees'. For instance, the resource created by the University of Oxford (**http://www.bodley.ox.ac.uk/olig/**) is a typical library Internet resource organised by subjects. In fact, many Internet directories are created by libraries or as library resources. The Internet directories or guides for engineering created by libraries may reflect the interests of the library's clients. A bonus of using these library resources is that the host library usually provides links to other resources.

A few libraries have produced rather sophisticated engineering-related subject guides: two notable ones are the Engineering Library at Cornell University and Heriot-Watt University Library. Keeping these guides up-to-date is a formidable and continuous task. Table 5-2 contains a number of leading engineering Internet resources created by libraries which you should not overlook, some of which are described in detail below. They are by no means the only library resources.

BUBL Information Services
http://bubl.ac.uk/link/subjects

BUBL (BUlletin Board for Libraries) Information Services is an Internet-based information service for the UK higher education community. It is located in the Andersonian Library of the University of Strathclyde, Glasgow, Scotland. Starting from a project at Glasgow University for training librarians, BUBL has been developed to become a UK national information service. The subject tree in BUBL was one of the early subject trees available on the Internet. It offers a comprehensive resource list with subjects organised by library classifications.

Name and Internet address

Bodleian Library at University of Oxford
http://www.bodley.ox.ac.uk/olig/

BUBL Information Service
http://bubl.ac.uk/link/subjects

Catholic University of America Library—Resources on the Internet
http://www.cua.edu/www/mullen/inetsubj.html

The Clearinghouse for Subject Oriented Internet Resource Guides
http://www.clearinghouse.net/

Edinburgh Engineering Virtual Library
http://www.eevl.ac.uk/

EEL's All Engineering Resources on the Internet
http://www.ub2.lu.se/eel/ae/

Engineering Electronic Library at Lund University
http://www.ub2.lu.se/eel/eelhome.html

Frank Potter's Science Gems—Engineering
http://www-sci.lib.uci.edu//SEP/engineer.html

Heriot-Watt University Library Major Subject Guides to Internet Resources
http://www.hw.ac.uk/libWWW/electron/subjects.html

Internet Connections for Engineering (compiled at Cornell University)
http://www.englib.cornell.edu/ice/ice-index.html

Librarian's Index to the Internet at Berkeley University
http://sunsite.berkeley.edu/InternetIndex/

LibraryWeb—Columbia University Library WWW Information System
http://www.columbia.edu/cu/libraries/subjects/index.html

Mansfield Subject Guides—Mansfield University
http://www.mnsfld.edu/~library/start.html#guides

The Mother-of-all-BBS
http://wwwmbb.cs.colorado.edu/~mcbryan/bb/summary.html

Netlink Server at Washington & Lee University
http://netlink.wlu.edu:1020/-su

Oxford Libraries Internet Gateway
http://www.bodley.ox.ac.uk/olig/

Penn Library Engineering Page
http://www.library.upenn.edu/resources/sciences/engineering/engin.html/

Research & Subject Guides at University of California
http://www.ucsc.edu/library/subject/index.html

Rice Info: Information by Subject
http://riceinfo.rice.edu/Internet/Subject.html

Subject Guide from De Montfort University
http://www.dmu.ac.uk/~pka/guides/guides.html

Subject Guides from MiamiLink
http:///www.lib.muohio.edu/res/subjres/

University of Alberta Library School Guides
http://www.ualberta.ca/~slis/guides/guides.html

University of Wyoming Libraries General Engineering Internet Resources
http://www.uwyo.edu/Lib/geneng.htm

WWW Resources at University of Kentucky
http://www.uky.edu/Subject/subject-catalog.html

Table 5-2 WWW library engineering resources (Concluded)

Edinburgh Engineering Virtual Library

http://www.eevl.ac.uk/

Edinburgh Engineering Virtual Library, known as EEVL, is an excellent Internet resource specifically targeted at engineering. Hosted at Heriot-Watt University Library, EEVL has many partners: University of Edinburgh, Napier University, Cambridge University, Imperial College of Science, Technology and Medicine, the Nottingham Trent University and the Institution of Electrical Engineers. The EEVL project commenced at the beginning of August 1995 and has now established a comprehensive database for engineering resources on the Internet. You can browse the database for resources under different subjects, and also search it. EEVL also hosts a search system for Usenet Engineering newsgroups that queries a 40-day archive of news articles.

EELS All Engineering Database Resources on the Internet

http://www.ub2.lu.se/eel/ae/

'All Engineering' is a database for Engineering Internet resources. It is generated by a robot searching the full text of several tens of thousands of engineering pages on the Internet and indexing the results. This database is an indexed Internet resource that allows you to browse through its collections alphabetically by resource title, by domain or country, and by the number of times a resource has been linked to or cited by all engineering pages in the database. You can also search the database to find relevant Internet resources. The 'All Engineering Database' complements the Internet resource offered by EELS.

Engineering Electronic Library at Lund University

http://www.ub2.lu.se/eel/
eelhome.html

EELS, an acronym for Engineering Electronic Library, is an information system for quality assessed information resources on the Internet, created by libraries at the Swedish University of Technology. Its subject tree contains over a thousand annotated and indexed Internet resources. EELS is an attempt to provide mainly technical universities with links to evaluated resources, so it is of particular value to engineers and engineers-to-be. EELS organises its resources using the subject classification scheme of Engineering Information Inc.

Gopher resources

In addition to those library Internet resources on Web servers, there are many resources on library Gopher servers world-wide. Gopher as a distributed document delivery service for both local sources and remote sites has long been a popular protocol for library Internet services. However, its inability to deliver multimedia information has seen its service gradually being taken over by the Web. Some of the library Gopher servers do not share the same currency as their Web servers. Some libraries started with Gopher subject trees and migrated to a Web server. Still, many Gopher library resources are worth a visit.

Table 5-3 lists a number of the principal Gopher resources created by libraries.

Name and Internet address

Gopher Jewels from University of South Carolina
gopher://cwis.usc.edu:70/11/Other_Gophers_and_Information_Resources/Gophers_by_
Subject/Gopher_Jewels

InterNIC Directory of Directories
Gopher://ds.internic.net/11/dirofdirs

Lund University, Sweden
gopher://munin.ub2.lu.se:70/11/resources

Subject Guide from Library of Congress
gopher://marvel.loc.gov/11/global

Subject Guide from (Texas A&M) University
gopher://gopher.tamu.edu:70/11/.dir/subject.dir

University of Michigan
gopher://vienna.hh.lib.umich.edu:70/1/

University of Southern California Santa Barbara
gopher://summit.ece.ucsb.edu/11/Resources

University of Texas—Austin
gopher://lanic.utexas.edu:70/11/subject

University of Virginia
gopher://gopher.lib.Virginia.EDU:70/11/subject

Table 5-3 Gopher library engineering resources

The increasing number of directories or subject trees on the Internet enticed efforts to index them—the index of indexes. Some libraries embarked upon indexing the Internet resources. From their pages, we can find not just one resource but a list of resources organised in specific ways. The Internet Resources Index at University of Illinois at Urbana-Champain (**http://www.ncsa.uiuc.edu/SDG/Software/ Mosaic/MetaIndex. html**) is such a resources index. This 'meta-index page' or a variation of it is also hosted by many other servers.

Internet projects by libraries worldwide

The Web and Gopher library Internet resources provide well-organised and indexed information on the Internet. Many of these resources are the results of projects carried out by libraries world-wide. As well as creating different Internet resources, libraries the world over have been engaged on projects for improving library services and library management, and providing new services for the Internet era. Most of these projects were initiated and executed by individual libraries or a library consortium.

Name and Internet address

DAISY—Dissertations Available on Internet SYstems
http://www.englib.cornell.edu/daisy.html

Digital Libraries, University of Houston
http://info.lib.uh.edu/pr/v6/n1/lbdiglib.htm

INFOMINE—Scholarly Internet Resource Collections at University of California
http://lib-www.ucr.edu/

NEEDS—National Engineering Education Delivery System
http://www.needs.org/

Networked Computer Science Technical Reports Library
http://cs-tr.cs.cornell.edu/

OHIOLINKS
http://www.ohiolink.edu/about/what-is-ol.html

Scholarly Societies Project, University of Waterloo
http://www.lib.uwaterloo.ca/society/overview.html

The Synthesis Coalition
http://synthesis.org/

TULIP: The University LIcensing Project
http://www.englib.cornell.edu/tulip/tuliphome.html

Table 5-4 Some North American library Internet projects

North American projects

Table 5-4 lists the major Internet projects completed by libraries in North America and their Web sites. By visiting these projects sites, you can gain an insight into the background, initiation, growth and future direction of library Internet services, as well as their benefits. Two of them are described below.

INFOMINE—Scholarly Internet Resource Collections at University of California
http://lib-www.ucr.edu/

INFOMINE is an initiative of the Library of the University of California. It aims to provide library users with a comprehensive virtual library and reference tool on useful Internet and Web resources of different disciplines. These resources encompass online databases, electronic journals, electronic books, bulletin boards, listservs, online library catalogues, articles and directories of researchers, and more.

Scholarly Societies Project

http://www.lib.uwaterloo.ca/
society/overview.html

Scholarly Societies Project, according to the Electronic Library at the University of Waterloo, was created to facilitate access to information about scholarly societies across the world. It was developed from a small collection of resources to become a very extensive resource for scholarly societies all over the world and for their publications. This project has also created a search engine for its own pages.

European projects

In European Union countries, a number of projects have been or are being carried out by libraries from educational institutions or by public libraries. Some of them have already borne fruit. The integration of Europe has been a catalyst for developing many library projects aiming to harmonise and standardise the library systems on the continent in order to cater for diversified and cross-cultural users, and the Internet has been a excellent vehicle for undertaking such an endeavour. Table 5-5 lists a selection of library projects from Europe,

Name and Internet address

BIBLINK
http://www.ukoln.ac.uk/metadata/BIBLINK/

BUBL
http://bubl.ac.uk/

Camile
http://www2.echo.lu/libraries/en/projects/camile.html

DECIDE
http://slsgate.sls.se/sls/decide.htm

DECIMAL
http://www2.echo.lu/libraries/en/projects/decimal.html

Desire
http://www.ub2.lu.se/desire/

Edinburgh Engineering Virtual Library
http://www.eevl.ac.uk/welcome.html

Electronic Library
http://ukoln.bath.ac.uk/elib/

EQLIPSE
http://www.dcu.ie/library/eqlipse/

EU EDUCATE
http://educate.lib.chalmers.se/

HyperLib Electronic Document Store
http://www.ua.ac.be/docstore.html

Internet Library of Early Journals
http://www.bodley.ox.ac.uk/ilej/

ITAUL Projects
http://educate.lib.chalmers.se/IATUL/projpart.html

LAMDA at University College London
http://www.ucl.ac.uk/Library/lamda/

NetLab at Lund University
http://www.ub2.lu.se/netlab.html

PORTICO at British Library
http://portico.bl.uk/

Table 5-5 Some European library Internet projects

some of which are described in detail below. Obviously few library projects have an exclusive focus on engineering. However, the improved service derived from these projects will eventually benefit users from all disciplines including engineering, science and technology.

BIBLINK

http://www.ukoln.ac.uk/metadata/
BIBLINK/

The BIBLINK project was initiated amid the growing aggregation of electronic publishing and the need for adequate bibliographic control over it. It aims to develop and improve national bibliographic services, through testing a 'demonstrator' service involving new links between publishers and national libraries or national bibliographic agencies. According to the project description, the demonstrator will involve the transmission from publishers of agreed minimum data on electronic publications, which will be used by the libraries to provide enriched and embedded catalogue and authority data on the document. These data will be re-transmitted to the publishers for distribution with the publications. BIBLINK plans to generate (among many outputs) data formats, transmission standards and demonstrator service for national libraries and for publishers in the United Kingdom.

DECIDE

http://slsgate.sls.se/sls/decide.
htm

DECIDE—Decision Support System for European Academic and Public Libraries, is a project undertaken by six academic institutions and commercial enterprises in UK, Spain and the Netherlands. The landscape change in library service since the advent of the Internet gives new urgency and meaning to developing a decision support system for automated library management. According to the project description, DECIDE embraces two primary goals: 'to define a comprehensive set of decision-making support requirements, approaches and methodologies which can be adapted to match a wide range of current and future needs in European academic and public libraries,' and 'to create a decision support system (DSS) prototype for integration into automated library management systems from different manufacturers.'

DECIMAL

http://www2.echo.lu/libraries/en/projects/
decimal.html

DECIMAL, short for 'DECIsion MAking in Libraries', is a project undertaken by a consortium of libraries that comprises partners from the United Kingdom, Spain and Italy. It is coordinated by the Department of Library and Information Studies, Manchester Metropolitan University. DECIMAL aims to develop a decision-support module for integration into established library management systems. The work is carried out on the library system Heritage, a product of Inheritance Systems Limited, which is a partner in the project.

EQLIPSE

http://www.dcu.ie/library/eqlipse/

EQLIPSE stands for 'Evaluation and Quality in Library Performance: System for Europe'. It is a project participated in by 10 libraries from seven EU countries and coordinated by the Library at the University of Central Lancashire, UK. The objective of EQLIPSE is to specify, develop and validate an open system to support quality management and performance measurement in libraries of all types. The project sets out to perform a number of tasks that constitute the fulfilment of the project's objective during its two-year duration. They are Library Requirements Analysis, Initial Functional Specification, Prototype System, Data Tools and Data Collection, Field Trials and Evaluation, and Integration in Libraries.

EU EDUCATE

http://educate.lib.chalmers.se/

EDUCATE is a project funded under the European Union Telematics for Libraries programme and was undertaken by six universities in Europe: Limerick University, Ireland; Chalmers University of Technology, Sweden; Imperial College of Science, Technology and Medicine, UK; Ecole de Ponts et Chaussées, France; University of

Barcelona, Spain and University of Plymouth, UK; all members of the International Association of Technological University Libraries. EDUCATE aims to help students, research workers and practitioners in the development of information literacy by producing a new type of model self-paced user-education course in the selection and use of information tools in Internet environment.

Internet Library of Early Journals

http://www.bodley.ox.ac.uk/ilej/

The Internet Library of Early Journals (ILEJ) project, aims to digitise substantial runs of 18th and 19th century journals, and make these images available on the Internet, together with their associated bibliographic data. This project is a joint effort by the Universities of Birmingham, Leeds, Manchester and Oxford.

LAMDA

http://www.ucl.ac.uk/Library/
lamda/

LAMDA is an experimental inter-library loans service. It aims to offer quick delivery of requested journal articles electronically. The project was set up by a number of academic libraries in London and Manchester in 1995, as part of the Electronic Libraries (eLib) Programme. This project addresses an acute problem in today's library service, namely the increasing demand for rapid document delivery of journal articles.

Portico at British Library

http://portico.bl.uk/

The Portico projects at British Library were set up to bring the Library online for its Internet users. Starting from a Gopher server, the Library now provides a large collection of World Wide Web pages, graphic images, audio files and databases. The Library's services and collections can now be delivered through electronic or normal mail.

Improved library services using the Internet

The advent of the Internet and, more importantly, that of the WWW, has opened an avenue for developing traditional library services to respond to the burgeoning demands of current and future needs of academic and commercial clients.

Bibliographic instruction

With the development of the WWW came the demand for information previously provided in print form to be now available in electronic form, where it could be retrieved from the workstation in laboratories or offices. However, retrieving information from the increasingly vast collection of electronic data requires both the knowledge of information sources and the skills to use those sources efficiently. Bibliographic instruction teaches the library user how to use a reference book, how to choose and evaluate information, how to think through problems ahead of time and how to organise research and get the most out of the time spent at the library.

University students and researchers are usually poorly prepared when confronting the complexities of information searching. Many do not understand the difference between a catalogue of a library's holdings and a periodical index which gets inside selected periodicals, or between popular and scholarly sources. Bibliographic instruction is particularly useful to students and researchers at all levels. It trains students in finding ways of efficiently exploiting the resources available in and through the library. The Internet has not only brought new information sources, but has also become a powerful forum for hosting and running bibliographic instruction.

Many university libraries have taken up this task and created useful bibliographic instruction resources. Some libraries even offer course-specific Web pages, hypertext tutorials of databases, and other unique features of the World Wide Web. They teach users information-seeking skills, aimed at improving efficiency and productivity. You can see an example of a library's bibliographic instruction programme from the University of Michigan Undergraduate Library at **http://www.lib.umich.edu/libhome/**

UGL/bi.html. Another example, shown in Figure 5.13, is at **http://sehplib.ucsd.edu/electclass/classroom.html**—the Electronic Classroom at the Science and Engineering Library of the University of California, San Diego.

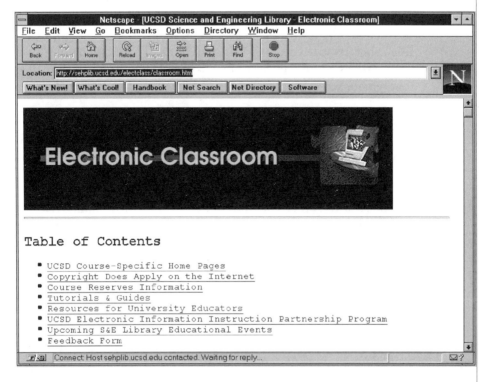

Figure 5.13 Electronic Classroom at University of California

Electronic cataloguing

The Internet has brought a new challenge to library cataloguing—how to cater for networked electronic information when traditional cataloguing is designed to accommodate physical items residing in libraries. The fact that a vast number of data resources available via the Internet are unverified and are of limited interest also reinforces the need for electronic cataloguing. Libraries, as traditional information providers, are in a unique position to index the information resources present on the Internet.

CHAPTER
5

In the past, there have been a number of cataloguing software systems developed for libraries. Systems such as INNOPAC, DYNIX and PALS have been adopted by many libraries world-wide as their cataloguing systems. For instance, a list of universities using INNOPAC can be found at **http://galaxy.einet.net/hytelnet/ SYS007.html**. The Gopher server at Yale University contains an instruction document for cataloguing systems, available at **gopher:// libgopher.cis.yale.edu:70/11/Instructions**. These cataloguing software systems are usually accessible from a Telnet protocol, provided that remote access is granted.

Electronic cataloguing can mean several things for a library. It can be the WWW variant of the traditional cataloguing which was designed to accommodate on-site collections in libraries—this is effectively the Web version of the Telnet protocol for access to a library. Or it can be the WWW cataloguing data for the resources available on the Internet which libraries gather and disseminate. Although a library may be interested in information on the Internet for particular disciplines, the resultant electronic catalogue may nevertheless supplement its catalogue of the library's holdings.

The Web catalogue of a library's collection entails the design of a search engine which works on the traditional catalogue as its database.

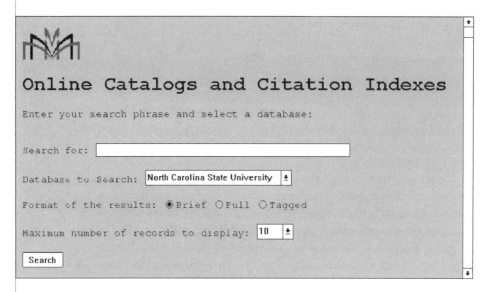

Figure 5.14 Search form at North Carolina State University Library

The Web interface for such a mechanism is usually a Web search form, much like that for many Web search engines. For example, Figure 5.14 shows the Web form developed by the North Carolina State University Library for interrogating their collections (**http://ncsulib4.lib.ncsu.edu/drabin/niso_forms**).

The online catalogue of the North Carolina State University Library provides bibliographic information, library location and circulation status for books, journals and other materials that have been processed by the Library since 1975, including items currently on order. Many items published before 1975 are also found in it.

Electronic publishing

With the World Wide Web, publishers, scholarly societies and libraries are nowadays forming partnerships in an effort to make electronic journals and books more readily accessible, easier to use and of a higher quality. Advocates of electronic publishing (also known as 'online publishing') have based their cases on the advantages of computer networking and electronic media over print publication, such as the speed of information dissemination, the relatively low costs of production and dissemination, and the ability to make the results of scholarly research more widely available than before.

The traditional sequence of scholarly publication usually entails six steps:

- author creation
- peer review organised by a publisher
- preparation by a publisher, including printing and shipping
- storage by a librarian
- cataloguing, indexing or abstracting by publishers or librarians
- utilisation by readers.

The advent of the WWW has brought the real possibility of significantly shortening this publication cycle. For example, the steps of preparation by a publisher and cataloguing/indexing can now be done by either the publisher (such as Contents Direct Source from Elsevier Science Inc.) or a commercial consortium (such as Ovid Technologies, producer of *Current Contents*, an index to periodicals backed up by document delivery) with real advantages in economy and in the timely and useful flow of information. This work can also be accomplished by the author's institutional library or professional engineering society. Printing, shipping and handling can be eliminated. In addition, the utilisation of publication materials can be made in appropriate ways at earlier and timelier stages in the process. That is, material for teaching or for informal discussion can be more widely and readily circulated while the peer review and formal publication processes continue.

Electronic publishing consists largely of three forms:

- electronic books
- electronic journals
- electronic newspapers.

With Web search engines such as WebCrawler, Lycos and Gopher, and search engines such as Jughead and Veronica, locating these electronic publications on the Internet is quite straightforward. There is a general recognition that electronic publishing as a means of information exchange is flourishing; however, there are still hurdles to overcome before electronic publishing can compete effectively with traditional publishing. To start with, the great variety of word-processors used today makes it nearly impossible to write filters to convert all the different formats to the HTML format used by the Web. As a result, authors are often forced to give up their word processing systems and instead deal with completely new and unfamiliar software.

Another shortcoming of electronic publishing yet to be overcome is the problem of the publications' availability to readers. This is largely due to the bottle-neck caused by a computer server transmitting excessive amounts of data to a few simultaneous users. Copyright and payment of royalties to authors need to be clarified, and a mechanism is needed for recompensing authors for their work. A payment system to both read online and print the document needs to be implemented.

These shortcomings of electronic publishing are being vigorously addressed. For instance, a Standard Generalised Markup Language (SGML) has been approved by the ISO as the new standard for electronic and database publishing. This language is sufficiently flexible to accommodate various functions in a hypermedia document, such as an animation of the vibration of a structure, or the sound of a turbine engine. In the meantime, the Web language HTML is inexorably moving toward greater expressiveness and greater conformance to the SGML standard. To overcome the billing and copyright problem for electronic journals, there is a strong proposal to charge for subscriptions.

As an example of electronic publishing, let's visit an electronic journal called the 'Public-Access Computer Systems Review' (PACS Review) at the University of Houston, **http://info.lib.uh.edu/pacsrev.html**, about end-user computer systems in libraries. It is distributed at no charge on the Internet and other computer networks. It publishes papers on topics such as campus-wide information systems, CD-ROM LANs, digital libraries, document delivery systems, electronic publishing, expert systems, hypermedia and multimedia systems, locally mounted databases, network-based information resources and tools, and online catalogues. It is published by the University of Houston Libraries.

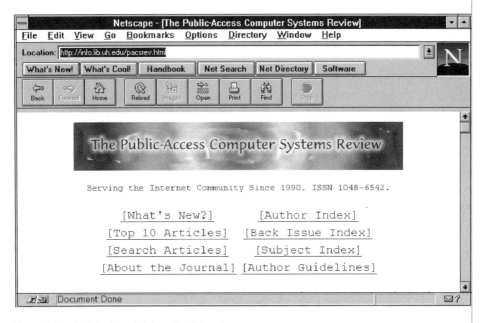

Figure 5.15 PACS Review at University of Houston

Another example of scholarly electronic publication is the 'Journal of Artificial Intelligence Research' at **http://www.cs.washington.edu/**

research/jair/home.html, a refereed journal published by University of Washington. It covers all areas of artificial intelligence and is distributed free of charge over the Internet. This journal offers AI researchers several advantages over traditional journals such as rapid publication of research results, no charge for distribution, and software for online search.

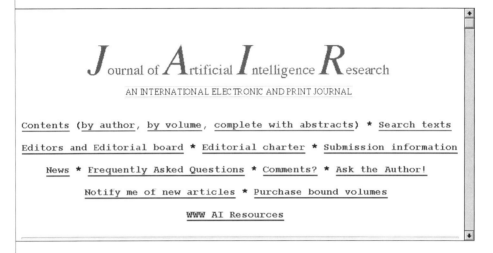

Figure 5.16 Journal of Artificial Intelligence Research

To find electronic journals related to engineering, we can use Web search engines such as Lycos and Infoseek. A thorough list of online engineering journals is provided by the Library of Heriot-Watt University at **http://www.hw.ac.uk/libWWW/faculty/genres.html #ejn**. The library has designed a subject tree in which numerous Web and Gopher sites for electronic journals are offered. More detailed discussion on electronic journals and online journals will be presented in Chapter 8.

Electronic ILL

The Internet provides an ideal venue for an electronic interlibrary loan (ILL) program. This is two-fold. A library user may file their ILL request electronically to the library, eliminating the necessity for physically delivering the request to librarians. For instance, the University of Sydney Library provides an 'Electronic Document Supply/Interlibrary Loan Request Form' at **http://www.library.usyd.**

edu.au/Services/Forms/index.html to enable academic staff, post-graduate students and final-year honours students to submit document supply/ILL requests directly from their offices. On the other hand, the library may submit the ILL request to other libraries from which publications are sought. Some libraries have already developed ILL forms on the Web to cater for requests from other institutions.

Digital libraries

A digital library, briefly, is a machine-readable representation of materials. Its service is an assemblage of digital computing, acquisition, storage and communications machinery together with the software needed to reproduce, emulate, and extend the services provided by conventional libraries based on paper and other material means of collecting, storing, cataloguing, finding and disseminating information. The documents involved in a digital library can be literary works, image databases, sound archives, scientific data archives (but not current experimental files), bibliographies and reference information, and can be in the format of text, image, sound, multimedia or data.

There have been a number of projects conducted by different libraries to develop an integrated and friendly digital library. An example is the Computer Science Technical Report (CSTR) Project (**http://www.cnri.reston.va.us/home/cstr.html**) carried out by the Corporation for National Research Initiatives (CNRI) and five research universities to build a large-scale, distributed digital library of computer science technical reports produced by project participants. The participating universities were Carnegie Mellon University, Cornell University, the Massachusetts Institute of Technology, Stanford University, and the University of California at Berkeley. The Library of the University of Houston hosts a Web page at **http://info.lib.uh.edu/pr/v6/n1/lbdiglib.htm** that includes a number of digital library projects conducted by university libraries (Figure 5.17).

Further reading

The first source for further reading will be a number of relevant online journals or magazines designed for library-related matters. Some of

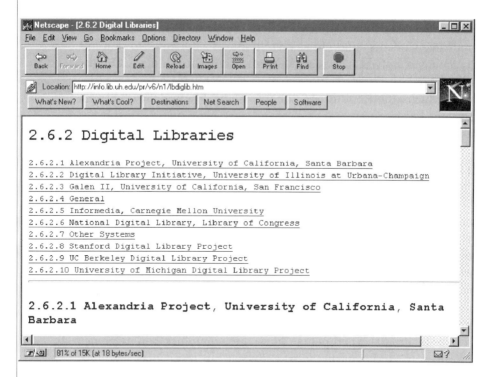

Figure 5.17 Digital library list at the Library of the University of Houston

these publications are online only, while others are the offshoots of their printed counterparts. In either case, you will find relevant articles in 'D-Lib Magazine' at **http://www.dlib.org/**, an excellent online magazine for stories, commentary, and briefings and a collection of resources for digital library research. The Web site also provides pointers to projects and collections concerning digital library research.

'ISTL', an acronym for 'Issues in Science and Technology Librarianship', is an online quarterly publication of the Science and Technology Section, Association of College and Research Libraries. Its Web site is at **http://www.library.ucsb.edu/istl/**. ISTL contains articles on issues strongly identified with library services in the Internet era. Recent articles cover Internet resources for a specific area of technology, the Science and Technology Libraries Discussion Group, online publishing, and creating electronic journal Web pages from OPAC records.

'LJDigital' at **http://www.ljdigital.com/** is an electronic offshoot of *Library Journal*, the oldest independent national library publication, founded in 1876. If you are interested in library public policy, technology and management developments you will find the journal helpful. LJDigital also covers reviews of books, audio and video, CD-ROMs, websites, and magazines. Another online journal on digital information called 'Journal of Digital Information' resides at **http:// joutnals.ecs.soton.ac.uk/jodi**/.

'MC Journal—The Journal of Academic Media Librarianship' at **http://wings.buffalo.edu/publications/mcjrnl/** is a peer-reviewed electronic journal covering all aspects of academic media librarianship, distributed free of charge on the Internet. 'NewsFlashes/Libraries' is an online newsletter updated weekly, containing brief news for the library community. Library users with inquisitive minds may also like to know some of the anecdotes in this newsletter.

The 'LITA Newsletter' at **http://www.harvard.edu/litanews/** is the demonstration World Wide Web version of the *LITA Newsletter* published quarterly by the Library and Information Technology Association, a division of the American Library Association.

'Internet Trend Watch for Libraries' at **http://www.itwfl.com** is a Web-based newsletter highlighting innovative Internet applications in libraries. The news appearing in the newsletter are compiled from library journals, computer publications, mailing lists, newsgroups and other resources.

If you are interested in more information on OPACS, 'Public-Access Computer Systems Review' at **http://info.lib.uh.edu/pacsrev.html** (PACS Review) constitutes a useful information source. PACS Review is an electronic journal about end-user computer systems in libraries, published by the University of Houston Libraries.

The 'Ariadne' newsletter at **http://www.ariadne.ac.uk/** is also a useful source of information. It describes and evaluates sources and services available on the Internet, and of potential use to librarians and information professionals.

There are various library-related resources available on the Internet for further reading. Naturally, many of these resources are compiled and hosted by libraries. For example, the 'Library-Oriented Lists and Electronic Serials' at **http://info.lib.uh.edu/liblists/liblists.htm** is hosted by the Library of the University of Houston (Figure 5.18), and contains a very extensive list of Internet sites related to library resources. The site also allows you to search this list.

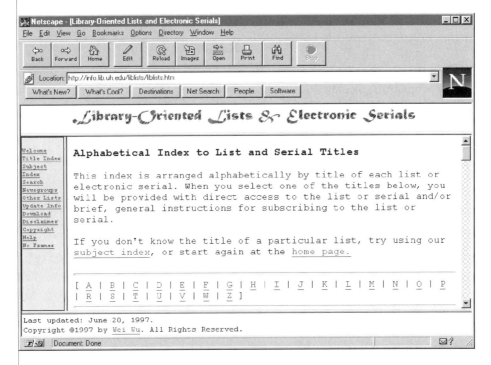

Figure 5.18 'Library-Oriented Lists and Electronic Serials' at the University of Houston

The Library of the University of Pennsylvania hosts a Web page entitled 'Libraries and Publishing' at **http://www.library.upenn.edu/ resources/infostudies/infostudies.html**.

Bibliography

Australian Libraries
http://info.anu.edu.au/ozlib/ozlib

Electronic Cataloging Instructions
gopher://libgopher.cis.yale.edu:70/11/Instructions

Electronic Classroom
http://sehplib.ucsd.edu/electclass/classroom.html

Electronic Publishing Standards
http://www.adfa.oz.au/Epub/McLean_Cook.html#RTFToC1

Innovative Internet Applications in Libraries
http://www.mtsu.edu/~kmiddlet/libweb/innovate.html

IPL Especially For Librarians Internet for Libraries
http://www.ipl.org/svcs/internet.html

LIBCAT—A Guide to Library Resources on the Internet
http://www.metronet.lib.mn.us/lc/lc1.html

Librarian's Index to the Internet
http://sunsite.berkeley.edu/InternetIndex/

Libraries and Publishing
http://www.library.upenn.edu/resources/infostudies/infostudies.html

Library Catalogs with Web Interfaces
http://www.lib.ncsu.edu/staff/morgan/alcuin/wwwed-catalogs.html

The Library Connection
http://www.ths.tased.edu.au/library.html

Library of Congress Z39.50 Gateway
http://lcweb.loc.gov/z3950/gateway.html

Library Resources on the Internet
http://www.lib.uwaterloo.ca/discipline/Libraries/

Library WWW servers
http://www.lib.washington.edu:80/~tdowling/libweb.html

Lund University Electronic Library
http://munin.ub2.lu.se/ub2.html

MiamiLink Main Menu
http://www.lib.muohio.edu/

CHAPTER
5

Oxford Libraries Internet Gateway
http://www.bodley.ox.ac.uk/olig/

A Pointer Page About Z39.50 Resources
http://ds.internic.net/z3950/z3950.html

Reference Resources from OhioLink
http://www.lib.muohio.edu/res/ref.html

The University of Waterloo Database Catalogue
http://www.lib.uwaterloo.ca/databases/catalogue.html

UC Berkeley Digital Library SunSITE
http://sunsite.berkeley.edu/

University of Sydney Library
http://www.library.usyd.edu.au/

The University of Waterloo Electronic Library
http//www.lib.uwaterloo.ca/

University of York Library and Related Resources
http://www.york.ac.uk/services/library/subjects/libint.htm

Worldwide Library Catalogues & Servers
http://sunsite.anu.edu.au/search/lib/world.html

WWW–to–Z39.50 Gateways
http://is.rice.edu/~riddle/webZ39.50.html

Don't forget to visit us at
http://dingo.vut.edu.au/~jimin/book.html

What is a research database?

Databases on the Internet are information warehouses. A database can be broadly defined as a collection of interrelated data of different types—there are full-text databases, image databases, abstract databases, and so on. A research database is one that collates research-related publications, abstracts, reports, patents, etc., and is often a collection of machine-readable bibliographic records. Such a record is a 'surrogate' for an actual document, published article, book or even audio-visual item. So a research database differs from reference databases for WWW search engines, which only furnish links or pointers to documents or Web pages. Nevertheless, 'research database' is a loose category, encompassing a type of document collection primarily for research purposes. Like other types of document databases, a research database categorises its collections; some typical ways of doing this are by author, title, by keywords, date, subject, etc. A research database is also characterised by its scope, usage cost, currency of information, search facility, documentation and online help.

In the late 1960s we began to see a few bibliographic databases available for online search. They were, and still are, provided by commercial vendors or producers. Charges for using them were a combination of subscription fees, connection fees and a per-minute fee for searching the database. That 'online' search then was different from the online search of today, mainly in that it was done through a specially linked line through a modem to a designated computer or terminal. Today 'online' can include any computer and any user over the Internet. The Internet technology evolution (or revolution) in the past decade has also witnessed enormous changes in database use and in the databases themselves. The primary change is the access to databases. Technological developments made it possible to access a database without using cumbersome terminals, visiting a library or pre-booking a service. Increased usage also enables database providers to provide a variety of services such as 'free-to-search' and 'pay-when-you-order'. The technology also allows new types of databases to be generated for a wide range of data such as video, sound, picture and animation data. A database using a hypertext system can conveniently join together bibliographic records for the same authors, the same topics or the same issues of a publication using hypertext links.

Old databases evolve or disappear and new databases emerge. As in the corporate world, restructuring, ownership change, alliance and consolidation have taken place during the short history of online databases. An early database such as DIALOG has endured the changing years (though its ownership has changed—it is now owned by Knight-Ridder, one of the large database producers). LEXIS/NEXIS has evolved from Mead Data Central and is now under the banner of Reed-Elsevier. At the same time, new databases have been appearing on the horizon, especially those featuring specialities. Among them are INSPEC database by the Information Services Division of the Institution of Electrical Engineers (UK) and SPIE database by the International Society for Optical Engineering. There have also been new assemblages of individual databases from large databases. Many individual specialised databases can be incorporated into several integrated databases. For instance, both UMI's Dissertation Abstracts Database and INSPEC have been embraced by FirstSearch and DIALOG.

You can browse through the publication *Directory of Databases* in the library to discover thousands of databases available through various means: the Internet, WWW or CD-ROM. Together, there are thousands of database providers and vendors providing online services. Only a small fraction of those databases are of engineering or technological significance. The databases covered in this book are some of those used by engineering academics, researchers and practising engineers.

There are a number of individual or integrated research databases on the Web to assist you in your literature searches. They include FirstSearch, Current Contents, UnCover, DIALOG, LEXIS/NEXIS and COMPENDEX. Their accessibility via Telnet is still workable but becoming outdated. FirstSearch's Web page is at **http://www.ref. oclc.org:2000/**, and UnCover's at **http://uncweb.carl.org/**. You can easily find their WWW locations and relevant WWW pages by using the WWW search engines introduced in Chapter 4. For instance, if you search using the keyword 'FirstSearch', the search engine should return with URL addresses relevant to the database, including the FirstSearch's home page at **http://www.ref.oclc.org:2000/** and gateways (or link points) from many institutions leading to the database which are usually just for their patrons.

An individual database may be one developed for a special discipline such as manufacturing technology or electrical and electronic engineering. It may also be one for a specific data sources such as journal articles or conference proceedings. INSPEC is a database for electrical engineering-related disciplines. Due to growing information flow and integration among different disciplines, multidisciplinary research work, and the growing number of sources of publications, it is increasingly impossible to rely on one database for a specific discipline to supply comprehensive information on a selected topic. This has led to the emergence of integrated databases such as FirstSearch and UnCover. An integrated database is a group of individual databases; you can choose whether to conduct your search within individual separate databases, or over a number of individual databases. Many of these integrated databases share the same individual databases, and as a result there is a significant degree of overlap between the search results.

No one database or information source will have all the answers, though you will often get the most and best results from subject-specific databases. For example, when searching for information on electrical engineering, choose INSPEC. The next stage would be to search a more general engineering database such as COMPENDEX. FirstSearch is an integrated bibliographic database, a collection of different databases brought together on one site, providing an opportunity to search databases of relevant or peripheral disciplines.

Many research databases accessible on the Internet are commercial ones. This means users have to be subscribers with either upfront payment or proportional payment for the usage (paying either for each record found or for time connected). These databases are called 'restricted' databases or 'subscription-based' databases. The mechanism by which they are policed is by restricting or authorising access by imposing a password or authorisation ID when you log in. Universities, research institutions, industries and other government or non-government institutions often obtain passwords or authorisation as an institutional subscriber. If you work for one of these, you should be able to access research databases that your institution subscribes to from any computer with an Internet connection. Likewise, the library catalogues of some professional institutions are available only to their members or on a subscription basis.

Other research databases offer free access. For instance, UnCover is a prominent and comprehensive example of this type. It will be discussed later in this Chapter. Many 'small' and specialised databases are the results of dedicated efforts in specific fields, and they are often freely accessed only by a small group of people with common interests. At the other end of the spectrum are certain databases that are expensive and therefore their usage has to be closely supervised—these databases are still not available freely on the Internet.

Accessing a research database from the WWW

Accessibility and convenience are the main advantages of searching databases via the Internet. You no longer need to make an appointment with the library or wait for a librarian or a systems officer to perform the search. All you need are a computer, an Internet browser such as Netscape Navigator and an Internet connection. Usually the online databases require no instructions or they provide online help, so you don't have to spend time poring over lengthy manuals. Thanks to the WWW, the information you want is only a few clicks away from your computer screen. For databases, this really is a remarkably efficient means of disseminating information.

A principal issue in using a database is that of accessing the data. Traditional database access is based on various programming interfaces such as C or FORTRAN. This requires the user to have some basic knowledge of computer programming. Other database access relies on a menu-driven interface that requires training and does not offer uniformity among different databases. A Graphical User Interface (GUI) can make database access much easier and friendlier. Though special expertise may be needed to set up the GUI, it is not required from the database user.

The advent of WWW has provided an ideal environment for GUIs as Web browsers interpret them with no effort on the user's part. As a consequence, browsers can be used to access many electronic resources, including databases containing bibliographical records in plain text or hypertext. Using a Web browser's built-in forms capability, you can access a database by simply filling in the form and submitting it. The way the interface operates between the database server and your computer is of little concern. You can retrieve information as if you had direct physical access to a library's computer catalogue, even though the database may be situated in a different continent of the globe.

The other advantage of Web access to research databases is the elimination of problems arising from hardware incompatibility. The hardware platform hosting the databases may be different from yours. With the aid of HTTP, any hardware interface and networking links are dealt with by the HTTP client and server. This cross-platform nature of database access spares you from the technical difficulties involved in using different operating systems and GUIs, allowing speedy dissemination of information from the database. It also relieves you of the need to purchase additional networking software to accommodate the database's platform.

The Web's HTML standard offers a common format for accessing a research database, sending instructions and viewing retrieved items, re-enforcing the cross-platform nature of the Web's access to databases. A database can reside on one hardware platform but be accessed by users from various platforms. Hypertext also adds a new dimension to the cataloguing of database records, by providing hyperlinks from retrieved records; for instance, from one record, you can follow hyperlinks to recent publications by the same author or authors.

Not all research databases are accessible via the Web yet, although most are evolving towards Web access. Some of them still rely on traditional Telnet access; others use a variety of protocols, ranging from Gopher to WAIS. In any case, since all protocols nowadays have direct Web gateways, accessing a database from a Web browser is becoming the norm.

Through the WWW, an HTTP server is able to run an external program from within an HTML document. A program can be one of several types, but it must be able to handle text-processing, and preferably is friendly for applications across platforms. It can also be a 'compiled executable program', that is, its execution is remotely controlled by the user's input through the HTML document—by selecting or activating links you send commands which are executed at the other end, as when you click on the 'search' button to begin a search. This program execution method is called the 'Common Gateway Interface', generally abbreviated to CGI. With CGI, the interaction between the server at one end of the communication channel and the user at the other becomes feasible. You can send commands and instructions to the server through a graphical user interface, and receive the retrieved data either in HTTP format or in some other format. This CGI method of interaction is particularly useful for communicating with an online database—all you need to do is to prepare a Web search form detailing information such as author, date, title or keywords and send the form to the database server. The outcome of the search will be returned to the local computer in a readable format.

Research databases for public access

The databases listed in Table 6-1 are open to public access. You can link to them directly using the Web gateway and search for information. Some databases provide an initial Web connection, leading to Telnet connection to the actual database. Passwords are prompted on the computer screen whenever they are necessary. The fact that these databases are open for public access does not mean that they are necessarily less comprehensive than those with restricted access. UnCover, for example, is a good all-round database. Other databases may be sponsored or administered by professional societies; therefore they are specialised and designed for the purpose of disseminating information within a professional community. In that sense, they are extremely comprehensive within specific fields.

Although databases can offer public access, the accessibility may not be completely unlimited. Certain databases may provide only partial bibliographic information about searched records; to obtain further bibliographic information you have to pay. This is one way for the information provider to make its operation commercially viable and sustainable. Some databases do provide fuller bibliographic information, but you are expected to purchase the hardcopy version of items retrieved and pay additional costs for swift document delivery.

Name and Internet address

ACM Database
http://www.acm.org/pubs/toc/Search.html

Advanced Technology Program
http://cos.gdb.org/best/stc/atp.html

AT&T InterNIC Database Services
http://ds.internic.net/ds/dspg01.html

Canadian Community of Science
http://cos.gdb.org/work/best-dbs-canada.html

CARL Libraries and Information Databases
http://www.carl.org:80/cgi-bin/getDatabase?14419+1

CEDB-ASCE Database for Civil Engineering
http://www.ascepub.infor.com:8601/cedbsrch.html

Community of Science Databases
http://cos.gdb.org/work/best-dbs.html

CORDIS Databases
http://apollo.cordis.lu/cordis/GLOBALsearch.html

CURL COPAC Database
http://curlopac.ac.uk/copac/

Distance Learning Institutions and Courses Database
http://www-icdl.open.ac.uk/icdl/index.htm

Educational Resources Information Center (ERIC)
http://www.aspensys.com/eric/index.html

European Commission Host Organisation
http://www2.echo.lu/echo/en/home.html

HyTelnet Databases and Bibliographies
http://galaxy.einet.net/hytelnet/FUL000.html

Informatics for Engineering and Science
http://liinwww.ira.uka.de/bibliography/index.html

Information Quest
http://www.eiq.com/

Marketplace Library Database
http://www.industry.net/c/buying_guide

NASA Astrophysics Data System (ADS)
http://adsabs.harvard.edu/

NASA Databases
http://galaxy.einet.net/hytelnet/NAS000.html

National Engineering Education Delivery System
http://www.needs.org/

National Science Foundation
http://cos.gdb.org/best/fedfund/nsf-intro.html

Netlib Database (mathematical software, papers, and databases)
http://www.netlib.org/

NTTC Databases
http://iridium.nttc.edu/brs/brs.html

Quakeline on the Internet
http://clark.eng.buffalo.edu/qklncnct.html

Resources on Global Internet
http://www.gi.net/GINS/resources/index.html

Scholarly and Professional Electronic Conferences
http://n2h2.com/KOVACS/

SPIE Database
http://www.spie.org/
http://www.spie.org/search/spie_ab_search.html

US Patents Database
http://ericir.syr.edu/Eric/

UnCover
http://uncweb.carl.org/

Water Resources Abstracts
http://h2o.usgs.gov/public/nawdex/swra.html

Table 6-1 Engineering-related databases for public access

Sometimes online database hosts may provide two tiers of search: the first and usually quick search is for browsing for information, and the second and usually advanced search caters for 'serious' users with well-focused objectives. Nevertheless, a database host is not necessarily the database producer. You will see later that many database providers offer access to databases produced by other companies, some of which also offer Web access to their products.

Table 6-1 lists engineering-related databases available for public access. Those most relevant to engineers are described below in detail.

ACM Database

http://www.acm.org/pubs/toc/
Search.html

This database contains abstracts of papers that have appeared in ACM publications. ACM stands for Association for Computing Machinery. Founded in 1947, it is an international scientific and educational organisation dedicated to advancing the art, science, engineering and application of information technology. The search form allows you to search for papers published in ACM journals. Queries are based on free-text searching in the summaries of papers held in the ACM publications database. Each summary contains title, author, journal, abstract, categories and subject descriptors from the ACM Computing Classification System, as well as the text of brief critiques published in Computing Reviews.

Advanced Technology Program

http://cos.gdb.org/best/stc/
atp.html

This is another Web page affiliated to the Community of Science Web site. The resident ATP (Advanced Technology Program) database is a product of the National Institute of Science and Technology, begun in 1990. The National Institute of Science and Technology aims to promote the economic growth and competitiveness of US business and industry by accelerating the development and commercialisation of promising, high-risk technologies with substantial potential for enhancing US economic growth. The ATP provides technology development funding through cooperative research agreements to single businesses or industry-led joint ventures.

The database accepts Boolean searches. The retrieved entries are ranked according to the appropriateness of each document with respect to the query.

Canadian Community of Science

http://cos.gdb.org/work/
best-dbs-canada.html

The Canadian Community of Science is an integrated part of the Community of Science (described on page 155), and like COS contains four major databases:

- The Canadian Community of Science Expertise Database is a database of expertise records from leading universities and R&D organisations in Canada.
- The Community of Science (COS) Funding Opportunities Database is conceived as an aid to the development of knowledge by linking researchers and research funding world-wide. The database includes information on funding opportunities announced by federal agencies, state/provincial and commercial organisations, non-profit foundations and professional associations.
- The Canadian Community of Science Inventions Database is a database of inventions made at universities and R&D organisations in Canada. Entries include invention titles, descriptive abstracts, key-words and contact information.
- The Canadian Community of Science Facilities Database is a database of facilities and resources at universities and R&D organisations in Canada.

CARL Libraries and Information Databases

http://www.carl.org:80/cgi-bin/
getDatabase?14419+1

This Website from CARL (the same company that produces UnCover) has links to a large number of bibliographic databases from 74 academic libraries, 74 public libraries, 8 special libraries (Figure 6.1), 4 school libraries and 20 magazine and reference databases. The library databases are mainly OPACs. You need authorisation before you can use the magazine and reference databases. The search page is well organised for selecting databases and submitting queries. The search types include 'Keywords', 'Author or name', 'Subject headings', 'Name headings', 'Title browse', 'Name browse', 'Subject browse', 'Series browse' and 'Call number', offering plenty of flexibility.

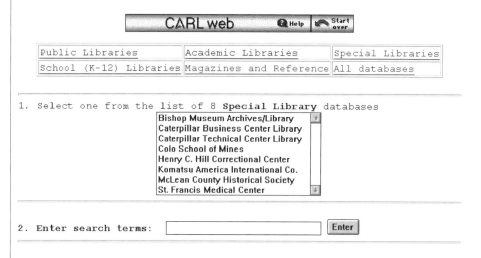

Figure 6.1 CarlWeb library databases

CEDB–ASCE Database for Civil Engineering

http://www.ascepub.infor.com:8601/cedbsrch.html

The Civil Engineering Database (CEDB) is designed to provide bibliographic information on all publications from the American Society of Civil Engineers (ASCE), one of the most important professional engineering bodies in America. The database covers ASCE documents published since 1975, nearly one million records in total. It provides access to all ASCE journals, conference proceedings, books, standards, manuals, magazines and newsletters.

Although theoretically in the realm of civil engineering, the database actually covers a wide range of engineering subjects which are either directly or peripherally related to civil engineering: aerospace engineering, architectural engineering, bridges, cold regions, computer practices, construction, earthquake engineering, education, engineering mechanics, environmental engineering, forensic engineering, geotechnical engineering, highways, hydrology, hydraulics, irrigation and drainage, management, materials engineering, structural engineering, transportation, urban planning, water resources, and waterway, port, coastal and ocean engineering.

You can search the database by a variety of fields. The default index is the 'Basic Index', which includes words from titles, keywords, abstracts, etc. You can also focus your search by searching only the title, keyword, or author fields. You can browse the 'Keyword List' on the Web page to help you select relevant terms.

```
ASCE'S Electronic Information Retrieval Service to
All Its Publications Published since 1975

Current Coverage: January 1975 - March 1997        Scout Report
                                                   SELECTION
─────────────────────────────────────────────────────────────
To start your search, enter one or more words for each category you are
interested in.

*note: please note the changes made to the Author's search

Full Text              [                                        ]
Author (Last, First)   [                                        ]
Title                  [                                        ]
Keyword Term           [                                        ]
Date Range             Start Date: [    ]   End Date: [    ]

[ Search ] [ Reset ]
```

Figure 6.2 ASCE database search form

Community of Science

http://cos.gdb.org/work/
best-dbs.html

The Community of Science (COS) World Wide Web server contains databases for information about scientific expertise, funded scientific research, and funding opportunities for research in the USA and Canada. COS is a consortium of research institutions established to provide a comprehensive directory of faculty researchers and scientists, and to connect academic and corporate researchers via the Internet and other electronic platforms. The large collection of profiles of faculty researchers and their interests and expertise at COS provides industries with an excellent base from which to identify prospective collaborators, license new technologies, leverage their existing R&D effort, and generally stay informed about the constantly changing world of basic science and academic research. COS also provides researchers with valuable information tools to assist them complete research work under way and secure funds for future projects.

Founded in 1988 at Johns Hopkins University, COS is now based in Baltimore. It was formed in direct collaboration with over 125 major research universities and other R&D organizations in the US and Canada. Each participating institution has its 'Institution Fact Sheet' on the COS Web site. Currently, COS contains three major databases:

- The Community of Science Expertise Database is a database of expertise records from leading universities and R&D organisations in North America. Entries include the name and address of the individual researcher, a description of his or her current research interests, past positions, memberships and associated keywords.
- The Community of Science Inventions Database is a database of inventions made at universities and R&D organisations in North America. Entries include invention titles, descriptive abstracts, keywords and contact information.
- The Community of Science Facilities Database is a database of facilities and resources at universities and R&D organisations in North America. Entries include the name of the facility, a descriptive abstract, keywords and contact information.

CORDIS Databases

http://apollo.cordis.lu/cordis/
GLOBALsearch.html

CORDIS is an acronym for the Community Research and Development Information Service, an information service run by the European Commission. CORDIS (also available at **http://www.cordis.lu**) provides information on all research and technological development activities in the EU through a complete collection of databases. It holds a list of thousands of European companies seeking partners to develop or exploit technologies and know-how. CORDIS's objective is to disseminate information on R&D to the widest audience possible with complete, up-to-date and easily accessible data helping research projects across borders. This central resource is crucial for industry, research organisations, universities or other organisations that are interested in taking part in EU-funded research programmes, seeking research partners or exploiting the latest research outcomes.

The CORDIS service was originally designed to be available online through a Windows-based interface called Watch-CORDIS. This Windows application supports a variety of hardware configurations and data communication settings, and is supplied free of charged via the CORDIS WWW service or from the CORDIS Help Desk. Later, direct WWW access to all CORDIS databases was made available. Full-text documents including work programmes and information packages and calls for proposals for all the research programmes will be available on CORDIS. In addition to online access, the CORDIS databases are also available on a CD-ROM, updated quarterly. Presently, the CORDIS resource contains nine databases: News, Acronyms, Documents, Programmes, Projects, Publications, Results, Partners and Contacts. You can find detailed descriptions of these databases at **http://www.cordis.lu/cordis/ cordn1000.html.**

The example in Figure 6.3 uses the keywords 'laser sensing' to search the CORDIS 'Publications' database. The CORDIS search form allows you to select one or more databases and use more than one keyword.

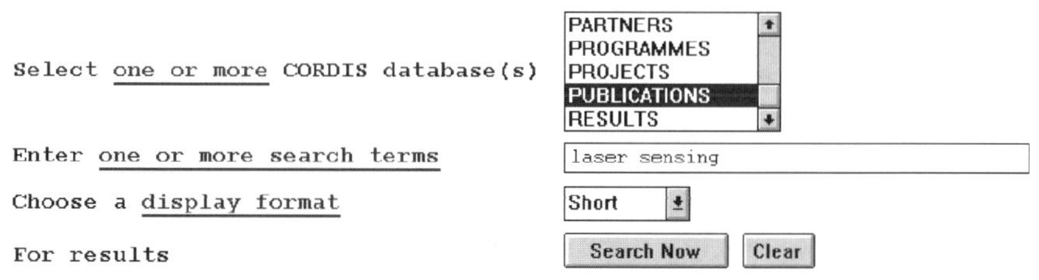

Figure 6.3 CORDIS database search form

This search, when carried out in April 1997, retrieved 12 publications, each having 'laser' and 'sensing' in its title. The search results Web page is shown in Figure 6.4.

Figure 6.4 CORDIS database search results

Since the titles are displayed as hypertext, by clicking on a title you can obtain further information, including its authors and an abstract.

Distance Learning Institutions and Courses Database

http://www-icdl.open.ac.uk/icdl/index.htm

'Distance Learning Institutions and Courses Database' and 'Distance Education Library' are two databases hosted by the International Centre for Distance Learning (ICDL). They contain information on institutions world-wide teaching at a distance, together with details of programmes and courses offered by some of these institutions, and references, including abstracts, to the literature relating to all aspects of distance education. They are freely accessible, provided you accept the copyright terms.

Educational Resources
Information Center (ERIC)

http://www.aspensys.com/eric/
index.html

The Educational Resources Information Center (ERIC) is a national information system affiliated to the US federal Department of Education. It provides a variety of services and products on a broad range of education-related issues. The ERIC databases contain bibliographic records of research reports, conference papers, teaching guides, books and journal articles relating to the practice of education, including engineering and technology education. ERIC databases can be accessed through a number of Web, Gopher, Telnet, or TN3270 sites. For instance, Syracuse University in New York maintains an 'ASKERIC' page at **http://ericir.syr.edu/** from where you can enter the ERIC search form. The Catholic University of America maintains a search page for ERIC databases at **http://ericae2.educ.cua.edu/search.htm**, shown in Figure 6.5.

Search ERIC Wizard

Search terms:

Set1	
Set2 AND	
Set3 NOT	

Limited to: `not limited` ▾ [Refresh]

[Submit to AE] [Submit to EDRS] [Clear]

[Look Up]

Look-up a new term:

Figure 6.5 ERIC search form

European Commission Host Organisation

http://www2.echo.lu/echo/en/
home.html

ECHO (European Commission Host Organisation) was set up in 1980 to encourage the development and promote understanding of information services in the European Community. Its Web site offers free access to more than 20 online databases (at **http://www2.echo.lu/echo/databases/en/dbindex.html**) in all Community languages. Databases accessible on ECHO cover four main areas: user support, industry databases and economy database, and the language industry.

Informatics for Engineering and Science

http://liinwww.ira.uka.de/
bibliography/index.html

This collection of Computer Science Bibliographies at the University of Karlsruhe in Germany is a free service. It contains scientific literature, mainly in computer science, from various sources, covering most aspects of computer science, but also includes literature from other disciplines. The more than 870 bibliographies are updated monthly from their original locations such that you'll always find the most recent versions here. The site offers both simple search and advanced search options. In addition, the bibliographies have been grouped into subject areas. Among them are 'Artificial Intelligence', 'Neural Networks' and 'Networking and Telecommunications'.

Information Quest

http://www.eiq.com/

Information Quest (IQ) is a new Web-based information access and retrieval service. The database covers over 7 million table-of-contents entries from over 12 000 journals since 1990. Though mainly designed for the research needs of librarians, information managers and business professionals, IQ offers full-text access to scientific, technical, medical and business electronic content—with new titles and journals added to the database on a daily basis. IQ also offers a personalised alert service to alert you of newly arrived information that matches your search criteria.

NASA Astrophysics Data System (ADS)

http://adsabs.harvard.edu/

The Astrophysics Data System (ADS) hosted at Harvard University is a NASA-funded project whose main resource is an Abstract Service, which includes three sets of abstracts:

- astronomy and astrophysics, containing approximately 255 000 abstracts
- instrumentation, containing approximately 460 000 abstracts
- physics and geophysics containing approximately 220 000 abstracts.

Each data record can be searched by author, object name (for astronomy only), title or abstract text words. In addition, ADS has extended the abstract service to include links to scanned images of over 40 000 journal articles appearing in most of the major astronomical journals. Click on the 'Articles' hyperlink on the ADS Web page for details. In addition to the Abstract Service, ADS provides access or pointers to astronomical data catalogues and data archives, thereby making data collected by NASA space missions available to astronomers.

National Engineering Education Delivery System

http://www.needs.org/

The National Engineering Education Delivery System, or NEEDS, lets you to search its database on course-related materials. You can search for bibliographic records in the NEEDS Database for courseware, course modules and software, and download courseware, course modules, and software from the Database. You can also download multimedia elements of courseware and course modules, such as images, movies and individual pages, and view listings of World Wide Web Courseware within the NEEDS Database.

National Science Foundation

http://cos.gdb.org/best/fedfund/
nsf-intro.html

The National Science Foundation (NSF) is an independent agency of the US Government in relation to overseeing federally funded research in the USA. Its database is affiliated to the Community of Science's Web site. The Foundation's purpose is to:

- Initiate and support, through grants and contracts, scientific and engineering research, programmes to strengthen scientific and engineering research potential, and education programmes at all levels; and appraise the impact of research upon industrial development and the general welfare.
- Award graduate fellowships in the sciences and in engineering.
- Foster the interchange of scientific information among scientists and engineers in the United States and foreign countries.

The NSF Grants database at **http://medoc.gdb.org/best/stc/ nsf-best.html** contains information about all NSF grants (from 1989 to the present). It also contains a complete listing, for each institution, of the amounts of grants awarded. You can search either the entire database, or alternatively, each category of the database can be searched separately. The NSF database embraces the following categories:

- Mathematical and Physical Sciences
- Biological Sciences
- Computer and Information Science and Engineering
- Engineering
- Education and Human Resources
- Geosciences
- Social, Behavioral, and Economic Sciences
- Polar Programs
- Science and Technology Infrastructure.

NTTC Databases

http://iridium.nttc.edu/brs/
brs.html

The National Technology Transfer Center in the US hosts a number of searchable databases. They include:

- 'Directory of Federal Laboratory and Technology Resources' (DFLT) for over 100 000 scientists and engineers working at US federal R&D facilities, addressing virtually every area of science and technology
- 'Federal and University Licensable Technologies and Patents' for access to licensable technologies and patents produced from over 700 federal laboratories and 114 US universities.

Some of the NTTC's databases are still accessible on the Web. Others, however, are being moved to a fee-for-service model, where the data itself continues to be free but the services necessary to provide electronic access will be charged for.

Quakeline on the Internet

http://clark.eng.buffalo.edu/
qklncnct.html

Quakeline is the database of the US National Center for Earthquake Engineering Research (NCEER). It contains bibliographic information on earthquakes, earthquake engineering, natural hazard mitigation and related topics. Quakeline includes records for various publication types, such as journal articles, conference papers, technical reports, maps, and videotapes. Access to Quakeline is through Telnet connection to the University at Buffalo Libraries' computerised system BISON (Buffalo Information System ONline). The Quakeline database is also available on CD-ROM.

SPIE Database

http://www.spie.org/

SPIE, the International Society for Optical Engineering, publishes a wide variety of materials for the engineering, scientific, and research communities, including journals, proceedings, monographs, news publications and guidebooks. Currently there are nearly one million abstracts of SPIE publications online. SPIE's Web page allows you to search for a specific paper or volume, or to browse the entire list of in-print publications by years, technology or volumes. The citations and abstracts you found can also be downloaded via FTP or automated e-mail server.

InCite is SPIE's index/abstract service providing access to SPIE's technical information databases through print and electronic indexes, electronic catalogue services, online paper citations and abstracts and related information services. You can find the InCite's search page at **http://www.spie.org/search/spie_ab_search.html** (Figure 6.6).

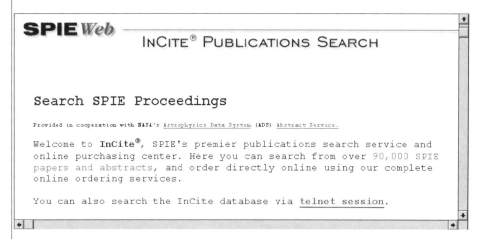

Figure 6.6 InCite Web page at SPIEWeb

UnCover

http://www.carl.org/carlweb/index.html

UnCover is an online periodical article delivery service and table of contents database provided by Colorado Alliance of Research Libraries at Knight Ridder Information Company. It contains a keyword index to some 17 000 English-language periodicals and magazines in all disciplines. UnCover provides an online order system for millions of articles from its collections. Articles appear in UnCover at the same time as the periodical issue is delivered to local libraries, featuring the extreme currency of index information provided. In addition,

UnCover offers a look at the periodical collections of some of the major university and public libraries in the United States, Europe and Australia.

The costs incurred by the user for its document delivery services helps to sustain the services the company provides. Articles ordered from UnCover are delivered usually by fax, together with an invoice for the cost of provision and a royalty fee. Payment can be made by credit card. Patrons outside the US and Canada may incur a fax surcharge. Libraries and other institutions can purchase gateway access and receive article discounts, dedicated ports, and, in some cases, customised screens and local periodical holdings display.

UnCover also offers a Reveal Alert service, which delivers tables of contents from the latest periodical issues directly to your email box. You can also set up stored search strategies with UnCover so that they are automatically run each week against new articles added to the database to generate the latest search results, which are then emailed to

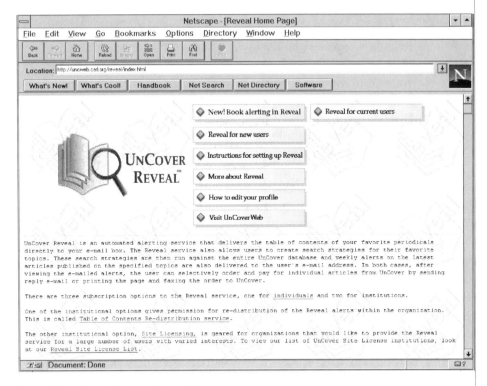

Figure 6.7 UnCover Reveal database Web page

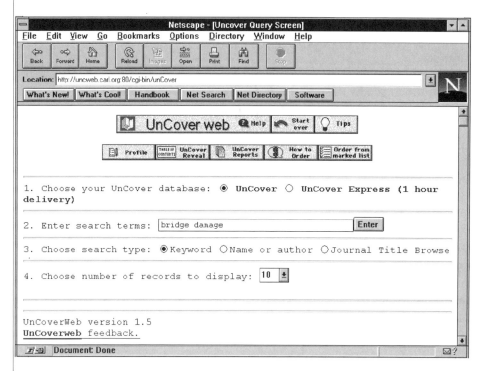

Figure 6.8 Search form for Uncover

you automatically. This service is particularly significant if you need to track the latest publications related to a specific topic. A small fee is payable: for instance, an annual fee of US$25 allows you to automatically receive the tables of contents of up to 50 journals and the results of search strategies via email on a regular basis.

UnCover can be used at any time without access restriction. However, if you're a regular user, it's beneficial to set up a personal profile to allow a speedy link to UnCover. Every time you connect to UnCoverWeb, you only need to enter your UnCover Profile Number assigned by the system and a password selected by yourself. If you want to use UnCover Reveal service, then you must set up a profile that includes your email address, so that search results can be forwarded to you. To create your own profile, you need to navigate fields to enter information such as your name, address, phone and fax numbers, payment information, etc. You can edit your profile at any time by clicking on the 'Profile' button located at the top of all the search result screens.

To illustrate the main search functions of UnCover, let's use the database without a profile. Figure 6.8 shows the UnCover's search page.

Using the keywords 'bridge damage', UnCover will retrieve more than 10 items, including those shown in Figure 6.9.

Mark for Order	7	Pandey, P.C. Multilayer perceptron in damage detection of bri Computers & structures.	[1995]
Mark for Order	8	Keating, Peter B. Focusing on Fatigue. Civil engineering.	[11/01/94]
Mark for Order	9	 News. Construction today.	[04/01/94]
Mark for Order	10	Zwerneman, Farrel J. Fatigue Damage to Steel Bridge Diaphragms. Journal of performance of constructe	[11/01/93]

Figure 6.9 Search results from Uncover

If you select Item 7, 'Multilayer perceptron in damage detection of bri', published in the journal *Computers & Structures*, detailed information about this paper and Web links to the authors' more recent papers and to the journal in which the paper appeared will be shown on the screen. This enables you to trace works on the same topic from the same authors and from issues of the relevant journal. This feature of UnCover is particularly useful if you are interested in following up the recent work of researchers in a focused field.

To conduct a successful Web search on UnCover, you need to follow a few designated steps:

■ First, select either the Full UnCover database or UnCover Express to search. The latter is a companion database that solely indexes all UnCover articles that can be delivered by fax within an hour. It is for people working against a close deadline. For a more rigorous search, you should use the full UnCover database.

■ Second, like other databases, UnCover allows you to search by topic, author name, or journal title.

■ Third, you need to enter a number in the 'Number of Records to Display' box before searching. Even with a small number selected, UnCover will offer more records on request when the selected number of items are displayed. UnCover allows a more sophisticated search using Boolean logic on the keywords.

The CARL Corporation, through its graphical Web-based user interface CarlWeb at **http://www.carl.org/carlweb/**, also provides a search service over a range of libraries and databases besides UnCover. These databases are from public, academic or special libraries or from other sources. Some of them are for restricted access, but others can be searched by Web users. A list of some reference databases on the CarlWeb is shown in Figure 6.10.

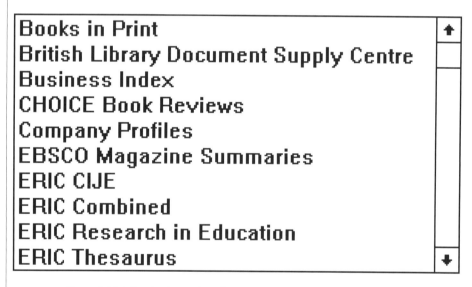

Figure 6.10 A few databases from CarlWeb

Water Resources Abstracts

http://h2o.usgs.gov/public/
nawdex/swra.html

This database contains data within the US Geological Survey Selected Water Resources Abstracts, from 1939 to date. You can enter general search query terms or mix a general query with specific field searches.

Research databases for online technical reports

Technical reports are scattered throughout the Internet. Some announce their presence on the Internet, but access is limited. By and large, engineering- and technology-related technical reports come from research institutions and universities, whose technical report sites are usually open for public access. Perhaps to no one's surprise, a large portion of engineering-related technical reports are related to electrical and electronic engineering. The host for technical reports can be a Gopher server, FTP server, WAIS server or even an HTML server. Files of technical reports come in various formats.

In Table 6-2 you will find a few Web sites for technical reports. Those most relevant to engineers are described below in detail.

Computer Science Technical Reports Archive

http://www.rdt.monash.edu.au/tr/siteslist.html

This is a sizeable list of mainly FTP servers that host technical reports. It contains more than 300 links arranged in alphabetical order. This site is based on the Department of Digital Systems at Monash University. There is no search option available.

Networked Computer Science Technical Reports Library

http://www.ncstrl.org/

NCSTRL is an international collection of computer science technical reports from academic departments and industrial and government research laboratories, made available for non-commercial and educational use. The NCSTRL collection is distributed among a set of inter-operating servers operated by more than 30 participating institutions. NCSTRL allows online searching on its collections, and most of the technical reports can be downloaded. NCSTRL is mirrored on many of its participating institutions such as the

Name and Internet address

All-in-One Search Engine
http://www.albany.net/allinone/all1rpts.html#TechRpts

Bibliographies of Technical Reports
http://donkey.cs.arizona.edu:1994/bib/Techreports/

Computer Science Technical Reports Archive
http://www.rdt.monash.edu.au/tr/siteslist.html

CSTR Project
http://www.cnri.reston.va.us/home/cstr.html

Database of TR Archive Sites, Monash University, Australia
wais://daneel.rdt.monash.edu.au/cs-techreport-archives

Engineering Technology Technical Reports from TradeWave galaxy
http://www.einet.net/galaxy/Engineering-and-Technology/Technical-Reports.html

Hypertext Bibliography Project Database
http://theory.lcs.mit.edu:80/~dmjones/hbp/

NASA Technical Reports Server
http://techreports.larc.nasa.gov/cgi-bin/NTRS

Networked Computer Science Technical Reports Library
http://www.ncstrl.org/

RECONplus
http://www.sti.nasa.gov/casitrs.html

Sony Technical Reports Archive
http://www.csl.sony.co.jp/techreport/

TRS at University of Maryland
http://www.cs.umd.edu/TRs/TR-no-abs.html

Unified Computer Science TR Index Database
http://www.cs.indiana.edu:800/cstr/

Wide Area Technical Report Service (WATERS)
http://www.cs.virginia.edu/~techrep/Techrep/doc/Contributors.html

Yahoo!'s Technical Reports List
http://www.yahoo.com/Science/Computer_Science/Technical_Reports/

Table 6-2 Engineering-related databases for technical reports

University of California, Berkeley at **http://sunsite.berkeley.edu/NCSTRL/index.html.**

NASA Technical Report Server

http://techreports.larc.nasa.gov/cgi-bin/NTRS

The NASA Technical Reports Server (NTRS) is a free service that lets you search the many different abstracts and technical report databases maintained by various NASA centers and programs. NTRS is both a front end for the various databases, and an official listing of the databases. You can select different combinations of databases to search, or simply follow links from the NTRS search form to other NASA Web sites for individual study. Technical reports from NASA covers a wide range of engineering disciplines. For instance, the largest technical report database in NASA is the CASI Technical Report Server, which hosts over 2 million records spanning areas of aeronautics, astronautics, chemistry, electronics and electrical engineering, mechanical engineering, quality assurance and reliability, structural mechanics and more. Obviously, NTRS is an ideal place to look for useful technical reports in almost any engineering and science discipline.

RECONplus

http://www.sti.nasa.gov/casitrs.html

This Web site is a new and improved version of the CASI Technical Report Server. It contains bibliographic citations for Scientific and Technical Aerospace Reports ('STAR' file series) produced since NASA was established in 1958, journal articles and conference proceedings produced since 1958 ('Open Literature' file series) and citations from the National Advisory Committee on Aeronautics (NACA) collection, NASA's predecessor organisation.

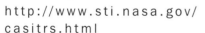

CHAPTER

6

Online Research Databases and Catalogues

SONY Technical Reports Archive

http://www.csl.sony.co.jp/
techreport/

The SONY TR Server at Sony's Computer Science Laboratory contains a rich collection of technical report servers on the WWW and on WAIS. The server for technical reports in Japan provides links to a number academic and government institutions that hold collections of technical reports.

Unified Computer Science TR Index Database

http://www.cs.indiana.edu:
800/cstr/

An automatically created index of technical reports available through nearly 200 anonymous FTPs all over the Internet. The collection exceeds the scope of mere computer science. This site permits simple index keyword searches. It is based at the Department of Computer Science, Indiana University.

Research databases with restricted access

Obviously, the production and maintenance of a worthwhile research database requires significant financial as well as human resources. So it is no surprise that many databases have to charge their users one way or another for the information they provide or for document delivery. This usually results in access being restricted to individual or institutional subscribers. The policing of access restriction is usually done by offering either individually authorised access to a database, or access for institutions which can transfer the access to their patrons. Even many databases with restricted access offer free trial periods for online searches. This should give you ample opportunity to examine the databases and their suitability for your own needs.

There are still numerous individual databases available. Many were created by professional societies, government departments, special industries and research organisations to fulfill specific missions to cover specific disciplines. These databases earn their own right to exist on the Internet. However, the trend towards forming amalgamated databases incorporating many specific databases is evident. Many specific databases have been incorporated into a number of large databases, so it is worth knowing the composition of large databases in order to avoid duplicating online searches and creating unnecessary costs.

Most restricted-access databases offer bibliographic information for their records. Some may even provide abstracts. This should give you the information you need to determine whether you need to acquire the hardcopy version. Under rare circumstances, databases offer full documents. In this case, all you need to do is to download the documents to your own computer for further perusal or printing. Such full document delivery is becoming a feature of many academic and scholarly publications.

Table 6-3 lists the names and Internet addresses of some prominent restricted-access databases with engineering relevance. Those most relevant to engineers are described below in detail.

ANSI—American National Standard Institute Databases

http://www.ansi.org/

The American National Standard Institute (ANSI) offers online searches of its databases. ANSI's Standards Information Databases (also referred to as 'SID') provide unique reference information on:

- American National Standards approved and under development
- contact information for accredited developers of American National Standards
- the availability of proposed European regional standards developed by CEN and CENELEC—European regional standards-developing committees
- US activities supporting the development of international standards by the International Organisation for Standardisation (ISO) and the International Electrotechnical Commission (IEC).

Name and Internet address

Academic Press Online Library
http://www.idealibrary.com/

ANSI—American National Standard Institute Databases
http://www.ansi.org/

Compendex
http://www.ei.org/eihome/services/cpx/cpx_menu.htm

Computer Science Bibliographies
http://liinwww.ira.uka.de/bibliography/index.html

Current Contents from Ovid Technologies
http://www.ovid.com/

DataStar
http://www.krinfo.ch/krinfo/products/dsweb/index.htm

DIALOG
http://www.corp.dialog.com/

Elsevier Science Database Services
http://www.elsevier.nl/inca/homepage/sah/spd/

FirstSearch
http://www.ref.oclc.org:2000/

INSPEC
http://www.iee.org.uk/publish/inspec/inspec.html

Internet Database Service from CSA
http://www.csa.com/ids.html

JournalsOnline
http://www.journalsonline.bids.ac.uk/JournalsOnlinepages/jo.html

MathSciNet
http://www.ams.org/mathscinet/

MELVYL
http://www.library.ucla.edu/catalog/melvyl.html

NetFirst
http://www.oclc.org/oclc/netfirst/netfirst.htm

NTIS—National Technical Information Service
http://www.fedworld.gov/ntis/ntishome.html

Orbit
http://www.questel.orbit.com/patents/readings/n_wrldpt.html

Questel-Orbit
http://www.questel.orbit.com/

Recent Advances in Manufacturing (RAM)
http://www.ntu.ac.uk/lis/ram.htm

SilverPlatter
http://www.silverplatter.com/

SPIN
http://www.infoed.org/

STN—Databases for Science and Technology
http://www.fiz-karlsruhe.de/stn.html/

UMI Dissertation Abstract
http://www.umi.com/hp/Support/DExplorer/

Table 6-3 Engineering-related databases with restricted access

SID consists of four different databases:

- American National Standards Database
- ANSI Accredited Standards Developer Database
- Database of US Participation in ISO Activities
- CEN and CENELEC Database.

The American National Standards Database contains information on approved American National Standards (ANS) and standards projects now under development. These standards represent the work of over 250 accredited standards developers. The American National Standards Database was developed by ANSI in April 1995 to track standards throughout the various stages of the development cycle. Records added prior to the April 1995 implementation may not contain complete tracking information.

The ANSI Accredited Standards Developer Database provides you with contact information about each of these organisations.

The database of US Participation in ISO Activities provides access to information on US Technical Advisory Group Administrators and Chairs for each ISO Technical Committee (TC) and Subcommittee (SC), including ISO/IEC Joint Technical Committee 1.

CEN and CENELEC are European regional standards-developing committees. ANSI receives copies of CEN and CENELEC drafts distributed for review, as well as notification of the initiation of new activities. The CEN and CENELEC Database can be used to monitor European standardisation activities.

COMPENDEX

http://www.ei.org/eihome/
services/cpx/cpx_menu.htm

COMPENDEX is an interdisciplinary engineering computer database produced by Engineering Information (Ei), Inc., containing references and abstracts for journal articles, conference papers, technical reports and books from 1970 to date, totalling over three million records. The database covers the technological literature in English in all engineering disciplines and major specialties, including mechanical, civil, environmental, electrical, structural, process, materials science, solid state physics and superconductivity, bioengineering, energy, chemical, optics, air and water pollution, solid waste management, hazardous waste, road transportation, and transportation safety and related technology. The database also extends its coverage to manufacturing, quality control and engineering management issues. Each year it indexes over 2600 journals and 500 conferences. COMPENDEX is available in different formats, including online, Internet and WWW, CD-ROM and print.

Apart from COMPENDEX, Ei also offers services on other abstract databases at **http://www.ei.org/eihome/catalog/data/database. htm**:

- Ei COMPENDEX®, the world's most comprehensive engineering database
- Ei ChemDisc®, the database for chemical engineering
- Ei CivilDisc™, the database for civil engineering
- Ei EEDisc™, the database for computer and electrical engineering
- Ei MechDisc™, the database for mechanical engineering

- Ei Manufacturing™, the database for integrated manufacturing engineering
- Ei Energy/Environment™, the database for energy and environmental engineering
- Advanced Materials, the database for engineered materials
- Ei Tech Index™, the database for technical research.

DataStar

http://www.krinfo.ch/krinfo/
products/dsweb/index.htm

DataStar is an online search service provided by Knight-Ridder Information, containing over 350 databases. These databases offer information ranging from a directory-type listing of companies or associations, to an in-depth financial statement for a particular company, to a citation with bibliographic information and an abstract referencing a journal, conference paper, or other original source, to the complete text of a journal article. As seen from its Web page, DataStar categorises its database collections into the groups listed in Table 6-4.

Technology is the most obvious choice for an engineering search. You can select from an attached list of databases before commencing an online search. Each retrieved item contains the information contained in the source database, as well as appropriate bibliographical details.

DataStar offers an online demonstration search service, providing a brief overview of the service. For instance, we can use the demo search within the 'Technology' group as shown in Figure 6.11.

By selecting all the databases on the screen and the 'Quick Search' option, we enter a search form where we can type search terms and select the part of the document to be searched. This can be the whole document, the title or the synonyms, summary, etc. After the search is completed, the bibliographic information of an item is returned together with the abstract. There is an example in Figure 6.12.

Depending on the database, the information retrieved may also contain relevant keywords, hypertext search items and links to further articles by the same authors.

Database collections and coverage

Business and Finance
General Company & Industry News, Market Research reports, Business Opportunities, Management & Economics, Company Directories, Company Financial Data, News by Country, Practice Files, Country Research reports, European Union Information, Mergers & Acquisitions

Chemicals
Chemical Industry, Company Directories, Chemistry, Toxicology, General Company & Industry News, Pharmaceutical Industry, Food Industry, Biotechnology Industry, Medical Research

Energy & Environment
General Company & Industry News, Chemical Industry, Toxicology, Energy & Environment

Food and Agriculture
Food Industry, Market Research reports, Agriculture, Veterinary & Food Sciences, General Company & Industry News, Company Financial Data, News by Country, Practice Files, Biotechnology Industry, Toxicology

Government and Regulations
Food Industry, European Union Information, Management & Economics, News by Country, Drug Legislation

Medicine
Medical Research, Medical Press, Medical Events, Toxicology, Chemistry

News and Media
General Company & Industry News, Management & Economics, News by Country

Pharmaceuticals
Pharmaceutical Industry, Drugs in Development, New Drug Products, Drug Patents, Drug Legislation, Pharmaceutical R&D, Pharmaceutical Company Directories, Practice Files, General Company & Industry News, Food Industry, Biotechnology Industry, Medical Research, Chemistry, Toxicology

Technology
Automotive and Aerospace Industry, Engineering, Computing & Information Science, Materials, General Company & Industry News, Pharmaceutical Industry, Food Industry, Biotechnology Industry, Medical Research, Chemistry

Social Sciences
Management & Economics, Social Sciences & General Reference

Table 6-4. DataStar database collections

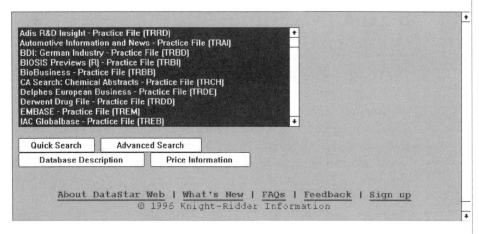

Figure 6.11 DataStar search form

```
Accession number & update
    4319105, C9302-3260J-002; 930101.
Title
    Use of electro-rheological fluids for adaptive vibration isolation.
Author(s)
    Randall-R-J; Tsang-W-F; Ed. by Culshaw-B; Gardiner-P-T; McDonach-A.
Author affiliation
    R Naval Eng Coll, Plymouth, UK.
Source
    First European Conference on Smart Structures and Materials, Glasgow,
    UK, 12-14 May 1992, p.399-402.
    Sponsors: Eur. Opt. Soc., SPIE, Smart Structures Res. Inst., IOP,
    Glasgow Dev. Agency, EEC, IEEE, IEE, OSA, IMechE, et al.
    Published: IOP, Bristol, UK, 1992, xvi+418 pp.
ISSN
    ISBN: 0-7503-0222-4.
Publication year
    1992.
Language
    EN.
Publication type
    CPP Conference Paper.
Treatment codes
    A Application; X Experimental.
```

Figure 6.12 DataStar search results

CHAPTER

6

DIALOG

http://www.corp.dialog.com/

DIALOG Information Retrieval Service from Knight-Ridder Information Inc. and MAID has been providing an online information service since 1972. Currently, DIALOG contains over 450 databases covering a broad range of disciplines. Documents from these databases are drawn from scientific and technical literature, full-text trade journals, newspapers and many other sources. Each database in DIALOG has a hypertext link to a document which explains the details of the database structure. A complete list of databases contained in DIALOG and the hyperlinks to their introductory documents can be found at **http://www.krinfo.com/dialog/databases/netscape1.1/blf.html#Contents**.

Elsevier Science Database Services

http://www.elsevier.nl/inca/homepage/sah/spd/

Elsevier Science has successfully developed a wide range of database products and services for online use, CD-ROMs, diskette, print, customised services and document delivery. Among the bibliographic databases are Geo Abstracts, Fluidex, World Textiles, and Current Awareness in Biological Sciences. These databases have been incorporated into some prominent integrated databases. For instance, Fluidex (the Fluid Engineering Abstracts Database) can be searched through DIALOG and ESA/IRS, and the World Textiles Abstracts Database is accessible from DIALOG.

FirstSearch

http://www.ref.oclc.org:2000/

FirstSearch is a menu-driven online reference service. Although it can be regarded as a single database, it is actually a collection of over 50 databases, some with bibliographic citations to journal articles, some with full text, for a broad range of subject areas. FirstSearch, as its name suggests, is an excellent source of bibliographic information for any literature search. The producer of FirstSearch, OCLC (Ohio College Library Center), was originally set up in 1967 to develop a computerised system to allow the libraries of Ohio academic institutions to share resources and reduce costs. Today, OCLC is one of the most prominent online information producers in the world, and serves numerous libraries in the USA and in other countries.

FirstSearch accepts the Boolean search operations 'AND', 'OR', 'NOT', and the adjacency operators 'WITH' and 'NEAR'. It allows you to refine searches to publication dates and record format. In addition, FirstSearch has a word list which allows you to choose and browse a list of available search terms associated with the selected word.

The FirstSearch Web page is shown in Figure 6.13.

As can be seen from its Web page, FirstSearch categorises its database collections into 14 areas, among them 'Engineering and Technology'. For this area, FirstSearch selects 11 databases, listed in Table 6-4. Most of these databases are produced by OCLC.

On entering the 'Engineering and Technology' area, you can select one of the 11 displayed (say the 'AppSciTechAb' database) by highlighting it and then pressing the 'Select Database' button (Figure 6.14).

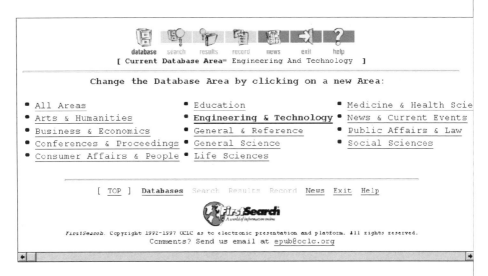

Figure 6.13 FirstSearch Web page

Databases produced by OCLC

Article1st
Index of articles from nearly 12 500 journals in science, technology, medicine, social science, business, the humanities and popular culture. 1990 to date.

Contents1st
Tables of contents and member library holdings for nearly 12 500 journals in many fields. January 1990 to date.

FastDoc
Index of articles that have a high percentage of citations, that can be ordered for online viewing or email delivery.

NetFirst
OCLC database for Internet resources, including Internet-accessible resources, World Wide Web pages and Listservs. Usenet newsgroups, FTP sites, Gopher servers and electronic publications to be added soon.

PapersFirst
Over 580 000 papers included in every congress, conference, exposition, workshop, symposium and meeting papers received at the British Library from October 1993 to date.

Proceedings
Over 19 000 citations of every congress, symposium, conference, exposition, workshop and meeting proceedings received at The British Library from October 1993 to date.

WorldCat
Over 326 million records of books and other material catalogued by OCLC member libraries in the US.

Other databases

AppSciTechAb
H W Wilson Company
Applied Science and Technology Abstracts covers more than 350 international English-language periodicals, involving engineering, mathematics, physics and computer technology.

Environment
Cambridge Scientific Abstracts
An index of comprehensive, multidisciplinary coverage of relevant fields across the environmental sciences from all the primary sources to 11 abstracts journals for the current year plus five previous years.

INSPEC
IEE
Scientific and technical journals and conference proceedings in physics, electrical engineering and electronics, computing and control, and information technology. January 1969 to date.

MicrocompAbs
Information Today Inc.
More than 75 popular magazines and professional journals on microcomputing in business, education, industry and the home. Includes news, articles, reviews and product announcements. January 1989 to date.

Table 6-5 Engineering-related databases in FirstSearch

This displays the search form for the databases selected. By default, the search is a 'Basic Search' that uses the query to perform a key-word search, without any limiting factors such as publication years. Alternatively, you can select an 'Advanced Search', which allows the search to be of subject, author or title types, and permits the search to be limited by publication dates.

Obviously, the 11 databases affiliated with the 'Engineering and Technology Area' are of direct engineering and technology relevance. However, others may have relatively remote connections to the category and should be used with discretion: databases listed under 'Engineering and Technology Area' may also appear in other areas. The databases listed in Table 6-5 could be useful for specific interests related to engineering and technology.

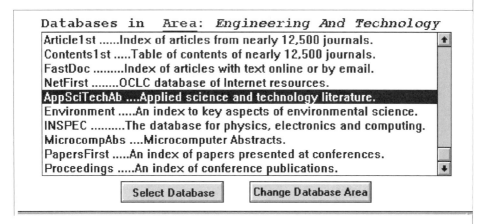

Figure 6.14 The FirstSearch database list

For instance, PerAbs, a product covering periodical abstracts produced by UMI, may contain articles of recent engineering design news. Diss, another UMI product covering dissertation abstracts, is certainly of acute interest to users wanting to trace up-to-date postgraduate research.

INSPEC

http://www.iee.org.uk/publish/ inspec/inspec.html

The INSPEC database, produced by the Information Services Division of the Institution of Electrical Engineers UK, provides access to the world's scientific and technical literature in physics, electrical engineering, electronics, communications, control engineering, computers and computing and information technology. Journals and conference proceedings account for approximately 98% of the references. The remainder are from government reports, patents (1970–76), monographs, theses and technical reports.

Presently, many large database hosts include INSPEC in their collections. They include DataStar, DIALOG, OCLC (in FirstSearch), Ovid (Current Contents), Questel-Orbit and STN. It is also available in print or on CD-ROM.

Internet Database Service

http://www.csa.com/ids.html

This well-established service is provided by the Cambridge Scientific Abstracts, an information provider respected throughout the world. It allows its subscribers access through the World Wide Web to more than 35 databases published by CSA and its publishing partners. These electronic files include the most up-to-date contents of the databases (updated before the print versions go to press), as well as archival data and retrospective searching.

The databases offered on the IDS cover a broad range of scientific disciplines. In relation to engineering, Table 6-6 quotes descriptions from the IDS.

Bioengineering Abstracts

This resource provides access to international research on all aspects of biochemical and microbial technology as applied to bioengineering. Principal areas of coverage are biomedical engineering and equipment.

Computer & Information Systems Abstracts

It permits access to thousands of scientific databases and hard-to-find conference literature, provides a comprehensive monthly update on the latest theoretical research and practical applications around the world.

Electronics & Communications Abstracts

Theoretical and applied research summaries in electronics and communications as well as business and marketing aspects in this database. Information ranges from medical, scientific and industrial applications in electronics to promising new technologies in communications.

Environmental Engineering Abstracts

This database addresses the growing challenges of pollution arising from industrial development and population growth. Pollution control and waste management are extensively covered with the emphasis on technological and engineering aspects of maintaining air and water quality, environmental safety, and alternative energy sources.

Mechanical Engineering Abstracts

This database provides the facts, figures, and discoveries engineers need in order to make faster, more authoritative decisions. The only abstracts database that surveys and summarises the worldwide literature in mechanical engineering, engineering management, and production engineering, it presents theoretical perspectives as well as specific applications.

Microcomputer Abstracts

A comprehensive source of information about products or services related to the field of personal computing. This database features cover-to-cover coverage of 90 of the most widely read microcomputer trade publications, magazines and professional journals. Included are thousands of reviews of software packages, microcomputers, peripherals and publications.

Solid State & Superconductivity Abstracts

This database presents global coverage on all aspects of theory, production, and application of solid state materials and devices. Specific topics include phase, crystal, and mechanical properties of solids, optical and dielectric properties, conductive and magnetic properties, exotic electronic structures and energy gaps, SQUIDs, flux structures, ceramics, and twinning phenomena.

Table 6-6 IDS databases

Like many other databases, the IDS allows searches on title and author name. In addition, it has a search facility called 'Words in any field' that allows you to search simultaneously on both titles and names. Furthermore, IDS accepts queries typed in a 'Box for experts', enabling field-specific searching and building of complex queries using specific field codes and Boolean operators ('AND', 'OR', 'ADJ', 'NOT'). The IDS query form is shown in Figure 6.15.

MathSciNet

http://www.ams.org/mathscinet/

MathSciNet is a searchable Web database providing access to over 55 years of *Mathematical Reviews* and *Current Mathematical Publications* from 1940 to the present. MathSciNet is a product of the American Mathematical Society.

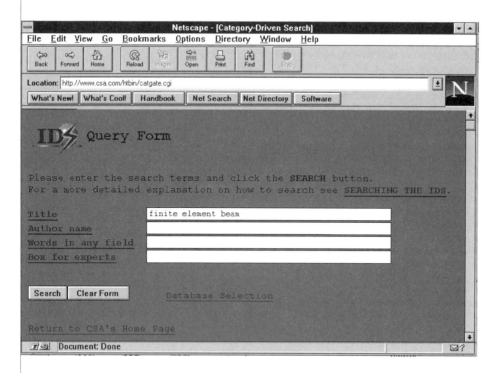

Figure 6.15 IDS database query form

NetFirst

http://www.oclc.org/oclc/netfirst/
netfirst.htm

NetFirst is another quality product from OCLC. By archiving and indexing Internet resources, this database aims to help library users to locate relevant Internet resources efficiently. As a result, it covers only those resources of interest to libraries and their users. Its diversity is ascertained by including all major Internet resources: Web pages, listservs, newsgroups, fee-based services and more. At present you can access NetFirst through FirstSearch.

NTIS—National Technical Information Service

http://www.ntis.gov/ntisdb.htm

The National Technical Information Service (NTIS) is the official resource for government-sponsored US and worldwide scientific, technical, engineering and business-related information, offering unparalleled bibliographic coverage of research in these fields. It is provided by the US Department of Commerce. Currently it holds nearly 3 million titles, with 100 000 new entries each year. The database's contents represents hundreds of billions of research dollars, and covers a range of important topics including agriculture, biotechnology, communication, engineering, science, transportation and space technology. The NTIS database can be accessed through CD-ROM, computer tapes and diskettes, audio and video cassettes and online.

Questel–Orbit

http://www.questel.orbit.com/

Questel-Orbit is an international online information company specialising in patent, trademark, scientific, chemical, business and news information. There are several categories in the database collection: Business, Chemical Information, Energy and Earth Science, Engineering, Health, Safety and Environment, Humanities and Social Science, Materials Science, Medicine, News, Patents, Science and Technology, and Trade Marks. Each category has recruited a number of databases, although categories may overlap. For engineering, Questel-Orbit contains a list of databases covering a broad range of disciplines. These include Aqualine, Dervent Biotechnology Abstracts, Chemical Abstracts, Chemical Engineering and Biotechnology Abstracts, COLD, Corrosion, Geomechanics Abstracts, GEOREF, ICONDA, INSPEC, Global Mobility database, NTIS, PASCAL (Science and Technology), COMPENDEX, TRANSIN and Weldsearch.

Some of these databases can also be searched elsewhere. However, Questel-Orbit is unique in providing information which is rare or exclusive. For instance, 'Orbit Online Products' assists individuals and companies in the petroleum industry by providing access to related worldwide literature at **http://www.questel.orbit.com/patents/readings/n_petro.html**. Major topics include the petroleum processes, fuels, environmental matters, storage and petroleum geology. In most cases, this information is drawn from such sources as journals, books, maps, theses, conference proceedings and government documents.

There are a number of databases exclusively available at Questel-Orbit, including 'Derwent World Patent Index/API Merged' produced by Derwent Publications Ltd. and the American Petroleum Institute Central Abstracting and Indexing Service. The TULSA/Petroleum Abstracts database is another example, produced by Petroleum Abstracts and covering 1965 to the present. This database has more than 500 000 references and abstracts to literature worldwide and patents related to oil and natural gas exploration geology, exploration geophysics and geochemistry, oil and gas production, reservoir studies and recovery methods, pollution, alternative fuels, and transportation and storage.

Recent Advances in Manufacturing (RAM)

http://www.ntu.ac.uk/lis/ram.htm

RAM is a bibliographic database for manufacturing and related areas. It was produced by the Library and Information Services (LIS) Department at the Nottingham Trent University in the UK, on behalf of Nottingham Consultants Ltd, the commercial arm of Nottingham Trent University. RAM covers manufacturing industry and management; systems and processes; planning and control, maintenance, monitoring and inspection; applied technologies; education and training; and books, conferences and videos. According to RAM, its Web subscription is soon to appear, but a subset (records from June 1996 onwards) of RAM is available for trial online searching until December 1997. This search service is hosted by the Edinburgh Engineering Virtual Library, known as EEVL (**http://www.eevl.ac.uk/ram/**).

SilverPlatter
http://www.silverplatter.com/

SilverPlatter is one of the largest database providers. Its Web site offers electronic access to quality bibliographic and full-text databases via the Internet. SilverPlatter offers over 230 electronic database titles published under the SilverPlatter label. They cover a wide range of subject areas including science, technology and engineering.

The complete list of databases currently listed in the SilverPlatter directory can be found at **http://www.silverplatter.com /catalog.htm**. Each database has an online introduction.

SPIN
http://www.infoed.org/

Sponsored Programs Information Network, or SPIN, is primarily a database of funding opportunities, with over 500 subscribers in the US, and increasing numbers worldwide. It is hosted by InfoEd. SPIN contains current and comprehensive information on thousands of funding opportunities for projects which cross all interest areas. Using 'SPIN Services and Links', you can locate funding for research and development, international projects, collaborative projects, fellowships, academic programs, exchange programs, travel, endowments, equipment, outreach and service delivery projects and more.

The nature of SPIN dictates that its customer orientation points to higher education institutions. SPIN can be accessed in a number of different ways: SPIN Micro, SPIN On-line, SPIN Gopher and SPIN WWW. To cater for a variety of institutional needs, SPIN's host

InfoEd has tailor-made several versions of SPIN: SPIN International, SPIN Corporate and SPIN 2-Year.

UMI Dissertation Abstract

http://www.umi.com/hp/Support/
DExplorer/

UMI's Dissertation Abstracts database is a central authoritative source for information about doctoral dissertations and master's theses. It currently contains more than 1.4 million entries, most of them being dissertations from North America. Each year, some 55 000 new dissertations and 7000 new theses are added to the database.

UMI's Dissertation Abstracts database is available via several integrated databases or database vendors such as FirstSearch, DIALOG, STN, Ovid, DataStar, etc. If you have access to one of these databases, you should be able to search the Dissertation Abstracts database online. Ovid Online, DIALOG and FirstSearch also allow you to order dissertations and theses online. Alternatively, for an additional cost you can search the Dissertation Abstracts database can through DATRIX (**http://www.umi.com/hp/Support/Dexplorer/ products/**), an individualised search service for the Dissertation Abstracts database.

Online databases for patents

Engineering and technology have historically been closely linked to patents. A patent is an official document from a government patent office which allows an inventor to exclude others, for a limited time period, from developing, selling or using a device, process or design. Although the concept appears to be regressive and restrictive, patents protect, encourage and nurture new inventions and ideas. There are different types of patents, but for engineers the most relevant ones are 'utility patents' and 'design patents'. A utility patent covers a new and useful device, process, composition of matter or improvement upon any of these; while a design patent covers the appearance of a manufactured article.

Just as there are now many research databases for academic publications, there have been a growing number of databases especially for patents. These databases are often accessible to public and are accessible via the Web. Nevertheless, some integrated research databases already comprise databases specifically for patents. In DIALOG and Questel-Orbit (described on pages 180 and 187), you can search the EPIDOS-INPADOC databases choosing PFS and PRS for European patents—see the description of the European Patent Office Database on page 193. However, nowadays you can search for patent information through many specialised patent databases, and you can often obtain free copies online. Alternatively, you can contact the appropriate Patent Office for hard-copies of the patents you want, such as the US Patent and Trademark Office at P O Box 9, Washington, DC 20231 or your national patent office.

The patents databases in Table 6-7 complement the patent information included in some integrated databases. All of them are described below in detail.

Name and Internet address

Biotechnology Patents and New Technologies
http://www.nal.usda.gov/bic/Biotech_Patents/

Canadian Patent Office
http://strategis.ic.gc.ca/sc_innov/patent/engdoc/cover.html

Chemical Patents Plus
http://casweb.cas.org/chempatplus/

European Patent Office Database
http://www.european-patent-office.org/

IBM Patent Server
http://patent.womplex.ibm.com/

QPAT–US
http://www.qpat.com/

US Patent Citation Database
http://cos.gdb.org/repos/pat/

US Patents at CNIDR
http://patents.cnidr.org/access/access.html

Table 6-7 Patents databases

Biotechnology Patents and New Technologies

http://www.nal.usda.gov/bic/
Biotech_Patents/

This small database is an extensive bibliography of articles and monographs related to biotechnology patents in recent years (1994 to date). The database provider is the Biotechnology Information Center of the US Department of Agriculture. This database is open for public access.

Canadian Patent Office

http://strategis.ic.gc.ca/
sc_innov/patent/engdoc/
cover.html

The Canadian Patent Bibliographic Database is produced by the Canadian Intellectual Property Office. It covers patents issued or applied for at the Office that have been made available to the public from 1 October 1989 to the present. It is updated monthly. Presently, the pilot product of this database is offered on the Web for public access in order to determine the best format for patent records and to assess the usefulness of online public access.

Chemical Patents Plus

http://casweb.cas.org/
chempatplus/

Chemical Patents Plus is a database attached to Chemical Abstracts Service (CAS). It offers the full text of patents of all classes issued by the US Patent and Trademark Office from 1975 to the present, as well as partial coverage from 1971 to 1974. Complete images of pages from patents are available for patents issued from 1 January 1994. To use this database you need a CAS account user ID and a password. Although searching and displaying patent titles and abstracts is free, you have to pay for other patent and related data. Chemical Patents Plus includes CAS Registry Numbers (for patent identification) and complete subject indexing for all chemical patents covered in *Chemical Abstracts*, based on either the US patent or an earlier foreign equivalent patent document within the same patent family.

European Patent Office Database

http://www.european-patent-office.org/

The European Patent Office (EPO) has in the past years established huge patent databases for patent information and documentation. Databases 'PFS' and 'PRS', produced by the EPO, are the largest patent databases in the world in terms of both the countries and time-span covered. Their contents are updated on a weekly basis. According to the EPO, approximately 25 000 and 40 000 documents are added to the PFS and PRS databases respectively each week. These databases are not yet accessible on the Internet, but you can access them through DIALOG (see page 180).

IBM Patent Server

http://patent.womplex.ibm.com/

IBM Patent Server is a World Wide Web server set up by IBM in 1996 for public access to patents issued in the US. It was initially established as an internal project to help IBM's own researchers, product developers and intellectual property attorneys perform basic searches of US patent data quickly and easily, but was eventually developed into a useful database for public use.

The Patent Server provides access to the bibliographic data and text of all patents issued by the United States Patent and Trademark Office (USPTO) from 1974 to the present; images within patents for the last 17 years; plus some patents issued between 1971 and 1973. There are over 2 million patents stored on the Server. You can retrieve both bibliographic data and full text of all patents. The Server supports simple keyword, phrase and patent number searches, as well as the use of Boolean operators. You can use 'Patent number', 'Title', 'Abstract', 'All Claims', 'Assignee', 'Inventors' and 'Attorney/Agent' to search the database. You can even display the scanned image of a patent on your computer screen. In addition, the Server provides hyperlinks to related patents, enabling thorough navigation and location of relevant patents and documents.

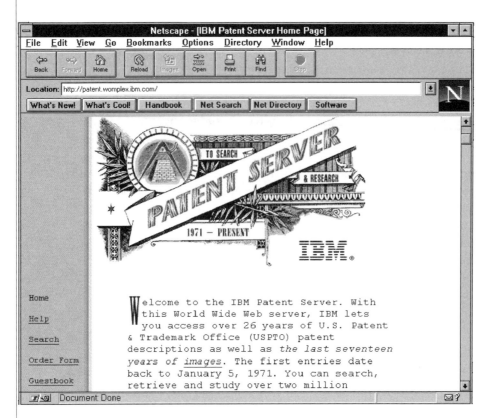

Figure 6.16 IBM Patent Server Web page

QPAT–US

http://www.qpat.com/

QPAT–US is a product of Questel–Orbit, a member of the France Telecom Group and a reputable global vendor in the electronic delivery of patent, trademark, chemical, business and general news information (see page 187). QPAT–US contains the full text of all US patents issued since 1 January 1974, with over 1.8 million records. In addition to the complete full-text database which is available to paying subscribers only, if you register you can search and display all of the patent abstracts contained in the database for free.

US Patent Citation Database

http://cos.gdb.org/repos/pat/

The US Patent Citation Database resides at the Community of Science Webpage, **http://cos.gdb.org/**, which also hosts a number of bibliographic databases, as described on page 155. The database contains fully indexed and searchable bibliographic files for approximately 1.7 million US patents issued since 1975, and is updated weekly. You can search using Boolean operators. You need a subscription to use this database.

The database provides information about each patent, such as number, dates, assignee, inventor, title, abstract, exemplary claims for recent years, and US and international classifications. You can search either by State or on the entire database. The collection also includes international patents, which warrants search by countries. In addition, the database tracks the 'lineage' of each patent— how each patent cites previous patents or is cited by subsequent ones. This feature is particularly useful, as it highlights a patent's technological impact, because a patent cited more frequently often suggests that it has a greater technological significance.

Refining your Query			Download Multiple Citations	
Range(s) Searched: 1995-1997 Query: (((Title=(twin-engine)) or (Abstract=(twin-engine)) or (Claims=(twin-engine)) or (Other Reference=(twin-engine))))				
Records Found: 1			**Records Displayed: 1**	
–	–	**Number**	**Title**	**Assignee**
☐	1.	05480107	x multi-engine jet configuration	–

Figure 6.17 US Patent Citation Database search results

US Patents at CNIDR

http://patents.cnidr.org/access/
access.html

This database, updated weekly, consists of the front pages of US patents (including design patents) dating back to 1976. It includes all bibliographic data, such as the inventor's name, the patent's title and the assignee's name, as well as the abstract, a brief description of the patent's contents. For online searching of the years before 1976, you have to rely on other databases such as the IBM Patent Server. However, if you know the number of a specific patent before 1976, then you can order a copy online by clicking on the 'sales' icon.

Other databases searchable online

The Internet's ability to host a diversity of resources foments a variety of online databases. Some databases are not designed to be bibliographic like INSPEC and FirstSearch. Yet they are relevant to and provide indexed information on engineering and technology. These databases can supplement those well-established commercial or noncommercial bibliographic databases.

Britannica Online

http://www.eb.com/

The Encyclopædia Britannica needs no introduction. Britannica Online is a good example of how technology helps to disseminate information and knowledge. It is an information service provided by Britannica Advanced Publishing, Inc., an Encyclopædia Britannica company. Offered by subscription to academic institutions in late 1994, Britannica Online consists of a fully searchable and browsable collection of authoritative references, including Britannica's latest article database, hundreds of articles not found in the print *Britannica*, *Merriam-Webster's Collegiate Dictionary* (10th edition), the *Britannica Book of the Year*, and thousands of links to other World Wide Web sites selected by Britannica editors.

Canada Institute for Scientific and Technical Information

http://cat.cisti.nrc.ca/screens/
mainmenu_eng.htm/

The Canada Institute for Scientific and Technical Information (CISTI) is an information provider in all areas of science, technology, engineering and medicine. As an information and technology diffusion service of the National Research Council of Canada, CISTI provides database services covering engineering, medicine and other areas. The CISTI Online Catalogue is now available on the Internet, though at present it caters for Telnet connections only.

Global Internet

http://www.gi.net/GINS/
resources/index.html

Global Internet's database consists of two parts: 'Internet Resources' and 'Software Resources'. The Internet Resources contains 'NetHappenings Mailing List', 'Web Announcements', 'Newsletter Mailing List', 'Searchable database of US Colleges and Universities', 'Directory of Scholarly Electronic Conferences' and 'Index of Places to Register Your Web Site'. These resources are modest in capacity, but constitute a good starting place if you are a new Internet user. The Software Resources contains 'Global Internet's Anonymous FTP Site', 'Global Internet's List of Internet Software for MACs and PCs', 'Software Announcements', 'Macintosh Software Announcements' and 'PC Software Announcements', announcements of new programs for the PC.

InterCAT—a Catalog of Internet Resources

http://orc.rsch.oclc.org:6990/

This is another searchable database from OCLC. InterCAT is a 'Catalog of Internet Resources' springing from the Internet Cataloging Project undertaken by OCLC. It contains bibliographic records for Internet resources that have been selected and catalogued by libraries worldwide.

Figure 6.18 InterCAT logo

ISIS from National Agricultural Library

`http://www.nalusda.gov/isis/`

ISIS is an online information service from the National Agricultural Library at the US Department of Agriculture. ISIS has two databases available to researchers for information retrieval: the NAL Online Catalog and the Journal Article Citation database. The NAL Online Catalog contains the most current bibliographic citations for books, reports, maps, journals/periodicals, audiovisuals, CD-ROMs and other electronic media. The Journal Article Citation database consists of citations reflecting journal/periodical articles, book chapters, reprints and other specialised materials indexed by NAL and its cooperators. This database is a subset of the AGRICOLA database (available on FirstSearch), in that AGRICOLA citations from January 1989 to the present are available. The Journal Article Citation database is the most current source of AGRICOLA indexing records. Both databases are updated daily.

Some major database providers and vendors

Probably all the major database providers and vendors have a presence on the Internet. Given a name, we can use a WWW search engine to locate them. Database providers produce and maintain databases which can be searched online or on CD-ROM. Some providers provide an online search interface as well as make their products available to database vendors. Others simply provide an introduction and description of their products and leave the entire interface between the user and the products entirely to their vendors.

Table 6-8 displays a list of some major database providers and vendors. From their Web addresses, we can find detailed information on their products, service, policy and update news. Most of these providers' and vendors' databases are relevant to engineering or technology. There are many more online databases, but they have not been listed here because they have little engineering significance.

Keep up with the latest on online databases

The online information industry is a dynamic one. Constantly there are corporate amalgamations, take-overs, changes, improvements, new products launches and more. To the user, many changes are not directly or immediately relevant, except that we should be optimistic that any commercial activity will benefit us in terms of providing better services for online database information. However, it is useful to be able to know the latest development in online databases when you feel the need or your curiosity is aroused. There can hardly a better

Name and Internet address

BIDS—Bath Information and Data Services
http://www.bids.com/

Brain Wave
http://alpha.n2kbrainwave.com/

The British Library
http://www.bl.uk/

Cambridge Scientific Abstracts
http://www.csa.com/

Canada Institute for Scientific and Technical Information
http://www.cisti.nrc.ca/cisti.html

Center for Networked Information Discovery and Retrieval
http://www.cnidr.org/

DIMDI
http://www.dimdi.de/homeeng.htm

Institute for Scientific Information
http://www.isinet.com/

Knight-Ridder Information
http://www.krinfo.com/

LEXIS NEXIS
http://www.lexis-nexis.com/

NERAC
http://www.nerac.com/index.html

NTIS—National Technical Information Service
http://www.fedworld.gov/ntis/ntishome.html

Ovid Technologies
http://www.ovid.com/

Questel–Orbit
http://www.questel.orbit.com/

SilverPlatter
http://www.silverplatter.com/

STN
http://www.fiz-karlsruhe.de/

H W Wilson
http://www.hwwilson.com/

National Information Services Corporation (NISC)
http://www.nisc.com/

Table 6-8 Online database providers and vendors

place to find out than on the Internet itself. You can bump into announcements of new services or products from various individual Web sites. The main sources of the information, however, are online magazines dedicated to databases and online services.

Online electronic journals and magazines are excellent resources for further reading. One notable choice is *Online* magazine, published by onlineinc.com at **http://www.onlineinc.com/onlinemag/index.html**. *Databases* at **http://www.onlineinc.com/database/index.html** and *Online Users* at **http://www.onlineinc.com/oluser/index.html** both contain updated news on online databases.

Another good sources of information is from relevant online discussion groups. For example, you could join a listserv group called DATABASE-L at the University of Sydney in Australia by sending an email message reading 'SUBSCRIBE DATABASE–L [yourname]' to **listserv@library.usyd.edu.au**, and receive regular updates on the latest discussions on online databases.

There are abundant tutorial materials or 'FAQs' (standing for 'Frequently Asked Questions') you can find online that constitute helpful readings on databases. For example, a 'Patent Searching Tutorial' has been composed by the Richard W. McKinney Engineering Library at the University of Texas at Austin, which you can find at **http://www.lib.utexas.edu/Libs/ENG/PTUT/ ptut.html**.

Bibliography

Bath Information and Data Services
http://www.bids.ac.uk/

Books on the Internet
http://www.lib.utexas.edu/Libs/PCL/Etext.html

A Consumers Guide to the Cost of Online Searching
http://sunsite.nus.sg/bibdb/access/iss04-05-/iss04-05-022.html

Database Magazine
http://www.onlineinc.com/database/index.html

Description of ASME's Civil Engineering Database
http://www.ascepub.infor.com:8601/cedbdesc.html

DIALOG Bluesheets
http://www.krinfo.com/dialog/databases/html2.0/bl0411.html

Directory of Publishers and Vendors
http://www.library.vanderbilt.edu/law/acqs/pubr.html

Electronic Cataloging Instructions
gopher://libgopher.cis.yale.edu:70/11/Instructions

Electronic Publishing Standards
http://www.adfa.oz.au/Epub/McLean_Cook.html#RTFToC1

Engineering Library—Cornell University
http://www.englib.cornell.edu/

Guide to COMPENDEX on INN-VIEW
http://scilib.ucsd.edu/electclass/Compendex.html

Home Page of ISI—Publisher of *Current Contents*
http://www.isinet.com/

InfoEd International Inc.
http://www.infoed.org/

INFOMINE—Scholarly Internet Resource Collections at University of California
http://lib-www.ucr.edu/

INSPEC Search Guide
http://www.englib.cornell.edu/instruction/inspec.html

International Electrotechnical Commission (IEC)
http://www.hike.te.chiba-u.ac.jp/ikeda/IEC/home.html

International Organization for Standardization (ISO)
http://www.iso.ch/

InterNIC Directory and Database Services (AT&T)
gopher://ds.internic.net/11/

Librarian's Index to the Internet
http://sunsite.berkeley.edu/InternetIndex/

The Library Connection
http://www.ths.tased.edu.au/library.html

Online Magazine
http://www.onlineinc.com/onlinemag/index.html

Online User Magazine
http://www.onlineinc.com/oluser/index.html

Patent Searching Tutorial
http://www.lib.utexas.edu/Libs/ENG/PTUT/ptut.html

Publishers' Catelogues
http://www.lights.com/publisher/index.html

Reference Resources from OhioLink
http://www.lib.muohio.edu/res/ref.html

UnCover
http://www.carl.org/carlweb/index.html

UnCover Blue Sheet
http://www.krinfo.com/dialog/databases/netscape1.1/bl0420.html

University of Waterloo Database Catalogue
http://www.lib.uwaterloo.ca/databases/catalogue.html

US Patent And Trademark Office
http://www.uspto.gov/

Don't forget to visit us at
http://dingo.vut.edu.au/~jimin/book.html

CHAPTER
6

CHAPTER

7

Engineering Education, Courseware and Professional Societies on the Internet

Engineering education and the Internet

The Internet has the potential to bring about a profound change in education for engineering, technology and science. Traditional approaches to teaching, lecturing and tutoring confined to classrooms and laboratories are beginning to be extended by new approaches using the more recent technology of online classrooms, multimedia courseware, distance courses, computer simulation, online workshops, media education and video conferencing. These changes enable educators to incorporate modern technology into engineering education. Internet-based instruction challenges the way in which engineering has been conventionally taught. Engineering education has relied heavily on hands-on work conducted in laboratories and the visualisation of materials and objects, as well as theoretical aspects of the discipline. Other disciplines not so reliant on practical and laboratory work can more readily adapt the Internet to their education. The teaching of literature and linguistics has flourished on the Internet—a fact evidenced by their voluminous online presence.

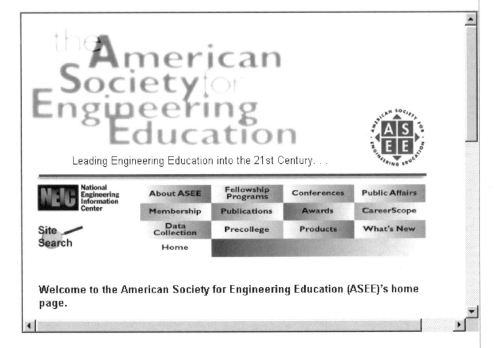

Figure 7.1 ASEE Web page

CHAPTER

7

However, the development of the Internet and computer software provides engineering education with an unprecedented opportunity to develop tools and simulation programs to study complicated engineering phenomena. With an appropriate computer language, the Internet can become a common platform that lacks the limitations of other computer platforms. A good example is the Java programming language; in recent years it has been used extensively to simulate engineering processes which otherwise may be difficult to study without hands-on work in the laboratory.

The rapid advance of technology requires practising engineers to remain continually abreast of it. This means constant development and updating of professional skills to enhance individual career prospects and improve professional competence. Universities and industries often form partnerships to make tertiary education accessible to practising engineers, and the Internet can serve as a venue for this. To advance their knowledge and develop skills relevant to their jobs and career interests, professional engineers and technicians

Figure 7.2 NSF Web page

can use the Internet to provide for their ever-present need to review and upgrade their expertise.

Name and Internet address

Accreditation Board for Engineering and Technology
http://www.abet.ba.md.us/

American Society for Engineering Education
http://www.asee.org/

ASEE/IEEE FIE95 Conference Proceedings
http://fairway.ecn.purdue.edu/FrE/asee/sect95/proc95.html

Association for the Advancement of Computing in Education
http://aace.virginia.edu/aace/

Center for New Engineers
http://www.cne.gmu.edu/

Courseware for Higher Education
http://libraries.maine.edu./umaine/Courseware/outline2.htm

Engineering Council
http://www.engc.org.uk/

Engineering Education Center
http://eec.psu.edu/

European Association for Education in Electrical and Electronics Engineering
http://cran.esstin.u-nancy.fr/EAEEIE/PresEAEEIE.html

European Society for Engineering Education
http://www.ntb.ch/SEFI/

International Association for Continuing Engineering Education
http://www.dipoli.hut.fi/org/IACEE/

National Science Foundation
http://www.nsf.gov/

National Science Foundation Engineering Education Coalitions
http://www.needs.org/coalitions/

Resources for Engineering Education
http://www.ctieng.qmw.ac.uk/

Table 7-1 Resources for engineering education

With the Internet as the platform and medium, some universities have formed coalitions or consortiums to promote and advance engineering education in this new technology age. These coalitions are often funded by government bodies or sponsored by publishing industries or professional societies. Their formation and presence on the Internet have in the recent years become a driving force in reforming and improving engineering education for university degrees and for tertiary education programmes.

The National Science Foundation (NSF) in the US is a leading funding body for engineering education. It funds the Engineering Education Coalitions Program that was developed to stimulate bold, innovative and comprehensive models for the tangible reform of undergraduate engineering education and to increase the retention of students, especially women and those minorities under-represented in engineering. This Program encompasses several coalitions involving more than 32 institutions. As stipulated by the NSF, the goals for its Engineering Education Coalitions Program are:

(1) to design and implement comprehensive, systemic, and structural reform of undergraduate engineering education; (2) to provide tested alternative curricula and new instructional delivery systems that improve the quality of undergraduate engineering education; (3) to create substantive resource linkages among engineering baccalaureate producing and pre-college institutions; and (4) to increase the number of baccalaureate engineering degrees awarded, especially to women, underrepresented minorities, and persons with disabilities.

The Synthesis Coalition is one of the very successful coalitions for engineering education under the NSF emblem. It is a union of eight American institutions: California Polytechnic State University at San Luis Obispo, Cornell University, Hampton University, Iowa State University, Southern University, Stanford University, Tuskegee University, and the University of California at Berkeley. Synthesis Coalition aims to 'design, implement and assess new approaches to undergraduate engineering education that emphasize multidisciplinary synthesis, teamwork and communication, hands-on and laboratory experiences, open-ended problem formulation and solving, and examples of "best practices" from industry.' Designed to rectify the plight of overburdened engineering programmes offered in higher education institutions with excessive compartmentalisation and general lack of excitement and motivation, the Synthesis Coalition seeks to develop and experiment with a variety of innovative curricula and delivery systems.

The Engineering Academy of Southern New England (EASNE) is another coalition from the NSF. Its objective is to integrate manufacturing concepts in the curricula for all engineering disciplines. It is designed to be a joint venture between government, university and industry. Engineering graduates of all specialties participate in integrated process and product development teams so that they can gain sufficient understanding of manufacturing principles, practices and processes. Industry partners in this programme from Southern New England share personnel, facilities and strategic planning and thus influence the engineering curricula of universities.

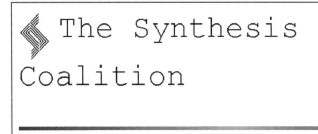

Figure 7.3 Synthesis Coalition Web page

SUCCEED, an acronym for the Southeastern University and College Coalition for Engineering Education, is another Engineering Education Coalition sponsored by the National Science Foundation. It is made up of the engineering colleges of eight south-eastern US universities and colleges. It aims to undertake a comprehensive

Name and Internet address

CAUSE
http://www.cause.org/

Coalition for New Manufacturing Education
http://www.mame.syr.edu/MET/supawards/ud.html

Consortium on Green Design and Manufacturing (CGDM)
http://greenmfg.me.berkeley.edu/green/Home/Index.html

Educom
http://www.educom.edu/

Engineering Academy of Southern New England
http://www.egr.uri.edu:80/ne/

Engineering Coalition of Schools for Excellence in Education and Leadership
http://echo.umd.edu/

Foundation Coalition
http://foundation.ua.edu/

Gateway Engineering Education Coalition
http://www-gateway.vpr.drexel.edu/

Greenfield: the Coalition for New Manufacturing Education
http://www.needs.org/coalitions/info/greenfocus.html

Institute for Academic Technology
http://www.iat.unc.edu/

Project Kaleidoscope (PKAL)
http://www.pkal.org/

Southeastern University and College Coalition for Engineering Education
http://succeed.engr.vt.edu/index.html

Southern California Coalition for Education in Manufacturing Engineering
http://heart.engr.csulb.edu/scceme/

Table 7-2 Resources for consortia and coalitions for engineering education

revitalisation of undergraduate engineering education for the 21st century by designing and implementing a fundamentally new and experimental engineering curriculum.

Engineering courses and courseware on the Internet

Traditionally, courses offered by universities are made known to school leavers through government promotional documents and university leaflets. School leavers can select a number of courses offered by domestic universities in their preference list and decide which course or courses to enroll in later. Inquiries to universities overseas for courses are usually met with a bunch of colourful brochures which you have to sift through for really relevant information on course enrolment. Another source of information can be universities' Open Days, when potential students receive first-hand information about courses offered and facilities available to support the courses.

Competition in education means that nowadays the survival of many academic institutions depends on the success of the courses they offer. Course advertisements in newspapers and other media by universities is indicative of how these institutions have felt the competition and have adopted business approaches to promote their own affairs. The advance of technology has created opportunities for various tailor-made short courses with specific focuses and targeted audiences. These short courses fulfill the need for engineers to receive continuous professional training. This scenario opens a new dimension for engineering education and for course design.

The Internet has provided an attractive venue for universities worldwide to promote and advertise their courses to a much wider domestic and international audience. It promises to link universities to potential students who otherwise would not be aware of the existence of these universities. Ample course information to enable an informed selection before enrolment can be made available on the Internet. For engineering companies or government organisations providing short courses for training or skill development, there can be no better and cost-effective ways of promoting their products.

The Internet can be used for more than just promoting courses; it can also be the venue for courses. It is a perfect means for distance education: courses can be offered on the Internet and students supervised, tutored and consulted through the Internet. Learning materials can be downloaded, instructions given via emails and assessment made online.

A shortcoming of the courses promoted or conducted on the Internet is that some of them seem to have a shorter life expectancy than other types of information on the Net. This is particularly true for specialised short courses. For universities, course information will usually be thorough and current, as there is a greater degree of stability involved.

For university educators and students, the Internet can be an ideal place to store lecture notes, tutorial materials, assignment sheets, instructions for laboratory practical, and other course materials. More than that, the WWW has enabled a Web server to host specially designed course materials that are interactive, multimedia, Internet-accessible. This was not possible before the Internet age.

The definition of 'courseware' is variable. The Web page of the University of Maine for engineering courseware at **http://libinfo.ume.maine.edu/Courseware/outline2.htm#eng** has defined courseware as 'the content and technique applied to instructional materials in electronic format', and consequently has listed the following categories constituting courseware:

- Class notes, scanned images, syllabi, textbooks, tutorials and assignments made available by instructors over the Internet and WWW.
- Fully developed, interactive products available commercially or as shareware from publishers, educational consortiums or individual authors and developers.
- A diverse body of applications used to develop instructional materials in electronic format.

Alternatively, engineering courseware can be seen as computer-based educational material that can be used to assist engineering learning and training. To accomplish this, engineering courseware should cover significant breadth of materials for different disciplines in its terrain. On the Internet, however, engineering courseware may not always earn an entire segment in lists of online resources available. This, ironically, is for two opposing reasons: engineering is too broad to be considered a single entity, and it is too limited to extend over a whole Web site. First, engineering is a broad category, especially taking into account the many cross-disciplinary areas that are flourishing. Second, many Web sites designed for courseware cater for wider interests than simply engineering and technology. A site exhibiting an abundance of such online courseware is the World Lecture Hall at the University of Texas, **http://www.utexas. edu/world/lecture/**, shown in Figure 7.4.

It contains a broad spectrum of courseware of titles ranging from 'Accounting' to 'Women's Studies'. Engineering-related courseware can be identified under several titles such as 'Science and Technology', 'Mechanical Engineering', 'Petroleum Engineering', 'Nuclear Engineering and Engineering Physics' and 'Industrial Engineering'.

National Engineering Education Delivery System (NEEDS) is a pioneer of online courseware creation, delivery and evaluation. NEEDS is the outcome of a project of Synthesis Coalition that is funded by the National Science Foundation with the aim of enhancing undergraduate engineering education through the use of computers. The NEEDS database is particularly important for anyone interested in engineering courseware. It provides access to a diverse range of engineering educational materials. Its collection includes computer-based instructional materials and other curricular materials

The World Lecture Hall (WLH) contains links to pages created by faculty worldwide who are using the Web to deliver class materials. For example, you will find course syllabi, assignments, lecture notes, exams, class calendars, multimedia textbooks, etc.

Here's a form to add your materials. For additions to the WLH, see What's New (13 August 97). And thanks to those who have contributed to our commendations page.

A	Accounting	Advertising	African (American) Studies

Figure 7.4 World Lecture Hall at the University of Texas

ranging from simple text to hypertext stacks to full-motion video. Like many other bibliographic databases, NEEDS can be searched by keyword, title, author or subject. The courseware and courseware elements from the NEEDS database can be downloaded and used to create or organise customised courseware modules.

Engineering case studies can make up a special part of engineering courseware. An engineering case study usually constitutes either an actual event or real problem with a degree of theoretical and technical complexity, or else an engineering activity that inspires learning about engineering principles, knowledge and practices. Its purpose is to demonstrate, from examples of engineering projects, how an engineer goes about performing tasks and obtaining results. Differing from lecture notes, engineering cases open a dimension where students master engineering theory in the context of real life. An engineering case commonly uses a well-programmed series of events which reflect the real engineering activity in order to explain an engineering principle or a practice so that the user can derive proper conclusions.

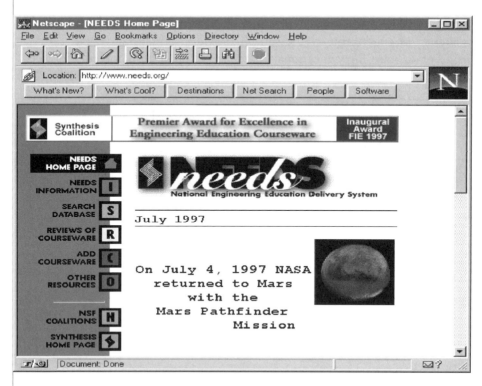

Figure 7.5 NEEDS database Web page

Name and Internet address

CASO's Internet University
http://www.caso.com/

Chemical Engineering Undergraduate Courses
http://www.che.ufl.edu/courses/che-undergrad.html

Edinburgh Engineering Virtual Library—Courseware and Training Materials
http://www.eevl.ac.uk:4321/search?query=&resourcetype=Courseware%2FTraining
+Materials

Engineering Courseware for Higher Education on the WWW
http://libinfo.ume.maine.edu/Courseware/outline2.htm#eng

Global Campus
http://www.csulb.edu/gc/index.html

Globewide Network Academy
http://uu-gna.mit.edu:8001/uu-gna/index.html

National Engineering Education Delivery System—NEEDS
http://www.needs.org/

Stanford Online
http://adept.stanford.edu./

Synthesis Courses on the Web
http://synthesis.stanford.edu/SynthCourses.html

Synthesis Curriculum: Computer-Integrated Civil and Environmental Engineering
http://synthesis.stanford.edu/CICEE.html

University of Buffalo Libraries

University Online
http://www.uol.com
http://ublib.buffalo.edu/libraries/units/sel/engineering/courseware.html

World Lecture Hall
http://www.utexas.edu/world/lecture/

WWW Information Sources for Engineering Short Courses
http://www.engr.utk.edu/dept/nuclear/TIW/engshort.html

Table 7-3 Internet resources for engineering courseware

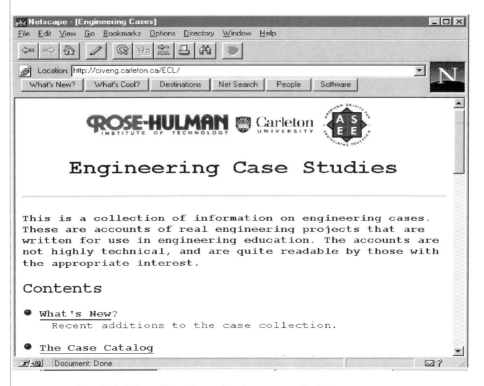

Figure 7.6 Carleton University engineering case studies Web page

The Internet makes it possible for good engineering case studies to reach a wider education community of interested users. The Carleton University Civil and Environmental Engineering in Canada hosts a Web site for extensive information on engineering case studies at **http://www.civeng.carleton.ca/ECL/**, shown in Figure 7.6.

Case studies on the Internet are not all from universities. Another breed of engineering case study found on the Internet comes from industry, R&D institutions and government organisations. There are more archive materials for special engineering cases than those designed in the academic world. These cases show the success and failure of engineering applications in the past. They constitute excellent real-life learning materials for practising and future engineers.

Table 7-4 is a small collection of online engineering case studies. Some Web sites allow you to download case studies but charge for this. You can find more case studies using the WWW search engines to search keywords like 'engineering' and 'courseware' together.

Distance education for engineering

The Internet also provides an excellent venue for distance education. In the pre-Internet era, distance education was conducted by mail; books and coursework and course materials were sent by post. Later, radio and television were used as a means of delivery. With the Internet a new dimension for distance education has been opened up. The original purpose of distance education has not changed much: it still means learning at a physical distance from universities and colleges for awards and degrees, as well as for courses, seminars and workshops. However, the methods of delivering distance education have changed. The Internet and the World Wide Web can provide a virtual learning environment and enhance accessibility to information and courses. In addition, they help to create a community of learners that was not previously possible in traditional classroom settings or through conventional methods of distance education.

Name and Internet address

Case Studies in Engineering Design
http://fulton.seas.virginia.edu/~shj2n/case/casehme.html

Engineering Ethics Cases
http://www.cwru.edu/affil/wwwethics/engcases.html

Ethics Case Studies for Undergraduate Engineering Courses
http://ethics.tamu.edu/

Information for Engineering Case Studies
http://www.civeng.carleton.ca/ECL

Manufacturing Systems Engineering Case Library
http://www.rpi.edu/locker/76/000776/trp/trp_case.html

Some Successful Case Studies
http://www.year2000plus.com/success.html

24 Numerical Case Studies over Selected Problems in Marine Engineering
http://www.dnv.no/ocean/bk/cas.htm

Table 7-4 Internet resources for engineering case studies

CHAPTER

7

Students or practising engineers are able to access online educational resources on the Web from anywhere and at any time (at least theoretically). Courses delivered on the World Wide Web can reach those of their customers who do not have physical access to the course providers. Online instructions can be given. The World Wide Web can also be valuable for collaborative learning, and courses designed to be highly interactive can facilitate group discussion. These activities can be supported by chat rooms, bulletin boards, listservs and other such Internet tools. Tests and examinations can be conducted online by using listservs, bulletin boards and other forums. Students can answer quizzes and examinations, or questions and solutions can be returned to the teacher by email. They can also submit assignments and project reports online.

With the Web, a greater variety of distance education courses becomes available. Distance courses that are electronic by nature, such as interactive multimedia courses, prosper only in the World Wide Web environment. The Internet has also found its niche in industrial training. Conventional industrial training materials can be been converted for re-use in distance education and training. Engineers are usually computer-literate; this makes it easy for them to adapt to an online training environment and teach themselves with minimal instructional intervention. Table 7-5 lists some Web sites where information on engineering-related distance education is available.

The size of distance education in the Internet era is reflected by the survey results from the US Market for Distance Learning Systems and Services, which show that in 1997 sales of distance learning equipment is expected to top $1 billion. This figure is up from $863 million in 1996, and is more than triple the 1992 figure (**http://www.syllabus. com/ntr07_21_97.html**).

An increasing number of universities are now offering education on the Internet. This is a timely reflection of both the internationalisation and commercialisation of education and the application of modern technology to education. The creation of Web pages for distance and continuing education exemplifies this endeavour. Universities are also ideal venues for offering short courses for professional development.

Name and Internet address
Distance Education for Dummies http://www.angelfire.com/mo/EmirMohammed/index.html
Distance Education Resource Sites http://miavx1.muohio.edu/%7Ecdcwis/distance_ed_index.html
Distance Education Technology http://www-distlearn.pp.asu.edu/
EUCEN—The European Universities Continuing Education Network http://alf.fe.up.pt/eucen/
EuroPACE 2000—A Virtual University http://www.europace.be/
International Association for Continuing Engineering Education http://www.dipoli.hut.fi/org/IACEE/
International Centre for Distance Learning (iCDL) http://www-icdl.open.ac.uk/
Iowa State University Engineering Distance Education http://www.eng.iastate.edu/ede/homepage.html
MASIE Center http://www.masie.com/
University Continuing Education Association http://www.nucea.edu/
University of Waterloo Distance and Continuing Education http://www.adm.uwaterloo.ca/infoded/de&ce.html
Worldwide Interactive Network, Inc. http://www.w-win.com/

Table 7-5 Internet resources for distance education

Engineering societies and associations on the Internet

Professional societies are very important communities and regulatory organisations for engineers. Being a member of one or more professional societies is a useful part of a practising engineer's professional life. A professional society can be an excellent information source for new technology developments, applications, regulatory issues conferences, workshops and seminars and career opportunities. It can also be a site for various professional events. Many prominent engineering societies produce their own magazines or technical reports for their members, as well as transactions and journal publications, and make them available on the Internet. Small societies can keep their members updated through electronic newsletters published on the Internet. In some societies, members can look for solutions to technology-specific problems through their technical databases.

The Internet has begun to break the geographical barrier between engineering societies and their members. A society's or institution's activities, publications and research can be made available to potential members such as university students. Figure 7.7 shows the Web page of the Society of Automotive Engineers (**http://www.sae.Org.80/ index.htm**), a professional society that has nurtured millions of engineers over the past decades.

Figure 7.7 SAE Web page

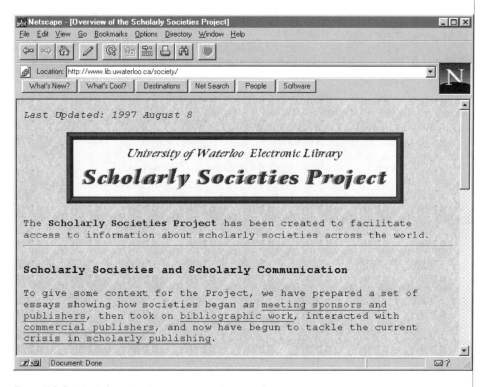

Figure 7.8 Scholarly Societies Project at the University of Waterloo

Many engineering Web sites contain lists of professional engineering societies, either in the same engineering discipline or in the same geographical location. Some of these fine lists are compiled by academics in universities or librarians in university libraries. The University of Waterloo in Canada embarked upon a project called 'Scholarly Society Project' to facilitate access to information about scholarly societies across the world. The Web site for this project at **http://www.lib.uwaterloo.ca/society/** (Figure 7.8) contains over one thousand scholarly societies, many of them societies for engineering, science and technology.

Table 7-6 shows some Web sites that list engineering societies on the Internet.

CHAPTER

7

Name and Internet address

Edinburgh Engineering Virtual Library—Engineering Societies and Institutions
http://www.eevl.ac.uk:4321/search?query=&resourcetype=Society%2FInstitution+Server

Engineering Associates & Institutes
http://www.aecinfo.com/eng/assoc.html

European Electrical and Electronics Engineering Societies
http://www.etec.polimi.it/eurel/

European Federation of National Engineering Associations
http://www.cri.ensmp.fr/feani/

IEEE Societies
http://www.ieee.org:80/society/

International Standards Organisations
http://www.ansi.org/resource.html

Professional Societies Engineering-Related Sites
http://www.interpath.net/~meps/meps/meplnks.htm

Scholarly Societies
http://www.lib.uwaterloo.ca/society/

Subject-based Internet Resources—Engineering Association
http://wally2.rit.edu/internet/subject/soc.html

Yahoo!: Science: Engineering: Organizations: Professional
http://www.yahoo.com/text/Science/Engineering/Organizations/Professional/

Table 7-6 Internet resources for engineering societies and associations

Name and Internet address

ACM
http://www.acm.org/

American Ceramic Society
http://www.acers.org/

American Chemical Society
http://www.acs.org/

American Institute of Aeronautics and Astronautics (AIAA)
http://www.aiaa.org/

American Society of Mechanical Engineers (ASME)
http://www.asme.org/

ANSI
http://www.ansi.org/

ASM International
http://www.asm-intl.org/

Institute of Electrical and Electronics Engineers (IEEE)
http://www.ieee.org:80/

Institute of Marine Engineers
http://www.engc.org.uk/imare/

Institution of Electrical Engineers (IEE)
http://www.iee.org.uk/

Instrument Society of America
http://www.isa.org/

International Society for Optical Engineering
http://www.spie.org/

National Association of Corrosion Engineers
http://www.nace.org/

National Society of Professional Engineers
http://www.nspe.org/index.htm

Society for Industrial and Applied Mathematics
http://www.siam.org/

Society of Automotive Engineers
http://www.sae.org:80/index.htm

Society of Experimental Mechanics
http://www.sem.org/

Society of Manufacturing Engineers
http://www.sme.org/

World Computer Society
http://computer.org/

Table 7-7 Some individual engineering societies

CHAPTER

7

In Table 7-7, the Web site addresses of some prominent engineering societies are listed. Their Web sites are excellent information sources for engineering students and researchers as well as for practising engineers.

Engineering standards on the Internet

Engineering standards have made a crucial contribution to the advancement and application of technology. They have also played an essential role in international economy and cooperation both within and between industries . Standards have a direct bearing on, among other things, our safety, quality of life and environment. With the Internet, various organisations for engineering standards have another avenue for publicising their presence. Both international standards organisations such as the International Organisation for Standardisation (ISO) and national standards bodies such as American National Standards Institute (ANSI) have sites on the Internet.

Both the ISO Web site at **http://www.iso.ch/infoe/stbodies.html** and the ANSI site at **http://www.ansi.org/resource.htmlcontains** contain a list of international and national standards bodies. The Web site for the Scholarly Societies Project at University of Waterloo in Canada (at **http://www.lib.uwaterloo.ca/society/standards.html**) offers a comprehensive list of Web sites of engineering standards, many of them linked to engineering societies. Table 7-8 lists the Web sites of a few prominent standards organisations. Other standards organisations affiliated to engineering societies can be found from the Web sites of their host societies.

Further reading

If you are interested in further material on engineering education on the Internet, it is advisable to visit regularly the sites of the consortia and coalitions listed in Table 7-2 for their recent publications, projects and activities. Many of them post published articles on their Web sites. A number of engineering education journals and magazines are available online. *Syllabus* is a journal full of rich materials and new trends, at **http://www.syllabus.com/syllmag.html**. Its archive of

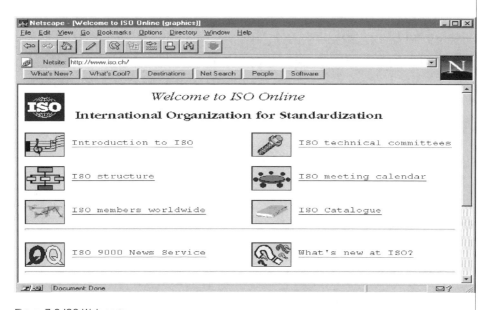

Figure 7.9 ISO Web page

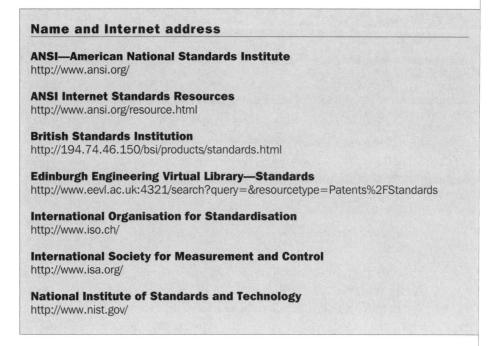

Name and Internet address

ANSI—American National Standards Institute
http://www.ansi.org/

ANSI Internet Standards Resources
http://www.ansi.org/resource.html

British Standards Institution
http://194.74.46.150/bsi/products/standards.html

Edinburgh Engineering Virtual Library—Standards
http://www.eevl.ac.uk:4321/search?query=&resourcetype=Patents%2FStandards

International Organisation for Standardisation
http://www.iso.ch/

International Society for Measurement and Control
http://www.isa.org/

National Institute of Standards and Technology
http://www.nist.gov/

Table 7-8 Internet resources for standards organisations

CHAPTER

7

Name and Internet address

ANSI—American National Standards Institute
http://www.ansi.org/

American Society for Testing and Materials (ASTM)
http://www.astm.org/

American Society of Agricultural Engineers Standards
http://www.asae.org/standards/

American Technical Publishers
http://www.ameritech.co.uk/

British Standards Institution
http://194.74.46.150/bsi/products/standards.html

Codes and Standards of ASME
http://www.asme.org/cns/

Cuscom Standards Services, Inc.
http://www.cssinfo.com/

IEEE Standards
http://standards.ieee.org/index.html

SAE Standards
http://www.sae.org:80/PRODSERV/STANDARD/standard.htm

Standards Developing Organisations
http://www.ihs.com/about/

Standards for the National Association of Corrosion Engineers
http://www.nace.org/std.htm

Standards of the Acoustical Society of America
http://asa.aip.org/standards.html

Standards of the Telecommunications Industry Association (TIA)
http://www.eia.org/eng/allstd/std/index.htm

Table 7-9 Internet resources for engineering standards

'News, Resources and Trends' amounts to an excellent anecdotal collection of recent information on distance education. *Deliberations* at **http://www.lgu.ac.uk/deliberations/** is another online magazine for academics, librarians and educators. *Education World* at **http://www.education-world.com/** is a Web resource containing a wealth of links to education-related sites, reviews of top education Web sites, information-sharing forums, links to state and federal education resources, and articles written by educators. Online proceedings of engineering education-related conferences may contain rich collections of interesting reading materials, such as the Proceedings of the ASEE 1995 Conference at **http://fairway.ecn. purdue.edu/FrE/asee/sect95/proc95.html**.

Search engines can be used either to search for queries such as 'engineering online education' or to browse the directories already grouped in categories. Many Web search engines are already stocked with their own directories, such as Lycos, WebCrawler and Infoseek. Each contains a wealth of online information on education.

Two databases devoted to education and relevant resources in education and in courseware are NEEDS (page 124) and ERIC (page 159). NEEDS is at **http://www.needs.org/**, and provides access to a diverse range of engineering educational materials. It can be searched by keyword, title, author or subject. The courseware and courseware elements from the NEEDS database can be downloaded. ERIC, at **http://www.aspensys.com/eric/index.html**, is a national information system affiliated to the US Department of Education. Its databases contain bibliographic records of research reports, conference papers, teaching guides, books and journal articles relating to the practice of education, including engineering and technology education.

The Web sites listed in Tables 7-8 and 7-9 constitute a useful collection of materials for engineering standards. Many of these sites either contain further reading material or provide links to more Web sites for materials related to engineering standards.

Bibliography

A Course to Help Students Prepare for College
http://www2.okstate.edu/lam2717/CollegePrep101.html

CTIEngineering Home Page
http://www.ctieng.qmw.ac.uk/

CyberEd
http://www.umassd.edu/cybered/distlearninghome.html

Distance Education
http://www.uidaho.edu/evo/dist4.html

Developing Accessible Engineering Courseware
http://FrE.www.ecn.purdue.edu/FrE/asee/fie95/4c5/4c55/4c55.htm

Distance Learning—A Faculty FAQ
http://www.microsoft.com/education/hed/online.htm

Education Electronic Journals
http://www.adm.uwaterloo.ca/infotrac/edujournals.html

Education Journal Annotations
http://www.soemadison.wisc.edu/IMC/journals/anno_AB.html

Education Journals
http://www.carfax.co.uk/subjeduc.htm

Engineering Library—Cornell University
http://www.englib.cornell.edu/

E-Zine-List from John Labovitz
http://www.meer.net/~johnl/e-zine-list/

Index to Education Network Resources
http://blair.library.rhodes.edu/educhtmls/educnet.html

INFOMINE—Scholarly Internet Resource Collections at University of California
http://lib-www.ucr.edu/

Internet University College Courses by Computer
http://www.caso.com/iu/articles.html

Introduction to Thermodynamics of Materials
http://uts.cc.utexas.edu/~kmralls/ME361/

Microsoft in Higher Education
http://www.microsoft.com/hed/

Privacy in a Networked Environment
http://www.cause.org/issues/privacy.html

Resources for Engineering Education
http://www.ctieng.qmw.ac.uk/Sites/genresources.html

Syllabus Magazine Archives
http://www.syllabus.com/

Time-Life Education
http://www.timelifeedu.com/

TradeWave Galaxy Engineering & Technology
http://galaxy.einet.net/galaxy/Engineering-and-Technology.html

Using the Internet for Teaching and Learning
http://www.library.nwu.edu/workshop/steffen/overview.html

Writing Engineering Cases
http://www.civeng.carleton.ca/ECL/cwrtng.html

**Don't forget to visit us at
http://dingo.vut.edu.au/~jimin/book.html**

Engineering Education, Courseware and Professional Societies on the Internet

CHAPTER

7

CHAPTER

Engineering Publications on the Internet

What is online publication?

Publishers on the Internet

Books on the Internet

Online journals

Online engineering journals

Online engineering publication projects

Further reading

What is online publication?

The Internet provides an excellent environment for academic and professional communities to publish the results of their research for their peers and for wider communities. It has enormous potential to provide and enhance access to information and to revolutionise the ways libraries and publishers conduct their business.

Web publishing, online publication, electronic publishing and electronic publication are terms often used on the Internet. These terms have never been satisfactorily defined, although many descriptions are available. However, all of them involve publications available on the Internet (with the possible exception that 'electronic publications' also include CD-ROM). These publications can be books, journals, magazines, reports, software or newsletters. Some are digital versions of printed ones, but others are authentic electronic publications with no printed counterparts. In this Chapter, the term 'online publication' is used to include all publications made available on the Internet.

Online publications come in different formats, ranging from simple text to multimedia, including audio and video. Some formats may be proprietary, in that the information can be accessed only by using special software. Other formats are more standardised, so that information may be viewed, read, and downloaded using simple computer software such as a Web browser.

Over their traditional printing counterparts, publications made online have a distinct advantage. They are not vulnerable to vandalism and negligence, nor will they deteriorate due to poor paper and binding quality. It is convenient to catalogue and document these publications, simply because their electronic records accord with library computer systems. Dramatic reduction in the physical space required also constitutes an excellent feature of electronic publications. The most important attribute of online publication is its readiness for online transfer. As a result, information from any libraries or collections can be shared, technically speaking, by anybody around the globe.

The increasing enthusiasm for online publication is accompanied by an eagerness to resolve a few of the thorny issues arising in this Internet era, including cultural impact, economic implications, standardisation of computer platforms on which publication is made and conversion of existing printed publications to electronic form. There are concerns that the quality of online scholarly publications will decline because the peer review process is different from the conventional one. The cost saving of online publication is still subject to debate. Some people remain doubtful about the hidden costs of electronic or online publications. The subscription cost of some online journals is no less than the cost of the printed version. Standardising the platform and format for online publication is still an ongoing issue for technologists, publishers, librarians and government regulators.

The other issue that needs resolving in this digital age is copyright. Copyright was designed to protect the interests of authors, and to reward their labour. Engineers, scientists and technologists are interested primarily in the progress of technology and science. Copyright laws have to pursue a balance between the public interest in access to works and copyright owners' interests in being able to profit from their works; and between society's need for the exchange of ideas and for the intellectual property rights of authors, publishers and copyright owners. In this age of information technology, more publications will be made available only in electronic formats, and may appear only online. In Australia, material on the Internet is protected by copyright; but in other countries, such as America, copyright protection is only afforded when the copyright symbol is actually on the work. This situation imposes an urgency for governments, academic and engineering communities and publishers to discuss a solution that protects authors' intellectual properties as well as promotes the progress of technology and science.

Online book publication is also emerging, after a transition from printed books to hybrid books with accompanying discs or even wholly on disc. Paperless books, when read on a computer, can be tailored to resemble printed books on the screen. However, this cosmetic effort cannot overshadow the substantive changes; that is to say, a book published online is usually in hypertext format, allowing the merging of different media. It also allows readers to determine what they want to learn and how. Online book publication has enabled traditional publishing companies to embrace information technology and multimedia tools in their business.

Standardisation, copyright, intellectual property and authors' royalties for their work are a few issues that need to be addressed. Other contentious issues, such as online delivery, storage and archive of online materials, also need to be satisfactorily resolved before online publication can become a formidable competitor (or supplement) to traditional printed publication. Leaving those aside, the small production run size is not an inducement for publishers to make substantial investment. The Internet has been a vibrant medium but it is non-regulated. Different computer file formats and operating system platforms can make online publication capital- and labour-intensive.

Publishers on the Internet

Publishers worldwide are making their presence felt on the Internet. Using WWW search engines, it is possible to find any publisher with a Web presence and make direct contact. Many of them would otherwise be unknown to readers and authors through conventional channels of communication. A Web site provides a publisher with a location to upload their publication list for browsing and searching, to

Figure 8.1 Oxford University Press Web page

Name and Internet address

AcqWeb's Directory of Publishers and Vendors
http://www.library.vanderbilt.edu/law/acqs/pubr.html

List of Publishers, University of York Library
http://www.york.ac.uk/services/library/subjects/libint.htm#pub

Publishers' Catalogues Home Page
http://www.lights.com/publisher/

Publishers List from Faxon
http://www.faxon.com/html/it_pl_am.html

Publishing Companies Online
http://www.edoc.com/ejournal/publishers.html

TitleNet and Inforonics, Inc.
gopher://gopher.infor.com/

WWW Virtual Library
http://www.comlab.ox.ac.uk/archive/publishers.html

Yahoo!'s List of Publishers
http://www.yahoo.com/Business/Corporations/Publishing

Table 8-1 Internet resources on publishers

advertise their recent publications and best-sellers, to establish direct communication with readers for feedback, and to put readers in contact with authors. It is also possible to order books from a publisher directly through its Web site. Table 8-1 shows a few Web sites that display lists of publishers.

Table 8-2 shows the Web sites of a number of publishers familiar to engineers, technologists and scientists because of their activity in their fields. Many more publishers can be found on the Internet by using search engines to search for such keywords as 'publishers'.

The publishers listed in Table 8-2 are publishers with broad publication interests, including engineering and technology. There are also other publishers who are more focused on, though not necessarily limited to, engineering and technology. Table 8-3 lists some of these publishers.

Name and Internet address

Academic Press
http://www.apnet.com/

Addison Wesley Longman
http://www2.awl.com/corp/

Association of American University Presses
http://aaup.pupress.princeton.edu/

Blackwell Publishers
http://www.blackwellpublishers.co.uk/

Cambridge University Press
http://www.cup.cam.ac.uk/

Coleman Research Corporation
http://www.crc.com/

Elsevier Science
http://www.elsevier.nl/

International Thomson Publishing
http://www.thomson.com/

Kluwer Academic Publishers
http://www.wkap.nl/

MIT Press
http://www-mitpress.mit.edu/

Oxford University Press
http://www.oup.co.uk/

Prentice Hall
http://www.prenhall.com/

Springer-Verlag
http://www.springer.de/

Thomson
http://www.thomson.com/

Wiley
http://www.interscience.wiley.com/

World Scientific
http://www.wspc.com.sg/

Table 8-2 Some individual publishers

CHAPTER

8

Name and Internet address

American Technical Publishers
http://www.ameritech.co.uk/

Athena Scientific
http://world.std.com/~athenasc/

Birkhäuser Boston
http://www.birkhauser.com/

Cambridge International Science Publishing
http://www.demon.co.uk/cambsci/homepage.htm

Crambeth Allen Publishing
http://www.capable.co.uk/

Engineering Press
http://www.engrpress.com/

Ernst & Sohn
http://www.vchgroup.de/ernst+sohn/indexeng.html

Morgan Kaufmann
http://www.mkp.com/default.htm

National Academy Press
http://www.nap.edu/

Thomas Telford
http://www.t-telford.co.uk/pu/puindex.html

Table 8-3 Some specialised engineering publishers

In addition to commercial publishers, there are those specialising in online publishing. They are usually not subsidiaries of commercial print publishers like those listed in Table 8-2. Their specialties often extend to Web-based interactive education courseware, online journals, conference and symposium proceedings, professional society publications and even books. For example, Commonwealth Network (**http://commonwealth.riddler.com/**) and University Online (**http://www.uol.com**) are two Web publishers. An extensive list of online publishers is maintained at **http://www.edoc.com/jrl-bin/wilma/pel**.

A comprehensive list of publishers world-wide can also be found at **http://www.lights.com/publisher/**,where a geographical index links you to publishers in different countries.

The Internet has also made it possible for numerous university presses to promote their publications. As the publishing arm of their parent universities, university presses have direct access to the fresh ideas and research produced by the scholarly community in universities. Publication of these ideas and research outcomes is very important for the scholarly and wider community. Having to survive in a commercial world, these presses are often in competition with the mainstream publishing circle. However, they do find their niche often by publishing specialised topics. The Association of American University Presses (**http://aaup.pupress.princeton.edu/**)is a co-operative organisation of over one hundred university presses in the US, Canada and other countries.

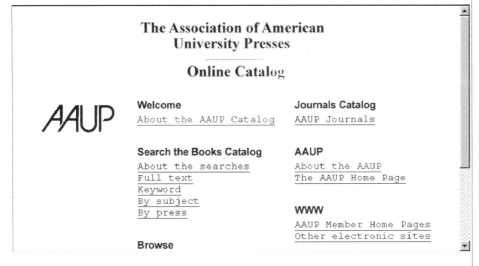

Figure 8.2 AAUP Web page

Various engineering societies are also publishers for their own professional communities, and their publications are usually directly targeted to an audience in a specialised engineering and technology circle. Many of these societies include their publications on their Web page, most commonly newsletters and online journals. For example, the World's Computer Society (affiliated to the IEEE) provides links

Figure 8.3 World's Computer Society Web page

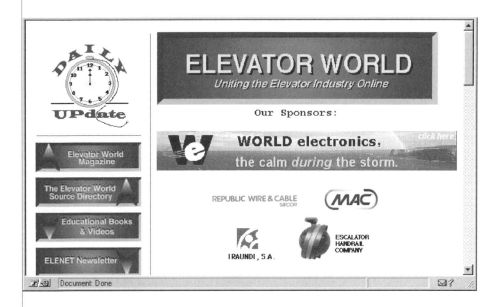

Figure 8.4 Elevator World Web page

Name and Internet address
American Institute of Aeronautics and Astronautics (AIAA) http://www.aiaa.org/
American Society for Testing and Materials (ASTM) http://www.astm.org/
American Society of Civil Engineers (ASCE) http://www.asce.org/
American Society of Mechanical Engineers (ASME) http://www.asme.org/
ASM International http://www.asm-intl.org/
Institute of Electrical and Electronics Engineers, Inc. (IEEE) http://www.ieee.org/pubs/
Institute of Marine Engineers http://www.engc.org.uk/imare/
Institution of Electronic Engineers (IEE) http://ioj.iee.org.uk/
International Society for Measurement and Control http://www.isa.org/
International Society for Optical Engineering http://www.spie.org/
Optical Society of America http://www.osa.org/

Table 8-4 Engineering societies as publishers

to a number of online journals and periodicals for computing professionals at **http://computer.org**.

Elevator World's Web site at **http://www.elevator-world.com/** is a good example of an industry body which publishes printed journals, books, standards and reports, and news about conferences, meetings and memberships. It also provides links to other relevant sites.

Table 8-4 gives a list of engineering societies which are also publishers in their associated disciplines. More engineering society publishers can be found on the Internet using Web search engines and such keywords as 'engineering society publisher' or 'engineering society publication online'.

Books on the Internet

Like journals, an increasing number of books are now being made available in part or in full on the Internet public domain. Online books, also called 'e-texts', are often either books published solely online, or digital replicas of printed books whose copyright has expired. They can also be printed books made partly available online. A few years ago, online books were largely stored using FTP or Gopher protocols, but nowadays more such books are being made accessible on the Web. They can be in ASCII (unformated text), GIF (graphical image) or HTML (Web browser) format for direct viewing online, or in other formats suitable for downloading for later viewing or printing. Be aware that files for books are often of considerable size, and can take a long time to download onto your computer. You can see an example of a complete book at **http://netlib2.cs.utk.edu/linalg/ html_templates/Templates.html**, where a book titled *Templates for the Solution of Linear Systems* has been made available on the Internet. Online books can also be conference proceedings, where a volume of full articles is made available. At **http://knuth.mtsu.edu/~itconf/**, proceedings of the past conferences hosted by Middle Tennessee State University are available online.

There are far fewer books online than journals. This could be due to many reasons, including the enormous effort it usually takes an author to make a publication available online. Many online books fall into non-engineering or non-technology categories. Technically, it would be much simpler to make a book of poems available online than a book on electronic circuits because of non-text features such as graphs and formulae. Nevertheless, a number of initiatives have been taken by libraries or institutions to make online books available.

Like online journals, academic libraries play an essential role in making online books available. For example, the Online Books Page at Carnegie Mellon University (**http://www-cgi.cs.cmu.edu/cgi-bin/ book/**) hosts a collection of online books covering a wide range of

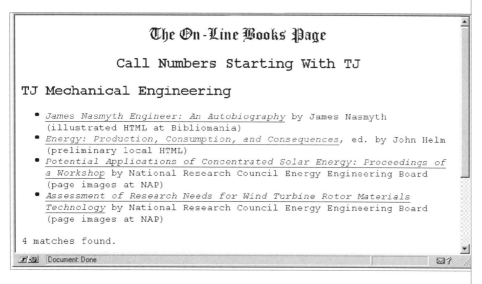

Figure 8.5 On-Line Books Page at Carnegie Mellon University

subjects: for example, Figure 8.5 shows books on mechanical engineering.

You can view and download these full-text online books: select the book entitled *Energy: Production, Consumption, and Consequences*, and you can view the full text of its contents.

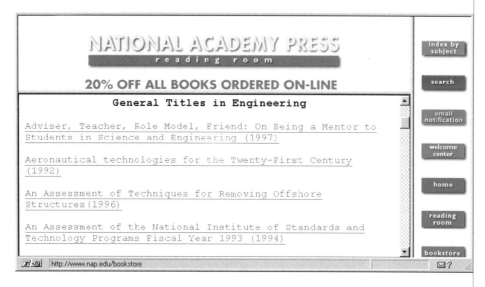

Figure 8.6 National Academy Press Web page

Commercial publishers are also interested in online engineering books. Most of the Internet resources provided by commercial publishers are, however, advertisements for conventionally published books. To promote their books, publishers also make part or all of some of their books available online. National Academy Press has created an online reading room (**http://www.nap.edu/readingroom/enter2.cgi?EG.html**, Figure 8.6) where you can select books, either from the list of titles or by searching, and read them using a Web browser (or alternatively by downloading files for local viewing).

Online journals

The Internet has attracted considerable enthusiasm among scholars and academia in the area of online journal publications. Scholars and researchers from all realms of study traditionally see journals as one of the main resources for the latest developments in their own disciplines. This is also true for practising engineers and technologists as new developments in technology take place more and more rapidly; in order to maintain their competitive advantage, it is essential to keep up to date on new developments. The Internet has made possible speedy information dissemination on the latest research and technology developments, and online journal publication is a major avenue for realising this possibility.

Technically, 'online publication' can be as unsophisticated as an article some individual has made available on the Internet. Indeed, some scholars have been loading their research findings, articles and course materials onto the Internet. These individual endeavours, however, are not subjected to the review process that most scholarly publications undergo, and as a result, the same recognition of quality and merit cannot be extended to them by the scholarly community. Standardisation of formats cannot be maintained over individual publications. It is also impossible to archive online publications made by individual scholars. Though it may appear to be difficult for potential readers to reach publications made by individuals, with the evolution of the Web and better and faster Web search engines, tracking down relevant online publications will become easier.

Unlike printed ones, online journals can recruit subscribers directly over the Internet, with the potential to achieve a wider base of readers.

However, it is a challenge for online journals to operate on a financially viable basis. Some online journals have imposed an 'access gateway' so that only subscribers can access journal articles. Subscription fees can also be solicited online, which indirectly applies pressure on the editors to ensure that the printed and online versions of their journals are of comparable quality. Many other online journals are operating on a free access basis, either affiliated to certain professional societies or operating on a non-profit basis.

Because of their electronic nature, online journals are readily available for full-text search. With a little additional software help, many online journals have already allowed users to search on their articles and collections. Clearly, this is a notable advantage over printed journals.

Ideally, an online journal should have a short production time with low costs, friendly formats for readers to access, view, download and copy articles, and wide dissemination among readers. For a scholarly publication, a respected review process is essential to add academic credibility. It is also important for the readers of online electronic journal to be able to access literature referenced in an article through hypertext links, if the literature is available online too. An online electronic journal has to be able to handle basically all the production technicalities a printed journal can. This involves different language characters, figures and charts, tables, colour images, mathematical formulas and notations, and possibly audio and video data. These technical issues have been dealt with well by many online journals in the Web environment.

Online journal publication has spurred libraries to undertake a new role. As well as carrying out their traditional function as a local information provider, libraries can now assume the role of an electronic publisher and online information provider. This is particularly prominent in universities, as academic libraries have a long tradition of dealing with paper journals. Combined with the information technology expertise and Internet infrastructure usually available in universities, libraries there are well positioned to become active publishers or archivers of online journal publications. An example of a university library's involvement in online journals can be seen at **http://ejournals.cic.net/**, the Center for Institutional Cooperation Electronic Journals Collection (Figure 8.7)—a prototype electronic journal management system coordinated by the

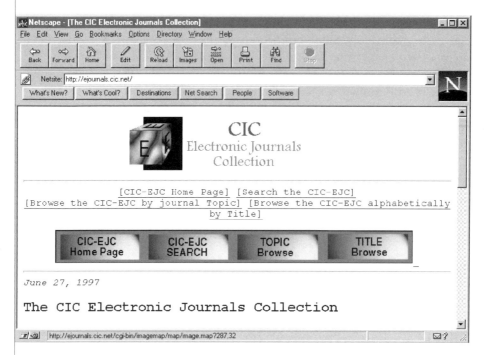

Figure 8.7 Electronic Journals Collection at CICNet

librarians of a number of American universities and the staff of CICNet Inc.

Public libraries, especially those large ones with considerable resources, have been actively involved in online publication. Their efforts include publishing online journals and magazines, digitising printed archive materials, indexing Internet resources on online publications and commissioning projects on online or electronic publications. The Library of Congress has been hosting an Electronic Texts and Publishing Resources Web page at **http://www.loc.gov/ global/etext/etext.html#publishing**. The National Library of Australia hosts a current listing of over a thousand Australian electronic journals, magazines, webzines, email fanzines, etc. at **http://www.nla.gov.au/oz/ausejour.html**.

Although printed journals from traditional publishers are not really online journals, their presence on the Internet has usually been made in the way of a table of contents, enabling interested users to browse through relevant journals and discover the latest developments in

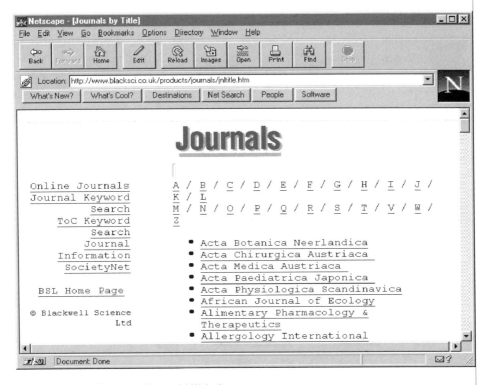

Figure 8.8 Blackwell Science 'Journals' Web site

topics of interest. Some publishers offer online search facilities for the contents and abstracts of the printed journals they publish. For example, Blackwell Science offers a search facility on its 'Journals' Web site at **http://www.blacksci.co.uk/products/journals/jnltitle.htm**.

More search facilities for printed journals can be found from most publishers' Web sites. The Library at Lund University, Sweden, has compiled a list of Web sites for searchable tables of contents of printed journals from different publishers at **http://www.ub2.lu.se/lub/services/ejournals.html**.

Many bibliographic database providers introduced in Chapter 6 offer a delivery service for printed articles by fax or by post after you have identified them through an online search. For printed journals available online, this service takes a different form—information vendors can make the full text of articles available online for subscribers to search, view, download and print full articles. For example, Bath Information and Data Services has a 'JournalsOnline'

CHAPTER

8

service at **http://www.journalsonline.bids.com/JournalsOnline**, which provides access to the full text of articles from a number of leading publishers of scholarly and academic journals, to which subscribers have full online access.

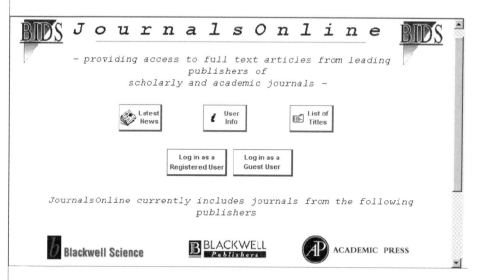

Figure 8.9 Bath Information and Data Services JournalsOnline

Many other bibliographic database producers or vendors such as FirstSearch (page 180) offer the same online service for printed journals. This greatly benefits engineers and researchers whose institutions are service subscribers.

Online and electronic journal publication has been subject to extensive discussion and debate among the librarian and scholarly communities. Many of these activities have proliferated on the Internet domain. Many Internet servers provide great reading or index resources for online journals or electronic journals; Table 8-5 lists some of these resources, some of which are described in detail below.

Name and Internet address
Academic and Reviewed Journals from Virtual Library http://www.edoc.com/ejournal/academic.html
Australian Electronic Journals by National Library of Australia http://www.nla.gov.au/oz/ausejour.html
Ejournal SiteGuide: a MetaSource http://www.library.ubc.ca/ejour/
Electronic Journals, Magazines and Newspapers http://www.ucalgary.ca/library/inetinfo/ejournals.html
Electronic Publications at University of Manitoba Libraries home page http://www.umanitoba.ca/libraries/units/engineering/epub.html
Electronic Journals— Libraries and Publishing http://www.library.upenn.edu/resources/ej/ej-library.html
Library-Oriented Lists and Electronic Serials http://info.lib.uh.edu/liblists/liblists.htm
National Science Foundation http://www.eng.nsf.gov/links/li00005.htm
Scholaraly Electronic Publishing Bibliography http://info.lib.uh.edu/sepb/sepb.html
Tables of contents, electronic journals and news, Lund University http://www.ub2.lu.se/lub/services/ejournals.html

Table 8-5 Internet resources for online journals

Academic and Reviewed Journals from Virtual Library

http://www.edoc.com/ejournal/ academic.html

This catalogue is the electronic journals home site for WWW Virtual Library. It contains lists of scientific, technical, medical and humanities journals, categorised as those 'peer reviewed', 'student reviewed' or 'not reviewed'.

CHAPTER

Australian Electronic Journals at National Library of Australia

http://www.nla.gov.au/oz/ausejour.html

This is a current listing of over a thousand Australian electronic journals, magazines, etc.—including overseas works with Australian content, authorship and/or emphasis.

Ejournal SiteGuide: a MetaSource

http://www.library.ubc.ca/ejour/

This guide from the University of British Columbia Library is not a huge list of individual online journals; instead it provides a selected and annotated set of links to sites for electronic journals, which in turn provide links to individual titles and/or to other collections of links.

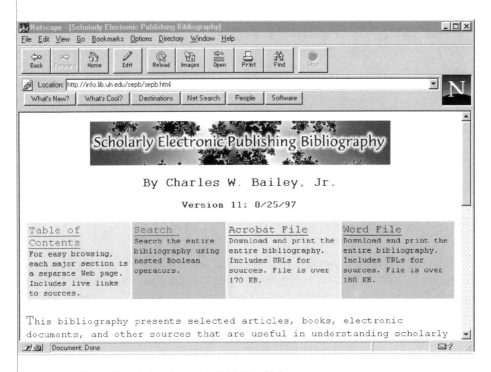

Figure 8.9 Scholarly Electronic Publishing Bibliography

Scholarly Electronic Publishing Bibliography

Scholarly Electronic Publishing Bibliography, created by Charles W. Bailey, Jr., is a resource listing selected articles, books, electronic documents and other sources that are useful in understanding scholarly electronic publishing efforts on the Internet and other networks. Many articles listed can be accessed online. You can search the entire bibliography using nested Boolean operators.

Online engineering journals

Broadly, online engineering journals consist of two types: those which replicate printed journals in part or in full, and those that are published purely online. Online journals of both types can support full-text search, an important advantage over printed journals.

Engineering journals from publishing companies

In the past, engineering journals were primarily published firstly by engineering societies and later by commercial publishers. Nowadays, many engineering, science and technology journal publishers are commencing web-based publishing programmes. We are also beginning to see an increasing number of printed engineering journals finding their double in Webspace. Some publishers are making all or most of their journals available online; others start Web publishing with a few pilot engineering journals. Table 8-6 summarises a few of the main commercial publishers who make available or publish engineering journals online, some of which are described in detail below.

Academic Press Online

http://www.idealibrary.com/

IDEAL is the online scientific journal library created by Academic Press to improve access to scientific and engineering journals on the Internet. Through licensing agreements with academic and industrial networks or consortiums of libraries, IDEAL brings research journals directly to your digital desktop. You can download articles, markedly

Name and Internet address

Academic Press Online
http://www.idealibrary.com/

Addison Wesley Longman
http://www2.awl.com/corp/

Association of American University Presses
http://aaup.pupress.princeton.edu/journals/

Blackwell Publishers
http://www.blackwellpublishers.co.uk/11.htm

Cambridge Scientific Abstracts
http://www.csa.com/print.html

Cambridge University Press
http://www.journals.cup.org/owa_dba/owa/journals

Elsevier Science
http://www.elsevier.nl/cgi-bin/inca/tree/browse.cgi? key=SSAF

HighWire Press
http://highwire.stanford.edu/

International Thomson Publishing
http://www.thomson.com/

Kluwer Academic Publishers
http://www.wkap.nl/kapis/CGI-BIN/WORLD/kaphtml.htm?JRNLHOME

MIT Press
http://www-mitpress.mit.edu/electronic.html

Springer-Verlag
http://www.springer-ny.com

Thomson
http://www.thomson.com/tcom/journals.html

Wiley
http://www.intersicence.wiley.com/

World Scientific
http://www.wspc.com.sg/journals/journals.html

Table 8-6 Individual publishers of online engineering journals

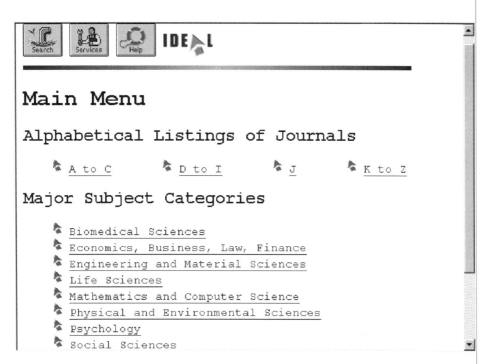

Figure 8.11 IDEAL at Academic Press

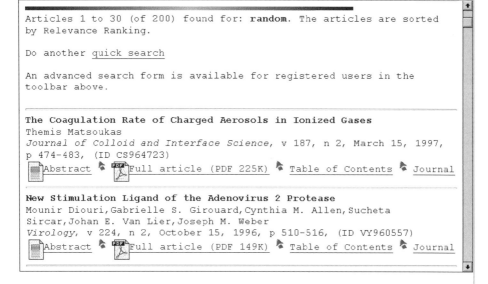

Figure 8.12 IDEAL search results

accelerating the speed with which you can be in contact with the latest development in your discipline. IDEAL's 'Subject Catalog' covers a wide range of areas, of which engineering is one section.

IDEAL allows you to search its journal article database. For password or institutional IP login users, full-text articles are available as well as the abstracts. For instance, using the search query 'random', you can search the IDEAL database and obtain results with articles from different journals published by Academic Press; they are not confined to engineering-related journals.

Cambridge University Press

http://www.journals.cup.org/
owa_dba/owa/journals

Cambridge University Press has embarked upon a development called 'Cambridge Journals Online' to make its engineering journals available free to everyone during the first phase of the site's

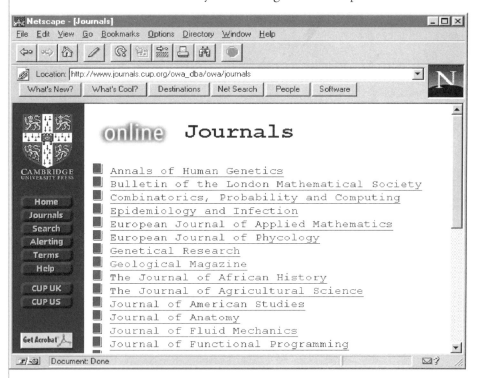

Figure 8.13 Cambridge Journals Online

development. The development aims to shape a model for future services the publisher provides for its journals. Currently, you can access a number of engineering journals from the Web site.

Elsevier Science

http://www.elsevier.nl/
cgi-bin/inca/tree/browse.cgi?
key=SSAF

Elsevier Science has compiled a list of the printed engineering journals it publishes on its Web site. From there, you can find contents, instructions for authors and related publications. In addition, Elsevier Science publishes a number of engineering-related electronic journals, which can be accessed from its Web site. For example, 'Intelligent Data Analysis' is an Internet-based journal published by Elsevier Science, accessed at **http://www-east.elsevier.com/ida/Menu.html**.

Figure 8.14 'Intelligent Data Analysis' Web page

HighWire Press

http://highwire.stanford.edu/

HighWire Press is an online publisher from Stanford University. According to its mission, it aims to foster research and instruction by

CHAPTER

8

providing a more direct link between the writers and readers of scholarly materials. It co-publishes Internet editions of science, technology and medicine journals. These Internet editions are presently available free, but are expected soon to be available only on subscription. Among frequently accessed journals and proceedings at HighWire Press are the *Proceedings of the National Academy of Science*, *Journal of Biological Chemistry* and *Science Magazine*.

Springer-Verlag

http://www.springer-ny.com

Springer-Verlag's online LINK program is designed for print and electronic journals. Journals published by Springer-Verlag across all disciplines will be offered electronically. Institutional subscribers can access the electronic full-text editions of printed journals. Several full-text formats have been used, including PDF, HTML, PostScript, and TeX. The Springer-Verlag Web site also facilitates full-text searching on journal articles.

Journals from engineering societies and research institutions

In addition to commercial publishers, a very useful source of engineering journals is the various engineering societies. Historically, engineering societies were responsible for publishing journals in their own disciplines. Some two decades ago, however, publication began to be overtaken by commercial publishers. The Internet has now enabled engineering societies to make their online journal publications available to the wider community of engineers and technologists. Visits to engineering societies' Web sites often reveal lists of journals published by them. Not all the journals found are online publications, however—for example, the Optical Society of America's Web site at **http://www.osa.org/**, called 'OpticsNet', provides Web links to the printed journals published by the Society. Subscribers to online journals can search via author, title, or subject for both current and back issues, as well as view, download and print articles, including figures, tables, and references.

Table 8-7 lists journals published by engineering societies and research institutions, some of which are described below.

Name and Internet address
ACM http://www.acm.org/pubs/journals.html
American Institute of Aeronautics and Astronautics (AIAA) http://www.aiaa.org/publications/journals.html
ASCE Journals http://www.pubs.asce.org/
ASME Journals http://www.asme.org/pubs/journals/index.htm
ASM International http://www.asm-intl.org/
Australian Journals of Scientific Research http://www.publish.csiro.au/journals/electronic.html
IEE Online Electronic Journals http://ioj.iee.org.uk/
IEEE Technical Journals http://www.ieee.org./pubs/pubs.html/
International Society For Measurement And Control http://www.isa.org/journals/
International Society for Optical Engineering http://www.spie.org/web/journals/journals_home.html
National Association of Corrosion Engineers http://www.nace.org/pubs.htm
Optical Society of America http://www.osa.org/

Table 8-7 Journals from engineering societies and research institutions

ASME Journals

http://www.asme.org/pubs/
journals/index.htm

ASME Journals is a Web site hosted by the American Society of
Mechanical Engineers offering its journals such as *Journal of Applied
Mechanics, Journal of Biomechanical Engineering* and *Journal of*

CHAPTER

8

Dynamic Systems, Measurement and Control. These journals contains peer-reviewed technical papers, technical briefs, discussions, editorials on philosophy and direction of emerging technologies, book reviews, calls for papers, issues devoted to specialised areas of vital technological advances and meeting notifications. Subscribers can order articles from these printed journals through the ASME online 'Periodicals Order Form.'

Australian Journals of Scientific Research

electronic edition

http://www.publish.csiro.au/
journals/electronic.html

The Australian Journals of Scientific Research are journals published by CSIRO, the Commonwealth Scientific and Industrial Research Organisation. Test versions are now available electronically on the World Wide Web. Free access to the full text of papers published in each journal is granted during 1997, but subscription will be required from 1998.

IEE Online Electronic Journals

http://ioj.iee.org.uk/

The Institution of Electrical Engineers publishes a range of journals on its Web site, including scholarly publications for research and technical developments, and IEE magazines and newspapers for practising engineers. The site allows searches across several journals, and contains browsable tables of contents for journals. Journals appear online in advance of print publication.

Online journals published or archived by university libraries

University libraries have been pioneering online journal publications. Many of these libraries provide on their Web sites extensive materials on, among other disciplines, engineering related online journals. Table 8-8 lists some of these sites.

Name and Internet address

BUBL Archive Journals
http://bubl.ac.uk/archive/journals/

Edinburgh Engineering Virtual Library Online journals and Newsletters
http://www.eevl.ac.uk:4321/search?query=&resourcetype=E-journal%2FNewsletter

Ejournal SiteGuide from University of British Columbia
http://www.library.ubc.ca/ejour/

Electronic Journals from Sydney University
http://www.library.usyd.edu.au/Ejournals/

Electronic Publications at University of Manitoba Libraries home page
http://www.umanitoba.ca/libraries/units/engineering/epub.html

Heriot-Watt University Library
http://www.hw.ac.uk/libWWW/irc/journals/njindex.html

Kresge Engineering Library University of California, Berkeley
http://www.lib.berkeley.edu/ENGI/ejrnls.html

Neiman Library of Exact Sciences and Engineering, Tel Aviv University
http://www.tau.ac.il/scilib/Lib_Project/ABfile/AB.html

Strathclyde University
http://bubl.ac.uk/journals/

University of California at San Diego Libraries
http://gort.ucsd.edu/newjour/

University of Colorado at Denver
gopher://ccnucd.cudenver.edu/h0/UCD/dept/edu/IT/ryder/itc_data/ejournals.html

University of Pennsylvania Library
http://www.library.upenn.edu/resources/ej/xej-news-indext.html

University of Waterloo Library
http://www.lib.uwaterloo.ca/society/full-text_soc.html

Table 8-8 Online journals published or archived by university libraries

Another source of electronic journals for engineering is various bibliographic databases. OCLC FirstSearch provides an 'Electronic Collections Online' service at **http://www.oclc.org/oclc/eco/** for its subscribers. The Internet Resources Catalog at **http://orc.rsch. oclc.org:6990/** is a database created by OCLC which can be used for searching online journals.

Online engineering publication projects

A number of Internet projects have been embarked upon by university libraries, institutions or engineering societies which aim to facilitate online publication of engineering- and technology-related journals, books, newsletters, tutorials and other publications. The outcome of these projects has been a wealth of online information for engineers, not to mention a significantly increased convenience in gaining access to materials they otherwise have to obtain through a lengthy process.

Name and Internet address

Australian Journals by National Library of Australia
http://www.nla.gov.au/oz/ausejour.html

The CD-ROM Acrobat Journals Using Networks
http://cajun.cs.nott.ac.uk/

Consortium Electronic Journal Project
http://www.ch.ic.ac.uk/clic/

DeLiberations: An Interactive Electronic Magazine
http://www.lgu.ac.uk/deliberations/home.html

A Digital Library of 18th and 19th Century Journals
http://www.bodley.ox.ac.uk/ilej/

Electronic support for Scholarly Communication
http://www.mpi-sb.mpg.de/~ohlbach/dictionary/stacks.html

The Journal of Information, Law and Technology
http://elj.warwick.ac.uk/jilt/

Network Publishing project—The HighWire Press
http://highwire.stanford.edu/

The Open Journal Project
http://journals.ecs.soton.ac.uk/

Project Muse from Johns Hopkins University Press
http://muse.jhu.edu/muse.html

The Superjournal Project
http://www.superjournal.ac.uk/sj/

Table 8-9 Online journal publication projects

Table 8-9 lists a number of Internet projects focusing on online publications, many of them involving engineering- and technology-related journals. Some of them have already appeared in this book in different contexts; others are described in detail below. These projects have varying objectives: they aim to index and archive online journals, to facilitate scholarly electronic publication, to foster joint venture with publishers or engineering societies or to categorise Internet resources related to online journals.

Consortium Electronic Journal Project

CLIC

http://www.ch.ic.ac.uk/clic/

This project is apart of the Electronic Libraries Program. It aims to establish a parallel electronic version of the Royal Society of Chemistry's journal, *Chemical Communications.*

DeLiberations: An Interactive Electronic Magazine

DeLiberations

http://www.lgu.ac.uk/deliberations/home.html

This project aims to establish an interactive electronic magazine with an associated archival database to support library staff, academic staff, educational developers and computing staff concerned with the innovative design and delivery of courses, particularly those with substantial electronic input.

The Open Journal Project

http://journals.ecs.soton.ac.uk/

The Open Journal project is intended to provide a framework for publishing journals on the World Wide Web in order to achieve maximum access to and from the publications. This involves hypertexting journals produced in HTML and PDF formats.

The Superjournal Project

http://www.superjournal.ac.uk/sj/

This project seeks to study the factors that make electronic journals successful and useful to the academic community. It has developed an application that makes clusters of electronic journals available to test sites of participating universities via the World Wide Web.

Library projects

In addition, many library projects introduced in Chapter 5 also contain an online journal component, which supplement the sources listed in Table 8-9. These sources often provide current information and resources on online journal publication; an example is the 'Archive Journals' from the BUlletin Board for Libraries (BUBL) at **http://bubl.ac.uk/ archive/journals/**.

BUBL Archive

BUBL Archive Journals

These publications are no longer issued or are no longer held by BUBL

Search the archive: [   ]   Search   Help

Alcoholism Treatment Quarterly
Annual Review of OCLC Research
Apple Library Users Group Newsletter
The Arachnet Electronic Journal on Virtual Culture
Art Libraries Journal
Art Reference Services Quarterly
Aslib Information
Assistant Librarian
Australian Library Journal

Figure 8.14 BUBL Archive Journals

The UK Office for Library and Information Networking (UKOLN) is a national centre for support in network information management in the library and information communities, based at the University of Bath.

UKOLN collates a comprehensive list at **http://www.ukoln.ac.uk/ services/elib/projects/** on all of the projects in the Electronic Libraries

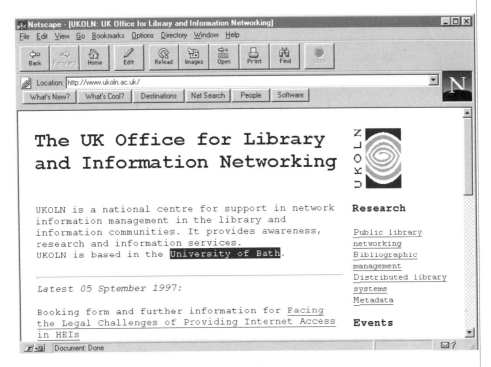

Figure 8.15 The UK Office for Library and Information Networking

Program funded by the Joint Funding Council's Libraries Review Group in the United Kingdom.

Further reading

'The Journal of Electronic Publishing' at **http://www.press.umich. edu/jep/**, published by the University of Michigan Press since 1994, is a useful resources for scholarly articles on digital publishing. It will soon begin quarterly publication. Articles the Journal solicits aim to widen our understanding of the emerging electronic-publishing field. Though the Journal is not specifically about engineering publication online, the general issues it covers, such as copyrights, economic, imaging, policy, technical matters and 'digital library' (issues related to online journals such as electronic texts), are applicable to all disciplines.

'First Monday' is an online journal that contains a wealth of articles on the topic of online publication in general as well as on the Internet and the Global Information Infrastructure. You can access this peer-reviewed journal at **http://www.firstmonday.dk/**. Its Web site offers a search engine that allows you search for articles published in the Journal using keywords.

'Electric Pages' is a monthly online journal from Graphics Research Laboratory that tracks the evolution of publishing on the Web. It can be accessed at **http://www.electric-pages.com/**.

'Current Cites' at **http://sunsite.berkeley.edu/CurrentCites/** is a monthly annotated bibliography of selected articles, books, and electronic documents on information technology. It contains many articles on electronic publishing.

'Scholarly Electronic Publishing Bibliography' at **http://info.lib.uh. edu/sepb/sepb.html** is created and updated constantly by Charles W. Bailey, Jr at the University of Houston. It contains a wealth of selected articles, books, electronic documents and other sources that are useful in understanding scholarly electronic publishing efforts on the Internet and other networks. Anyone with more than a passing interest in online publication should find many useful readings from this site. Many articles included have hypertext links to other items in the bibliography. The site also provides a search facility that enables you to search for articles and resources related to (among other topics) electronic publishing.

Bibliography

Academic and Reviewed Journals
http://www.edoc.com/ejournal/academic.html

Alex: A Catalog of Electronic Texts on the Internet:
http://www.lib.ncsu.edu/staff/morgan/alex/alex-index.html

The BookWire Index—Publishers
http://www.bookwire.com/index/publishers.html

Directory of Publishers and Vendors
http://www.library.vanderbilt.edu/law/acqs/pubr.html

The Electronic Journal on the Internet (Kristin Hede Kubly)
http://knuth.mtsu.edu/~itconf/papers96/EJOURNAL.HTM

Electronic Journals, Texts and Publishing
http://www.warwick.ac.uk/ETS/edu-tech/EP/

Electronic Publishing Programs in Science and Technology—Part 1: The Journals
http://www.library.ucsb.edu/istl/96-fall/brown-duda.html

Electronic Publishing Programs: Issues to Consider
http://www.library.ucsb.edu/istl/96-fall/brown-duda2.html

Electronic Publishing Research Group
http://www.ep.cs.nott.ac.uk/

Electronic Publishing Standards
http://www.adfa.oz.au/Epub/McLean_Cook_ToC.html

Electronic Text Center at the University of Virginia
http://etext.lib.virginia.edu/

Electronic Texts and Publishing Resources at the Library of Congress
http://www.loc.gov/global/etext/etext.html#books

Fair Use in the Electronic Age: Serving the Public Interest
http://arl.cni.org/scomm/copyright/uses.html

Frequently Asked Questions—Subscribing to Electronic Journals
http://newton.iop.org/Support/EJ/faqejs.html

The Hypertext Bibliography Project
http://theory.lcs.mit.edu:80/~dmjones/hbp/

Internet Related Magazines,
http://www.sau.edu/CWIS/Internet/Wild/Internet/Journals/jnindex.htm

National Science Foundation Papers and Journals
http://www.eng.nsf.gov/links/li00005.htm

On the Road to Electronic Publishing (Andrew Odlyzko)
http://math.albany.edu:8800/hm/emj/papers/road

Online Publishing: Threat or Menace?
http://www.press.umich.edu/jep/works/fillmore.threat1.html

PWS Publishing
http://www.pws.com/default.html

Reports from AVCC Working Party for Electronic Publishing
http://www.adfa.oz.au/Epub/summary.html

Scholarly Electronic Publishing Bibliography
http://info.lib.uh.edu/sepb/sepb.html

The SGML/XML Web Page
http://www.sil.org/sgml/sgml.html

Some Thoughts about Electronic Magazines on the Web
http://www.edgorg.com/mags.htm

Tables of Contents, Electronic Journals and News, Lund University
http://www.ub2.lu.se/lub/services/ejournals.html

Text Encoding Initiative
http://www.uic.edu/orgs/tei/

WebCom Web Publishing Guide
http://www.webcom.com/~webcom/html/

**Don't forget to visit us at
http://dingo.vut.edu.au/~jimin/book.html**

Appendix

Engineering career information
on the Internet

Glossary of Internet terms

File and data formats on the
Internet

Engineering-related computer
software on the Internet

Internet domain names and
country/region codes

Introduction to Boolean
operators

Engineering career information on the Internet

One of the Internet's most useful applications for engineering students and practising engineers is for finding online information about professional careers. This is a luxury that job-seekers a decade ago did not have. However, the vast career and employment opportunities listed on the Internet can sometimes deter users from embarking on finding useful information.

There are several differences between career and employment information on the Internet and that in other media such as newspapers. First, the information in newspapers is usually current; in contrast, the information on the Internet can vary from current to obsolete. You need to sift through, and if necessary, check the currency and validity of the career information located. Secondly, information in newspapers is largely compact and classified—it is easy to discover

Name and Internet address

Alpha Systems
http://www.jobbs.com/

Careermine
http://www.info-mine.com/careermine/

Engineer Employment Network
http://www.engineernetwork.com/

Engineering Job Source
http://www.engineerjobs.com/

Engineering/Manufacturing Jobs Page
http://www.nationjob.com/engineering

EngineerWeb
http://www.engineerweb.com/

A National Index of Engineering Jobs
http://www.EngineeringJobs.Com/

National Society of Professional Engineers Web Classifieds
http://www.nspe.org/em-home.htm

Table A-1 Online information on career opportunities in engineering

Name and Internet address

Aussie Careers Guide
http://www.northnet.com.au/~achamber/

The Australian Resume Server
http://www.herenow.com.au

Careers Online
http://www.careersonline.com.au

EmploymentNet Australia
http://www.employment.edu.au

Employment Opportunities Australia
http://careermosaic.jobs.com.au/cmaust.html

International Academic Job Market
http://www.camrev.com.au/share/jobs.html

JobNet in Australia
http://www.jobnet.com.au

Jobs-careers.com—Engineering
http://engineering.jobs-careers.com/

Table A-2 Online information on career opportunities in Australia

all relevant information together. On the Internet, however, classification is not the norm. Although there are Web sites dedicated to career and employment resources, a vast number of other Web sites can also contain relevant information for a particular job seeker. Third, on the Internet it is possible to find specific companies or institutions that require the expertise, experience and knowledge a particular job-seeker has.

There are many Internet sites that provide guidelines for finding career information online. The Riley Guide for Employment Opportunities and Job Resources on the Internet at **http://www.dbm.com/jobguide/** is a renowned site for online job-hunters. The site includes a list of 'General Recruiters' and 'Major Recruiting Sites', not to mention 'Resources for Specific Occupational Areas' such engineering and technology.

Name and Internet Address

4works
http://www.4work.com/

ACS Career Services
http://www.acs.org/careers/

CareerLine
http://www.acm.org/member_services/career/careerline.html

Career Magazine
http://www.careermag.com/

Career Paradise
http://www.emory.edu/CAREER/

Career Resource Center
http://www.careers.org/

Career Resource Homepage
http://www.eng.rpi.edu/dept/cdc/homepage.html

Career Talk
http://www.careertalk.com/career_links.html

International Business Network
http://www.interbiznet.com/

JobHunt
http://www.job-hunt.org/

JobWeb
http://www.jobweb.org/

Online Carer Center
http://www.occ.com/

Yahoo!: Business and Economy: Employment
http://www.yahoo.com/Business/Employment

Table A-3 General career information online

Another site of interest is **http://www.washingtonpost.com/ parachute/**, which contains an online reference guide and annotated Internet address list for job-seekers and those seeking a change of career. This Web site is based on a chapter in the 1998 edition of the book *What Color Is Your Parachute?* authored by Richard Nelson Bolles. 'Career Magazine' at **http://www.careermag.com/** also offers a wealth of career-related information for general reading.

Many Web sites have been developed for engineering job-hunters and those seeking a career change. Table A-1 shows a number of sites for general engineering job opportunities. They often contain timely information on job opportunities, classified job information or companies where openings exist. Many engineering societies also post relevant career information on their Web sites.

Most sites listed in Table A-1 contain career information in North America. For those interested in career information in other countries, there are also plenty of relevant Web sites. For example, Table A-2 presents a list of sites for career information in Australia.

Table A-3 shows a list of Web sites where you can find online reference guides, annotated Internet address lists, career planning information, résumé preparation advice and other relevant information.

Glossary of Internet terms

Table A-4 defines Internet terms used in this book.

There are many more Internet glossaries on the Internet itself. Because of the Internet's currency, many terms from different glossaries may have different definitions. Table A-5 shows a few Web sites for Internet glossaries.

Term and definition

Archie
An Internet tool for finding files stored on anonymous FTP sites.

ASCII
American Standard Code for Information Interchange—a computer coding standard for all upper- and lower-case Roman letters, numbers, punctuation, etc.

BBS
Bulletin Board System—a computer system allowing people to upload and download files. It is often used as a discussion venue.

Browser
A client program that is used to browse various kinds of Internet resources.

Client/server
A computer technology that separates computers into two categories: clients or servers. The 'client' is the computer requesting information, and the 'server' is the computer that delivers it. A client may need a program specially designed to work with one or more specific kinds of server programs: A Web browser is a specific kind of client program.

Database
A collection of inter-related data of different types in a computerised format.

Download
To transfer information from the Internet to your own computer. This information can be an electronic mail message, a computer program, a data file, a graphic, etc.

Email
Electronic mail—a means of sending messages electronically over a computer network.

FTP
File Transfer Protocol—an Internet tool that allows you to retrieve and send files between two computers in the same network. 'Anonymous FTP' enables the transfer of publicly available computer files.

Gateway
A computer that forwards and routes data between two or more networks. It provides both a physical link and a protocol translation program for doing so.

Gopher
A menu-driven computer interface on the Internet that allows users to access a large number of resources stored on the Internet.

Host computer
A computer in a network that directly provides service to a user.

HTML
Hypertext Markup Language—the coding applied to text files that allow them to appear as formatted pages on the World Wide Web.

HTTP
Hypertext Transport Protocol—the protocol computers on the Internet use to transfer hypertext documents.

Hypertext
Text that contains links to other documents.

Internet
A computer network interconnecting numerous computer hardware or local computer networks.

IP
Internet protocol—the Internet standard protocol that provides a common layer over dissimilar networks, used to move 'packets' of information among host computers and through gateways if necessary.

Jughead
Jonzy's Universal Gopher Hierarchy Excavation And Display—another Gopherspace searcher for getting menu information from various Gopher servers.

Listserv
An electronic discussion group or conference using email to communicate.

MIME
Multipurpose Internet Mail Extensions—a set of standards for attaching non-text files such as graphics to standard Internet mail messages.

Netscape Navigator
A graphical World Wide Web browser for Macintosh, Microsoft Windows, Amiga and other operating systems.

Network
A set of computers that are governed by the same protocol for exchanging information among themselves.

OPAC
Online Public Access Catalogie—a term used to describe any type of computerised library catalogue.

Packet switching
A method used to move data around on the Internet by first breaking up the data into chunks and sending each chunk to the given address, and then assembling the chunks back together at the destination. This method enables many users to use the same data transmission lines at the same time.

Protocol
A standard that defines the method of communication among computers.

Table A-4 A brief Internet glossary—continued over

Search engine
A tool that allows keyword searching for relevant sites or information on the Internet.

Shareware
Computer software that is distributed through public domain channels for 'trial-and-buy' use.

TCP/IP
Transmission Control Protocol/Internet Protocol—a combined set of protocols that perform the transfer of data between two computers.

Telnet
A protocol that allows a network user on one computer to log on to a computer in a distant location in order to use its programs or data files.

TN3270
A version of Telnet that provides IBM full-screen support.

URL
Universal Resource Locator—a standard for addressing an object on the Internet, especially on the World Wide Web. An 'Internet address' is a URL.

USENET
A distributed bulletin board system for Internet newsgroups.

Veronica
Very Easy Rodent-Oriented Net-wide Index to Computerized Archives—an Internet tool that allows you to search by keyword through Gopher titles and directories.

WAIS
Wide Area Information Server—an Internet protocol for searching a variety of databases on the Internet from a single local computer by looking for specific keywords in documents.

WWW
World Wide Web—an Internet hypertext system for information distribution and retrieval. It links documents, FTP sites, Gopher sites, WAIS, and Telnet, and integrates files in text, graphics, sound and other formats.

Z39.50
A national standard from the US National Information Standards Organization (NISO) that defines a protocol for computer-to-computer information retrieval. This protocol provides the framework for OPAC users to search remote catalogues on the Internet using the commands of their own local systems.

Table A-4 A brief Internet glossary

Name and Internet address

Basic Internet Terms
http://www.geocities.com/FashionAvenue/4869/desc.html

A Glossary of Computer Oriented Abbreviations and Acronyms
http://www.access.digex.net/~ikind/babel.html

Glossary of Terms for Internet Resources
http://galaxy.einet.net/hytelnet/GLOSSARY.html

ILC Glossary of Internet Terms
http://www.matisse.net/files/glossary.html

Internet Glossary
http://www.santel.lu/SANTEL/DOCS/internet_glossary.html

Internet Glossary
http://www.squareonetech.com/glosaryf.html

Internet Glossary—Pacific Lutheran University
http://www.plu.edu/www/libr/guides/glossary.html

Internet Terminology and Definitions
http://www.rci.rutgers.edu/~au/workshop/int-def.htm

The Marketing Manager's Plain English Internet Glossary
http://www.jaderiver.com/glossary.htm

The McGraw-Hill Internet Training Manual—Internet Glossary
http://www.marketing-coach.com/mh-guide/glossary.htm

Web Dictionary of Cybernetics and Systems
http://pespmc1.vub.ac.be/ASC/INDEXASC.html

Table A-5 Resources for Internet glossaries

File and data formats on the Internet

While you are using the Internet, you may have to download files of different types. Inevitably, you have to deal with files with various kinds of suffixes, which usually indicate the file type (barring any misuses or abuses). Different computer platforms use different file types. Table A-6 lists the file types frequently used for Microsoft Windows, the most common platform. For information on more file types or file types for other platforms, visit **http://help-site. com/fileformats/** and **http://wotsit.simsware. com/**.

File name suffix, file description and software needed to operate

.aiff
Sound file in binary
An audio player

.au
Sound file in binary
An audio player

.dat
Video CD
XingMPEG player

.doc
MS-Word file in binary
MS-Word application or WordView.

.exe
Executable file in binary
Download and run directly

.gif
The most common graphics format
A graphics viewer such as Lview Pro

.gz
The Gnu for UNIX systems
WinZip to view and extract files

.html or .htm
Hypertext Markup Language file
A Web browser such as Netscape Navigator

.hqx
Macintosh file encoded into 7-bit text
BinHex13 or WinZip to convert to PC file

.jpg or .jpeg
A 24-bit graphic format
A graphics viewer such as Lview Pro

.jfif
A 24-bit graphic format
A graphics viewer such as Lview Pro

.mpg or .mpeg
Standard movie/video format
An MPEG viewer such as VMPEG

.mov
QuickTime movie
QuickTime

.pdf
Adobe Acrobat Portable Document Format
Adobe Acrobat Reader

.pic
Graphic format
QuickTime Picture Viewer

.ps
PostScript file
Ghostscript

.sit
Stuffit Archive
UnSit

.tiff or .tif
high quality image format
A graphics viewer such as Lview Pro

.txt
ODS (Optical Data Systems) plain text file
A file editor or word-processor

.wav
Windows Wave format for sound
An audio player such as MS Media Player

.zip
A common DOS and Windows compression format
WinZIP

Table A-6 Some common file types found on the Internet

The software required to read, view or edit the different types files listed in Table A-7 can be found on the Internet. Some of it is 'freeware', that is, it can be distributed and used freely. Other software is 'shareware', which means it can be used on a try-and-buy basis. You can download it from the Internet and enjoy a fixed period of trial time before deciding to acquire a licensed copy or to cease using it. Table A-7 lists these software names and the Web sites from which they are available. If the Web sites listed here are slow or do not function, try searching some software sites such as **http://www.shareware.com/** to

Software name, function and Internet address

Adobe Acrobat Reader
To read Adobe Acrobat PDF files
http://www.adobe.com/Software/Acrobat/

Ghostview/Ghostscript
To view PostScript files on screen
http://www.cs.wisc.edu/~ghost/index.html

Lview Pro
To view files of a variety of graphics formats and to convert between different formats
http://www.lview.com/

MPEGPlay
A MPEG viewer
ftp://papa.indstate.edu/winsock-l/Windows95/Graphics/mpegw32h.zip

Multimedia Xplorer
A comprehensive multimedia viewer for sounds, movies, graphics and more
http://www.moonsoftware.ee/zips/mxplo131.exe

PolyView
A graphics viewer and converter
http://www.polybytes.com/v290/polyv290.exe

QuickTime
To create and view synchronised graphics, sound, video, text and music
http://quicktime.apple.com/

RealPlayer
Real-time audio and video player
http://www.real.com/products/player/playerdl.html

VMPEG
An MPEG viewer
ftp://ftp.cica.indiana.edu/pub/pc/win3/desktop/

Word Viewer
To display MS Word documents without having to open MS Word software
ftp://ftp.microsoft.com/Softlib/MSLFILES/WORDVU.EXE

Waveform Hold and Modify (WHAM)
Edit, convert, and play WAV, VOC, IFF, AIFF, au, raw files
ftp://ftp.winsite.com/pub/pc/win3/sounds/wham133.zip

WinZip
To compress or uncompress many different archiving and compression formats
http://www.winzip.com/winzip95.exe

Table A-7 Some online software for different file types

find other sites (there are usually many more) where the software is available, and download from there. For additional information on more software for different file types, you can visit **http:// cws.internet.com//32menu.html** or **http:// www.matisse.net/files/ formats.html**.

Most engineering-related online publications, if not compressed, appear in several common formats: HTML, ASCII, PDF or PS formats. If a publication is in HTML or ASCII format, it can be read directly within the Web browser. If, however, it is in PDF (Portable Document Format) format, you will need to download and install the Adobe Acrobat Reader to view it. If the publication is in PostScript (PS) format, it can either be downloaded and printed on a printer that has a PostScript function, or alternatively you can install Ghostscript software and view the publication on your computer screen.

However, many files you download from the Internet are compressed and therefore their true file formats are not immediately obvious. File compression takes advantage of the fact that the binary sequences of ones and zeroes often contain repeated patterns. They can be coded specially by a compression program so that the file can be converted into a new one with brief descriptions of the original file's patterns, thereby achieving great storage savings. The new file can be much smaller than the original one. Compression can also be operated on a group of files. Some people use the words 'pack' or 'zip' to mean 'compress'.

If a file is compressed, then after downloading it you must uncompress it before you can discover its true file format and use it. 'Uncompress' is also called 'extract', 'unzip' or 'unpack'. There are several ways a file can be compressed before being put on the Internet. Depending on the way it is compressed, you can use different software to uncompress it: WinZip at **http://www.winzip.com/** is the most common software for compressing and uncompressing compressed files. You can find online help at **http://www.winzip.com/faq.htm**.

Engineering-related computer software on the Internet

The Internet has provided a perfect venue for promoting, supporting and sharing engineering software. Many well-known engineering software companies have been using the Internet to advertise their products, promote demonstration or scaled-down versions of their software for free use and provide customer support. Researchers from academic institutions and engineers from industry can make their copyright-free software available on the Internet for their peers to evaluate or use.

When downloading software from the Internet, it is important to understand the difference between freeware, shareware, and commercial software. Freeware is software often written by enthusiasts and distributed at no charge on the Internet. They can also be demo versions of some commercial software. There is little limit on how you can use freeware. Shareware is software for which the author reserves certain rights for licensing, distribution and royalty. It is usually allowable to use it for a trial period only. Some shareware is a scaled-down version which can be upgraded to full capabilities and be given full customer support upon registration. Commercial software is commercially available for purchase; its presence on the Internet is usually for advertisement, software upgrade or support purposes.

Much software online is compressed for speedy transmission. After downloading to your computer, it needs to be uncompressed using appropriate software such as WinZip (**http://www.winzip.com/**). Software downloading can be done conveniently from within a Web browser.

Name and Internet address

ATN Shareware
http://hulk.oit.unc.edu/shareware/

Benchin's Software Review
http://www.benchin.com/

The CWSApps List from Stroud
http://www.icorp.net/stroud/

Database of Software Products and Companies
http://www.softwareage.com/ACGI/FindProduct.html

Download.com
http://www.download.com/

Filepile
http://filepile.com/nc/start

FILEZ
http://www.filez.com/

Galt Shareware Zone
http://www.galttech.com/sharware.shtml

Inter-Links Software Archives
http://alabanza.com/kabacoff/Inter-Links/downloads.html

Jumbo Download Network
http://www.jumbo.com/

Links to Various Software Archives
http://www.csc.fi/math_topics/FTP/index.html

Shareware.com
http://www.shareware.com/

SoftInfo —Software Search
http://www.info-partners.com/softinfo/search.htm

SoftSearch
http://www.softsearch.com/

Software.net

http://software.net/

Software Repository
http://www.coast.net/SimTel/

Software Sharing Resource Library
http://ssrl.rtp.com:443/Harvest/brokers/reuse/query.html

WiNDeX
http://win95.daci.net/

WinSite
http://www.winsite.com/

Table A-8 Some Web sites for online software

Name and Internet address

Archon Engineering Desktop Software for Civil & Mechanical Engineers
http://members.aol.com/archonrrs/index.html

ASME MechEng File Archive
ftp://ftp.mecheng.asme.org/pub/

Benchin Engineering Software
http://www.benchin.com/$index.wcgi/cat/1069

Bowling's Automotive Programs
http://devserve.cebaf.gov/~bowling/auto.html

Netlib Repository for Mathematical Software
http://www.netlib.org/

Civil Engineering Software Center
http://www.engr.uky.edu/CE/KYPIPE/index.html

Database on Irrigation & Hydrology Software
http://www.wiz.uni-kassel.de/kww/irrisoft/irrisoft_i.html

Earth Science Software
http://www.rockware.com/

Engineering Software
http://hqnet.org/fsn/robedsvc/1engsys.htm

Engineering Software
http://www.engineers.com/engsoft.htm

Engineering Software Center
http://www.he.net/~esc/

Engineering Software Database at ASME
http://www.mecheng.asme.org/

Hot New Products —Engineering Software
http://www.industry.com/c/mn/_hlf/

Internet Software Guide for Engineers
http://www.100folhas.pt/software/menu.html

Mathematics Archives
http://archives.math.utk.edu/

Software for Structural Analysis
http://www.vtt.fi/rte7/feminfo/femsivu1.htm

US Environmental Protection Agency Software
ftp://www.epa.gov/pub/

Yoyodyne
http://yoyodyne.tamu.edu/

Table A-9 Some Web sites for online engineering software

There are many software archive sites and software search sites on the Internet, and Table A-8 lists some of them. Most of these Web sites offer facilities for searching for particular software or a type of software. Alternatively, you can search for software using Archie search engines (when you know the file name) or WWW search engines (when you know keywords).

The software you can find on the Web sites in Table A-8 is not primarily engineering- and technology-related, although some of it contains

Name and Internet address

Guide to Available Mathematical Software
http://gams.nist.gov/

Java Educational Engineering
http://www.gamelan.com/pages/Gamelan.educational.engineering.html

JavaWorld Free Software Zone
http://www.javaworld.com/javaworld/common/jw.software.html

The Numerical Algorithms Group
http://www.nag.co.uk/

Numerical Methods
http://www.math.psu.edu/dna/num_methods.html

PGPLOT Graphics Subroutine Library
http://astro.caltech.edu/~tjp/pgplot/

The Standard Template Library for C++
http://www.cs.rpi.edu/~musser/stl.html

Visual Basic
http://www.microsoft.com/vbasic/

Table A-10 Some Web sites for programming software

engineering information. There are other Web sites which contain mainly engineering-related software. These sites may not be large compared with those designed for general purposes, but they can be especially interesting for engineers and researchers. For example, the professional software collection at **http://www.benchin.com/** links to much engineering-related software in automotive, electrical, mechanical, aviation and aerospace, chemical and other common categories. Table A-9 lists a few Web sites for engineering-related software.

There is also a class of Web sites where software related to numerical analysis and computer programming is made available. This software may not be specifically for engineers, but much of it can be used in engineering applications. Some computer routines are generically applicable and can be readily used in new programming for solving engineering problems. Table A-10 lists some software Web sites for numerical analysis and computer programming.

Internet domain names and country/region codes

Domain code and domain name	
com commercial	**int** international
edu educational	**mil** US military
gov government	**net** network infrastructure
	org non-profit organisation

Table A-11 Internet top-level domain names

Country/region and code

ae United Arab Emirates	**ba** Bosnia-Herzegovina	**bw** Botswana
ad Andorra	**bb** Barbados	**by** Belarus
af Afghanistan	**bd** Bangladesh	**bz** Belize
ag Antigua and Barbuda	**be** Belgium	**ca** Canada
ai Anguilla	**bf** Burkina Faso	**cc** Cocos (Keeling) Islands
al Albania	**bg** Bulgaria	**cf** Central African Republic
am Armenia	**bh** Bahrain	**cg** Congo
an Netherlands Antilles	**bi** Burundi	**ch** Switzerland
ao Angola	**bj** Benin	**ci** Ivory Coast (Côte d'Ivoire)
aq Antarctica	**bm** Bermuda	**ck** Cook Islands
ar Argentina	**bn** Brunei	**cl** Chile
as American Samoa	**bo** Bolivia	**cm** Cameroon
at Austria	**br** Brazil	**cn** China
au Australia	**bs** Bahamas	**co** Colombia
aw Aruba	**bt** Bhutan	**cr** Costa Rica
az Azerbaijan	**bv** Bouvet Island	**cu** Cuba

Table A-12 Internet country and region codes (ISO Standard 3166)—continued over

Internet Resources for Engineers

cv
Cape Verde

cx
Christmas Island

cy
Cyprus

cz
Czech Republic

de
Germany

dk
Denmark

dj
Djibouti

dm
Dominica

do
Dominican Republic

dz
Algeria

ec
Ecuador

ee
Estonia

eg
Egypt

eh
Western Sahara

es
Spain

et
Ethiopia

fi
Finland

fj
Fiji

fk
Falkland Islands (Malvinas)

fm
Federated States of
Micronesia

fo
Faroe Islands

fr
France

fx
France

ga
Gabon

gd
Grenada

ge
Georgia

gf
French Guiana

gh
Ghana

gi
Gibraltar

gl
Greenland

gm
Gambia

gn
Guinea

gp
Guadeloupe

gs
South Georgia and the
South Sandwich Islands

gq
Equatorial Guinea

gr
Greece

gt
Guatemala

gu
Guam

gw
Guinea-Bissau

gy
Guyana

hm
Heard and McDonald
Islands

hn
Honduras

hk
Hong Kong

hr
Croatia (Hrvatska)

ht
Haiti

hu
Hungary

id
Indonesia

ie
Ireland

il
Israel

in India	**kr** South Korea	**mc** Monaco
io British Indian Ocean Territory	**kw** Kuwait	**md** Moldavia
iq Iraq	**ky** Cayman Islands	**mg** Madagascar
ir Iran	**kz** Kazakhstan	**mh** Marshall Islands
is Iceland	**la** Laos	**mk** Macedonia
it Italy	**lb** Lebanon	**ml** Mali
jm Jamaica	**lc** Saint Lucia	**mm** Myanmar
jo Jordan	**li** Liechtenstein	**mn** Mongolia
jp Japan	**lk** Sri Lanka	**mo** Macau
ke Kenya	**lr** Liberia	**mp** Northern Mariana Islands
kg Kirghizia	**ls** Lesotho	**mq** Martinique
kh Cambodia	**lt** Lithuania	**mr** Mauritania
ki Kiribati	**lu** Luxembourg	**ms** Montserrat
km Comoros	**lv** Latvia	**mt** Malta
kn Saint Kitts-Nevis	**ly** Libya	**mu** Mauritius
kp North Korea	**ma** Morocco	**mv** Maldives

Table A-12 Internet country and region codes (ISO Standard 3166)—continued over

mw
Malawi

mx
Mexico

my
Malaysia

mz
Mozambique

na
Namibia

nc
New Caledonia

ne
Niger

nf
Norfolk Island

ng
Nigeria

ni
Nicaragua

nl
Netherlands

no
Norway

np
Nepal

nr
Nauru

nu
Niue

nz
New Zealand

om
Oman

pa
Panama

pe
Peru

pf
French Polynesia

pg
Papua New Guinea

ph
Philippines

pk
Pakistan

pl
Poland

pm
Saint Pierre and Miquelon

pn
Pitcairn

pr
Puerto Rico

pt
Portugal

pw
Palau

py
Paraguay

qa
Qatar

re
Réunion

ro
Romania

ru
Russian Federation

rw
Rwanda

sa
Saudi Arabia

sb
Solomon Islands

sc
Seychelles

sd
Sudan

se
Sweden

sg
Singapore

sh
Saint Helena

si
Slovenia

sj
Svalbard and Jan Mayen
Island

sk
Slovak Republic

sl
Sierra Leone

sm
San Marino

sn
Senegal

so
Somalia

sr
Surinam

st
São Tomé and Príncipe

sv
El Salvador

sy
Syria

sz
Swaziland

tc
Turks and Caicos Islands

td
Chad

tf
French Southern and
Antarctic Territories

tg
Togo

th
Thailand

tj
Tajikistan

tk
Tokelau

tm
Turkmenistan

tn
Tunisia

to
Tonga

tp
East Timor

tr
Turkey

tt
Trinidad and Tobago

tv
Tuvalu

tw
Taiwan

tz
Tanzania

ua
Ukraine

ug
Uganda

uk
United Kingdom

um
United States Minor
Outlying Islands

us
United States of America
(If a URL has no country
code, 'us' is implied.)

uy
Uruguay

uz
Uzbekistan

va
Vatican City State

vc
Saint Vincent and the
Grenadines

ve
Venezuela

vg
Virgin Islands (British)

vi
Virgin Islands (US)

vn
Vietnam

vu
Vanuatu

wf
Wallis and Futuna Islands

ws
Samoa

ye
Yemen

yu
Yugoslavia

za
South Africa

zm
Zambia

zr
Zaire

zw
Zimbabwe

Table A-12 Internet country and region codes (ISO Standard 3166)

Introduction to Boolean operators

Boolean searching has been adopted by some online databases and by many library catalogues which can be searched on the Internet. Boolean searching differs from other keyword searching in that it allows the use of Boolean operators 'and', 'or' and 'not'. With these three operators, you can be more precise on what to search and can extract more exact information from the search.

and

The 'and' operator enables you to search for every entry or record that has both the keywords you have entered somewhere in the same entry or record. To find information on 'engineering drawing', we can enter the Boolean search query:

engineering and drawing

or

If you use the operator 'or', the search engine will retrieve every record that has at least one of the keywords you have entered words in it. Both do not have to appear. This is a broad search, and may retrieve many more records than using the 'and' operator.

An example is:

(engineering society) or (engineering organisation)

In this example, the parentheses ensure that the words inside are treated as a single phrase.

not

The 'not' operator allows you to exclude a term from the search, so that the search engine finds everything the database has the first keyword but nothing that mentions the second.

An example is:

(civil structures) not (bridges)

Boolean operators can also be used in more sophisticated ways than these examples show. For example

(color imaging) and (digital or photoelastic)

will find records that include the words 'digital' or 'photoelastic' as well as the words 'color imaging'.

To make the best use of Boolean searching, you need to check with each database to ascertain which search functions it accommodates.

Index